Fragile Minds

An Advocate's Story

Diane Lane Chambers

Copyright © 2022 Diane Lane Chambers

Ellexa Press LLC, Conifer, CO

All rights reserved. No part of this book may be reproduced or transmitted in any form or by any means, electronic or mechanical, including photocopying, recording, or by an information storage and retrieval system—except by a reviewer who may quote brief passages in a review to be printed in a magazine, newspaper, or on the Web—without permission in writing from the publisher.

Book Design by YellowStudios (YellowStudiosOnline.com)

Paperback ISBN 978-0-9760967-8-8
Library of Congress Control Number 2022904133

First Edition

"Freedom to be insane is an illusory freedom, a cruel hoax perpetrated on those who cannot think clearly by those who will not think clearly."
—E. Fuller Torrey

Contents

Author's Note ix
Preface xi

Part 1

Chapter 1. Cherokee House 3
Chapter 2. Pocahontas And A Jewelry Box 15
Chapter 3. Will You Stay In My Family's Life? 27
Chapter 4. Total Craziness 33
Chapter 5. Textbook Schizophrenia 45
Chapter 6. Matters of Importance 53
Chapter 7. A Call From Denny's 57
Chapter 8. A Step Up 63
Chapter 9. Who Was Keeping Tabs? 67
Chapter 10. What Are We Doing Wrong? 71
Chapter 11. Wreaking Havoc 79
Chapter 12. The Psych Ward 87
Chapter 13. A New Suitcase 91
Chapter 14. I'm Sorry. Its the Privacy Laws 97
Chapter 15. It's the Law 107

Part 2

Chapter 16. The Revolving Door 115
Chapter 17. Repercussions of Deinstitutionalization 119
Chapter 18. It's Not Just Racing Thoughts and Spending Sprees 125
Chapter 19. Psych Ward Distractions 131

Chapter 20. Golden Brook	137
Chapter 21. Relentless Torment	147
Chapter 22. No Home To Return To	151
Chapter 23. Hallucinations	155
Chapter 24. Be Free and Fly Away	167
Chapter 25. On Edge	177
Chapter 26. Having Hope	183
Chapter 27. A Fragile Mind	187
Chapter 28. Crashing	195
Chapter 29. Somewhere Out There	203
Chapter 30. Scared	207
Chapter 31. Out of Balance	215
Chapter 32. A Quiet Rage	219
Chapter 33. A Fragile Mind Has Limits	229

Part 3

Chapter 34. Unbalanced People	237
Chapter 35. On A Crusade	241
Chapter 36. Blatantly Absent	247
Chapter 37. Not A Weakness of Character	253
Chapter 38. A Voice in the Fight	261
Chapter 39. Numerous Red Flags	265
Chapter 40. Time to Act	271
Chapter 41. Fighting for Families	279
Chapter 42. No Agreement In Sight	289
Chapter 43. Too Few of Us	297
Chapter 44. Not Giving Up	303
Chapter 45. Unfounded Fears	311
Chapter 46. Advocating for Reform	315
Chapter 47. Something to Feel Good About	325
Chapter 48. Sense of Accomplishment	333
Chapter 49. To The Finish	345

Epilogue	353
Acknowledgments	355
About the Author	357
Notes	359

Author's Note

This book is a memoir. While the story about me is true, out of respect for the privacy of others and the oath of confidentiality I have taken to practice my profession, the names, situations, and particulars of other people in this book are fictional. Where I have used real names, it has been with their permission. In addition, I have made every effort to ensure the accuracy of the academic information contained in this book. Any errors, inaccuracies, omissions, or inconsistency herein is unintentional, as well as any slighting of people, places, or organizations.

Preface

*Depression, anxiety, and panic attacks are NOT a sign of weakness. They are signs of having tried to
remain strong for too long.*
—Stuff's video, Facebook, May 27, 2017

Where does mental illness come from? Is it part of us from the beginning, brought forth from the womb, or does it fall upon us, conceived from life's tribulations and traumas? After all, there is no routine blood test that can diagnose mental illness. Researchers say that mental illness is genetic or tends to run in families, and my family is no exception. Among my relatives there is schizophrenia and others of us who struggle with anxiety and depression.

My own struggle with anxiety and depression snuck up on me. Like so many people, I didn't recognize it until it was full blown. I was 51 years old. I knew something within me was off-kilter, but I had no clue what it was. I just couldn't sleep. I couldn't sleep because my heart would not stop pounding. I thought about going to the ER many times but never did. What would I tell them, I thought, as I lay back the seat in my car exhausted, trying to nap in between my interpreting assignments. But sleep would not come. It went like this for months. My memories are hazy of how or when it all started, but looking back on what I'd been through in the four years leading up to it, it's not a surprise that I eventually crashed.

I'd been diagnosed with breast cancer and upon finishing treatment I'd gotten involved with several breast cancer groups. I started meeting scores of women diagnosed with the disease and making friends with many, some of whom died. They lost their fight against the disease and I lost their friendship.

One of these women was my neighbor, Sue. I drove her during the snowy month of January to her chemotherapy appointment. We were breast cancer buddies. I was a four-year survivor, and she was an eight-year patient. I was writing a book about breast cancer, and she allowed me to include her story in the book. I took Sue to her appointment because she was unable to drive herself. She'd been recently hospitalized three times, and now she was afraid to drive.

"I'm too shaky," she said.

It was an hour-long drive to the oncology clinic from the mountains where we lived. On the way, Sue talked about her fears. She worried about how her husband would manage with their two young children if she died. She worried that her eight-year-old daughter wouldn't remember her. A few times she paused, wincing in pain from the ascites, the fluid that had built up in the sacs around her lungs. She apologized for not being talkative. She hurt too much.

At the clinic, Sue settled into a reclining chair and removed her wig. Not a hair was left on her head. She slid a soft turban over her bald head to keep warm. After her IV was hooked up, she asked me to open a can of Coke for her. She couldn't do it herself because of the peripheral neuropathy in her hands from all the chemo she'd had. We talked for a while, and then she said she wanted to rest.

I'd been to infusion centers before with my other friend, Harriette, who'd had metastatic breast cancer for 12 years. Since I met Harriette at the Association for Breast Cancer Survivors two years before, I'd been writing about our friendship and her life as an athlete dealing with metastatic breast cancer. Sitting around infusion centers with cancer patients was nothing new to me. It was something women of the breast cancer sisterhood did for each other.

In February, Sue called again, asking if I could drive her to her chemotherapy appointment. A few weeks later, when I called to check on her, there was no answer. I called again the next morning and got her answer machine. I left a message, asking her to call me back. I hung up feeling uneasy. I knew she didn't go out much. She was too sick.

That night, I was already asleep when the phone rang at 10 p.m. At that hour, I knew it had to be for something important. I sat up in bed and reached for the phone. When the caller identified himself as Sue's husband, I knew it wasn't going to be good news. I'd never met or spoken to him before. He was very polite, saying he was responding to my phone message. He said he'd taken Sue to the hospital.

"It was another episode of the fluid building up. We've been down this road many times," he explained, "But the doctor said, 'I can't give her any more chemo; it's going to kill her.' So he stopped the chemo and she just went to sleep."

Sue's husband said he had gotten their two kids there just in time before she slipped away that afternoon. I fell apart after I hung up the phone, sobbing next to my husband.

At Sue's memorial service, I sat in the back of the church behind all the young mothers her age who were in attendance. Many had brought their children. I cried through the entire service. I looked around at the 200 attendees, and no one else was crying like I was. Maybe they'd already shed their tears at home or they were shedding them discretely. As far as I could tell, none of them were going through tissues like I was. So why couldn't I stop crying? I thought it was about Sue's eight-year-old daughter. Her big brown eyes. The innocent child and her slightly older brother, who were now suddenly motherless. It was that, but maybe it was something more.

Six months later, I participated in the Race for the Cure with my daughter and her roommate. Like many others, I wore a sign pinned on the back of my pink survivor's T-shirt that said, "Walking in Memory of_____." I'd written in Sue's name.

We were supposed to be walking with Harriette and her daughter Cyndi, who used a wheelchair, but the swarms of people made it impossible for us to find them. We fell into the sea of walkers heading off to the starting line. There was no loudspeaker as I'd envisioned, nor a gunshot into the air for the takeoff. It was only the people walking, a stream that soon grew into a powerful wave of people rolling peacefully along. Our energy focused up the hill ahead of us, and around the curves where bands played intermittently to keep the crowd of 63,000 methodically moving.

We finished the 5K, never spotting Harriette, but later we met up with her as we'd planned at a restaurant where she'd made reservations for the 10 most important people in her life. She had something she wanted to tell us. By the time we got to the restaurant I had a horrible headache. I had the feeling that I shouldn't even be there, but I knew this wasn't a time when I could not show up.

"This day is a celebration," Harriette told us after we'd removed our sunglasses and visors and settled in with our drinks around the table. "I wanted you all to be here with me today."

Then she told us the news she'd been expecting to hear for the last 12 years. The cancer had spread to her lungs and her liver. Harriette knew what this meant. She and I had talked about it many times. I gulped around the lump in my throat and dabbed at the tears filling my eyes. I had known I would hear this someday, but I'd been in denial. I couldn't imagine that Harriette, my best friend, was going to die.

My headache began pounding so loud I couldn't hear the others talking around the table. I felt nauseous. Waiting for our food, I guzzled my Diet Coke, hoping it would calm the nausea while I smiled politely at one of our friend's husband who was complaining about the president. Before our food arrived, I had to run out of the restaurant. I vomited in the alley.

Harriette died a few weeks later. I thought I'd been prepared for her death, but it was harder than I expected. Just over a month later, I lost Bert, an elderly deaf-blind man whom I'd worked closely with for nearly six years. He'd been an inspiration for me and was the reason I took up writing.

They say there's a link between stressful events and susceptibility to illness. The death of a loved one is one of the top 10 stressors. I hadn't realized it, but the death of my father shortly after my cancer diagnosis, coupled with the loss of two friends from breast cancer, and then my beloved Bert, had taken a huge toll on me. I began spiraling downhill, aware that something was very wrong with me, but I had no idea what it was.

Depression was not something that even remotely occurred to me. I thought depressed people wore pajamas and stayed in bed all day. They had mussed hair and didn't wash the dishes or clean their houses. I got up every morning and went to work. I set up a new business and published a book. I never thought for a moment that I had depression, but I was acutely aware that I had anxiety.

My stomach was in knots. I couldn't eat and was losing weight. I didn't want to see or talk to anyone. I quit working. Through it all, my husband saw me struggling and was sympathetic. He thought it was menopause. "You have all the symptoms," he said.

"Yeah," I agreed, but still I knew it was something else. Going through menopause can't be this bad. I was hardly functioning. I was at the end of my rope and I needed help.

I believe the physician's assistant saved my life, as I have learned that going without sleep for a long period can bring on a psychotic break. I understand now how close I had been to a breakdown. Looking back, I am humbled to think I could have become a patient in one of the psychiatric hospitals where I occasionally worked.

I began to study and read every article or book I could find on mental illness. I wanted to better understand myself, my family, the deaf clients I work with, and the other patients in these mental health facilities. Early in my career, I had encountered clients who were mentally ill, but I had not worked with them in an informed manner. In retrospect, I probably hadn't been as effective in my interpreting as I could have been had I been better educated about this affliction.

Things were different now. I was more aware and knowledgeable, and when I went to assignments at community mental health centers, to group homes, and the locked wards in psych hospitals, I could put faces onto what I was learning about mental illness. I could see things through a different lens.

Over time, I learned how our government's mental health system works. I became aware of the woeful lack of supervised housing options for those afflicted with serious mental illness, the inadequacies of community mental health services, and the lack of accommodations for deaf and deaf-blind patients and clients. As an American citizen with knowledge of this oft-hidden problem, and frequently ignored population, I felt compelled to speak up. It was this path that led me to become an advocate for mental health and reform of our laws. One of the ways I could do this was to write this book.

Diane Lane Chambers

PART 1

1

Cherokee House

September 2006

In an old Denver neighborhood near the railroad tracks, I found Cherokee House. "It's a group home for men with mental illness," the coordinator had said. Other than the client's name, it was all the information I had when I pulled up in front of the three-story Victorian house. I'd worked in residential settings before, though never one like this. While I was hesitant at first to accept this assignment, I decided to give it a chance.

A man with shoulder-length black hair and dark-rimmed glasses stood on the sandstone sidewalk watching as I stepped out of my car into the afternoon heat.

"Interpreter?" he signed.

Nodding with my fist, I signed, "Yes."

I realized he was my client, Carlos, and guessed him to be in his late 30s. He gestured for me to follow and led me around the house to a side door. With an overwhelming smell of disinfectant inside the house I struggled to breathe, though Carlos didn't seem to notice it. He led me through the kitchen to a room that served as the office and introduced me to the evening mental health worker.

"Thanks for coming," the man said. "I'm filling in tonight for the regular person. We'll all meet in the living room."

The men sat on couches arranged in a square around a coffee table. Carlos joined them while the substitute and I sat on wooden chairs.

"Tonight we're gonna talk about hepatitis," he told the group. "What do you guys know about it?"

My heart skipped a beat. I should have inquired what the meeting would be about. I would have prepared and read up on the subject. None of the men responded to the substitute's question.

He read from a sheet of paper, "Hepatitis C is especially dangerous for men, who are less able to fight off the virus once they've been infected. The symptoms are fatigue, yellowing of the whites of the eyes…those most at risk are people who get a tattoo or body piercing… have HIV or AIDS, or engage in anal sex…"

I signed for Carlos, thinking how important this information was for these men to discuss, since they might be vulnerable, except, there was no discussion. The substitute finished reading the printout and called it a wrap. I was stunned that the meeting was over so quickly. I was just getting warmed up and didn't these guys have any thoughts or questions about hepatitis?

Nobody said a word.

So, now what? I wondered. I'm scheduled for two hours. Carlos got up from the couch and scuffed into the kitchen with his shoelaces untied. I followed and watched while he filled a bowl with Cool Whip from the refrigerator. I sat across from him at the table as he ate spoonfuls of the white creamy stuff until one of the other clients, who looked barely out of his teens, came in wearing a football jersey. "Hi. My name is Casey."

Casey took advantage of my interpreting to get to know Carlos. "Who's your favorite Bronco?"

Carlos put another spoonful of Cool Whip into his mouth, then laid the spoon on the table and signed, "I like the LA Rams."

"My favorite is Ashley Lelie," Casey said and asked more questions. "Who's your favorite football team? Who did you want to win the last Super Bowl? Do you know…? Did you hear…?"

Carlos barely answered the barrage of questions, intent on eating his Cool Whip. Oblivious, Casey couldn't seem to slow down long enough to wait for the answers. He kept talking, and I kept signing. Carlos didn't seem much interested. He used his fingers to clean the inside of the bowl to get the last licks of the sweet cream. Casey continued his monologue until my arms ached. I was starting to dread this job. *Is this what I would be doing every week?*

Finally, I suggested to Casey, "How about I teach you fingerspelling and then you can talk to Carlos yourself?"

He agreed, so Carlos and I showed him how to form each letter using his fingers. It surprised me how quickly Casey picked up the fingerspelled alphabet. Like an autistic-savant, Casey seemed to know everything there was to know about sports, but interpreting his one-way conversation bored me. Fortunately, we were rescued from the kitchen conversation by the substitute worker.

"Time for meds," he called. I followed Carlos to the office where the clients lined up and waited until he got his medication before calling it a day.

* * *

The following week, I met the regular mental health care worker, Verna. The first thing I noticed was her commanding presence. When she called the guys to the meeting, her drill sergeant voice nearly knocked me to the ground. "Grooooooop," she yelled.

With the glass in the windows vibrating, I expected the clients to come running from all directions, but they must have been used to her roar. Instead, they filtered into the living room, one by one, and settled on the couches as they had done last week.

With everyone present, Verna began: "While we have the interpreter here, does anyone have anything to ask Carlos?"

"Yeah," one of them said. "What's in that jar you brought to dinner?"

Carlos still had the jar in front of him on the coffee table. It was filled with a yellow liquid.

"It's a chemical," he signed. "You add things to it, to make it change colors."

I spoke what he signed and everyone remained silent.

"May I see it?" Verna asked.

Carlos picked up the jar and carried it to her. With all our eyes intent on Verna and the jar, she opened the lid, careful not to spill it, and cautiously smelled the contents.

"Okay," she said.

We all let out a sigh of relief, reassured that the yellow liquid was not what we'd feared. Someone else asked Carlos if he wanted to get a job and what kind of work he was looking for.

Carlos nodded. "Maybe a janitor," he signed.

As the meeting progressed, I learned the names of the clients and became familiar with their personalities. Miguel, a nice-looking guy, sat across from Carlos with glazed eyes and folded arms. Almost catatonic, he looked as though he were ready to fall asleep. Jesse, slumped on the couch next to Miguel in one solid color of navy blue, moved like a sloth. Whenever he stirred just a bit, I thought he was about to say something, but he never did. He'd only offer a shy grin.

On the opposite end of the couch a young man, who looked like Johnny Depp, sat with his legs folded Indian-style. As soon as Verna noticed she reminded him of the rules, "At least one foot on the floor, at all times, Nick."

He appeared to not hear her. Nick was too busy combing his fingers upward through his hair, making it stick straight up. He carefully folded the middle part down and forward, leaving the sides spiked to where he looked like a devil.

Just then, an older man with a mop of gray and black hair limped in from the kitchen, grumbling about being late. He said Carlos had closed the kitchen door, so he didn't know it was time for group.

"Ernie, it wasn't Carlos," Verna said, "the doorstop is missing. It closes by itself."

Unconvinced, Ernie slid onto the second couch next to a heavy-set man, named Ronnie, bumping his elbow into Ronnie's rib.

"Ouch," Ronnie yelped. Yet instead of getting angry, he laughed. "Ernie cracks me up."

Perhaps now because Carlos finally had an interpreter for the community meetings, Verna took the time to remind the guys that one of the rules for living in the group home was to be out of the house during the day, working on getting themselves back into the community. During group they are to report what they did all day.

"Ronnie," she started, "What did you do today?"

"Saw the doctor."

Verna wrote his answer on a yellow legal pad and asked the next guy the same question.

"Went to see my case manager," he said.

The third client reported that he went downtown.

Carlos signed, "I went to Kmart."

No one seemed to want to talk about what they did. They appeared more interested in Carlos, now that they had someone to interpret for them.

"Have you ever been able to hear?" Damien asked.

"No," Carlos signed.

"Where were you before you came here?"

"In the hospital." Carlos gestured with his hand, tapping his finger against his thumb next to his ear, and I interpreted, "I hear talking in my head."

"But, I thought you couldn't hear," Damien said.

"He can't hear," Verna said. "He thinks in signs, not words."

Besides being loud, tall, and broad-shouldered, qualities which I suspect contributed to her ability to maintain order in a house full of men, Verna had a soft, understanding side to her.

"Do you actually hear things, or are they just thoughts?" Joel, another client, asked.

Verna tried again on Carlos' behalf. "He can read and write to communicate," she replied, without answering Joel's question.

It was a good question though. Many people, including me, wonder how a deaf person can experience auditory hallucinations. It triggered Demonde, one of the more outgoing clients, to pipe in, "Can you hear God and angels singing?"

"No," Carlos signed.

"I hear voices," Damien said. "I'm paranoid schizophrenic. I think the people on TV and the radio know me, and they're talking to me."

"I hear voices sometimes, too," Joel added.

Joel, one of the few who worked, did various odd jobs for people, for 10 dollars here and 10 dollars there. He had an old van parked out front that was stuffed full. He acted like he was the supervisor of the group, reporting on the others' wrongdoings. He occasionally laughed at Ernie, whom they all called the old man. Whenever they teased him, Ernie just grumbled.

When there were no more questions for Carlos, Verna asked him if he had any questions for them. Carlos turned to Jesse, who had been silent the entire time slumped down next to him, and signed, "Why didn't you go to church on Sunday?"

Jesse perked up and smiled. The others laughed. "Jesse?" they asked.

"You go to Franciscan Friends," Carlos signed.

"He goes there for lunch, and for coffee," Verna explained. "It's a place for homeless people to go for food and stuff during the week. Jesse doesn't attend church there."

Jesse smiled. Unlike the other clients, I gathered that Carlos, being deaf, hadn't heard about the community services they offered there.

My second week at Cherokee House had gone well, with me getting to know the residents a bit more. The one thing that surprised me was how energetic some of them were. I had envisioned "a group home for men with mental illness" to have more sedentary types. But I was seeing that there were many faces to mental illness and varied lives behind the faces.

* * *

Until my episode with anxiety and depression, I hadn't been interested in working with people afflicted with mental illness. In college, it was my dream to become a physical therapist. I'd always been active in swimming, tennis, biking, and hiking, and I wanted a career helping people through physical rehabilitation. With life's twists and turns, however, I ended up graduating with a degree in recreation therapy. At 21 years of age, set on finding a job in that field, I found two openings for recreation therapists in the classifieds. One was at Beth Israel Hospital in Denver, the other was at a nursing home in Lakewood.

When I found out that Beth Israel was a psychiatric hospital, I didn't even apply. I didn't know much about mental illness, but my impression was that the people afflicted were scary and smelled bad. So, that left the nursing home as my only option. I drove my used Volkswagen across town to the nursing home to apply. Full of confidence I climbed the narrow steps leading to what I thought was the front door. It was unlocked so I stepped inside, but instead of finding an office with a receptionist to greet me, I saw a long, empty hallway stretched before me. I started down the hall, suddenly overcome by the stench of urine. With my confidence waning I held my breath and slowed my pace. When a janitor soon appeared at the end of the hall, he called out to me, "Can I help you?"

"No," I said. "I was just leaving." I quickly turned around and sped back to my car. I got a job as a waitress instead.

I also got a second job as an assistant at a summer day camp for disabled children. Some children at the camp were deaf and used American Sign Language (ASL) to communicate. It was the first time I'd seen ASL, and it was awkward not being able to communicate with the deaf children. As soon as that summer ended, I enrolled in a sign language class.

My life changed during the very first class. I took to learning the language like metal to a magnet and was soon on the path of becoming a sign language interpreter. Since that day, I haven't had a single regret about not becoming a physical therapist.

My early reluctance toward working in mental health changed after going through breast cancer when I turned 46. I was a wife and mother, with a 17-year-old son and a 19-year-old daughter, enjoying my career as an ASL interpreter when I was diagnosed.

It's common for cancer patients to experience anxiety, and I was no different. Though once my treatment was over and I was on my way to recovery, it dissipated. Unfortunately, it returned after the deaths of several friends and my father, manifesting this time as full-blown, incapacitating, anxiety and depression.

Today, I am mentally and physically healthy. I'm no longer naïve about mental disorders, nor am I shy around those who are afflicted by them. So, when they offered me the assignment at Cherokee House, I accepted.

* * *

Signing with Carlos one evening before the meeting at Cherokee House, I noticed Zach watching me. Probably the sweetest and most outgoing of all the residents, Zach had a bright smile to go with his energy.

"I love to watch the sign language," he told me. "Do you interpret at other places, too?"

"Yes. All kinds of places," I replied.

"Is Carlos your favorite?"

I couldn't tell if Zach was serious or kidding. I answered with a smile and a chuckle.

I'd met hundreds of people as a freelance interpreter, but never thought of any one person as "my favorite." I guessed I felt for Carlos the same way a teacher might for her student. In fact, these weekly meetings at Cherokee House did have the feel of a classroom. These guys were trying to learn how to behave and function in society, so they could stay out of jail and live their lives despite having a mental illness.

My husband, Jim, was not fully comfortable with me working at a house full of men with mental illness. He thought it might be dangerous.

"It's not what you think," I assured him. "The men are stabilized on medication. They're mannerly and respectful and well supervised."

I told him that Verna, while crude at times, kept a firm hand over the guys. She allowed no disrespect or misbehavior. The guys respected her and asked her permission to go places, always accounting for their whereabouts. During the day they were to be out of the house engaged in some sort of activity. They couldn't just stay home and sleep all day. Verna also made sure they stuck to their curfews and did their daily chores. Verna knew each of her boys and didn't let them pull any wool over her sharp eyes. Nevertheless, I carried my husband's cautionary words with me whenever I went to work.

"Be careful," he'd say.

I heard his caution as I interpreted for Carlos when I noticed that Tyrell was back.

An attractive, 20-something, Tyrell was at Cherokee House several weeks ago for a brief time and then disappeared. I'd been wondering where he went and then someone said he was in the hospital. The guys had been going to visit him, but no one mentioned what he was in the hospital for. I recalled him talking a lot about God, stuff I couldn't follow—let alone interpret for Carlos. Tyrell had been disrupting the group. Come to think of it, Verna had mentioned once that Tyrell hadn't been taking his meds. Now I felt him staring at me as I signed.

Not that I was worried, but after the house meeting when it was time for meds, I felt reassured seeing Tyrell in line. No one was forced to take medication at the group home, though it was prescribed for each client. Their medication was stored in individual plastic containers and locked up in the office. It was the client's responsibility to come at the set times to take it. Rather than doling out pills, Verna would hand them their box and monitor each client, while he opened the bottles. The law required that she record the date and time of each medicine they swallowed. Clients who were noncompliant in taking their meds risked getting kicked out of the house.

Carlos took his turn, but instead of disappearing afterward as the others did, he stayed and watched the rest of them swallow their combinations of mood stabilizers, antipsychotics, stimulants for ADHD, or antidepressants. Depakote, lithium, Risperdal, and Zyprexa. Carlos knew them all and knew who took what.

* * *

Tyrell and another resident named Randy got into an argument one evening right before the meeting, about work.

"I'm getting my education first, so I can get a 'good job,'" Randy boasted.

Leaping out of his seat, Tyrell immediately went into offense against Randy for his better-than-thou attitude, "Physical labor is better than other work," he argued, getting louder and more agitated the more he thought about people not valuing laborers. Tyrell worked part-time at a warehouse.

Because I'm required to interpret everything I hear, including arguments between residents, I was signing their conversation to Carlos. More clients showed up as their argument was gaining heat. Fearing myself smack in the middle of a fight ready to break out, my heart started racing.

Fortunately, Verna showed up just in time and put a stop to it: "All right, that's enough. Let's get to the topic we're supposed to be discussing."

Verna sat down and everyone went quiet.

"Who can tell me the characteristics of schizophrenia?"

"Flat emotions," Eli called out from the corner of the brown couch where he always sat. Usually silent during the meetings, he wasn't that night.

"Do you think you have flat emotions, Eli?" she asked.

"Not much," he said. "But I can't remember the last time I felt really sad or really happy." He mentioned that his father had a mental illness as well.

As I signed for Carlos, I glanced at Eli, noticing his beard and huge stomach, and the way he looked through his glasses that sat at the end of his nose. I felt pangs of sadness for him. Looking back at Carlos, I saw Ronnie out of the corner of my eye, sitting in the opposite corner of the couch with Eli. With his own sizable belly, he and Eli were like matching bookends. Verna, eager to stay on topic, asked Ronnie to name another characteristic of schizophrenia. But he couldn't think of any, even though he's living with the disease.

Nick, usually quiet, spoke up. "Hearing voices," he said.

"Yes, that's one," Verna affirmed.

"I used to hear voices, but I don't anymore," Nick added. "I had an episode while I was in college, and I got arrested and put in jail. Then I was in a mental hospital for six months before I came here. Nick believes that drugs and stress brought on his schizophrenia.

He told the group, "Sometimes I feel like quitting my meds. But they say I could have a relapse if I stop."

Nick said his goal was to get a job or go back to school so he could move out of the group home. Knowing little about him, I felt optimistic for Nick that he would have a successful life if he stayed on track with his medications. Sadly, I didn't feel the same optimism about some of the others. I wasn't even sure about Carlos.

One grossly overweight man sat apart from the guys with earphones on listening to music. Once in a while he attended the house meetings, but no one talked to him, nor did he ever speak. Earlier, he was outside smoking.

Admittedly, out of all the clients, he was the one who scared me. His eyes always followed me as I came and went from Cherokee House.

I never asked Verna questions about the clients. The only time I learned things about them was when someone volunteered information, or if Verna mentioned something to me in confidence. No one had ever said anything about the heavyset man, but as the weeks passed I saw him lift his hand just a bit and wiggle his fingers at me when I arrived. It was several months before he finally said, "Hello."

"Hello," I replied, still not knowing his name.

People with schizophrenia are often quiet and withdrawn. They're not usually violent like the ones whose name makes the news headlines.

"And they don't like changes in their routine or strangers in their houses," Verna told me one evening after the house meeting. She said, "At first, the guys didn't want an interpreter coming into the group. They couldn't understand what you were here for. They asked, 'Why is she coming? When will she be done?' They didn't like it."

Verna said she expected this, and that's why she had requested that the same interpreter come every week. That way the guys would be comfortable speaking up during group. Different interpreters would be too disruptive, and Verna didn't want anything that might get them stirred up. She knew that something small could set one person off and trigger trouble in the whole house. I was grateful for Verna's caution and understood the need to keep things consistent.

Truth be told, in the beginning I wasn't exactly smitten with these guys or the house, either. With the overwhelming smell of disinfectant and the floors and bathrooms still looking dirty after they'd been cleaned, I didn't care if I continued as the regular interpreter or not. But I came with an open mind, and since that first night, I'd been the regular interpreter and had come to like working there.

2

Pocahontas And A Jewelry Box

Since my friend, Harriette, passed away two years ago from breast cancer, I'd been keeping in touch with her 41-year-old disabled daughter, Cyndi. We usually talked over the phone, but today I was in her neighborhood. So, I called to say I'd stop by to see her new home.

The door was unlocked when I arrived. Pushing it open I stepped inside a compact living room with an adjoining mini kitchen calling out, "Hello."

"I'm back here," she hollered.

With a bathroom and a bedroom, her condo was only three rooms, yet it seemed like all the space she needed. Cyndi spent a lot of time in bed. Due to long-term use of steroids for her asthma, her bones had become so fragile she couldn't walk. Without assistance from her certified nursing assistant (CNA) she couldn't even transfer herself out of bed into her wheelchair in the morning or back to bed in the evening.

I found Cyndi on her bed watching reruns of *Dr. Quinn, Medicine Woman* starring Jane Seymour. I noticed her dark hair was clinging in oily strands to her head. And that's when something peculiar caught my eye. Cuddled up with Cyndi was a kitten with huge brown eyes. At once I felt struck with Cupid's arrow. "Where did you get her?" I asked, sliding onto a chair next to the bed.

"One of my CNAs brought her. Her name is Pocahontas."

As soon as I sat down the kitten crawled from her cozy spot next to Cyndi, jumped off the bed, and to my delight hopped right onto my lap. I thought she was the perfect pet for Cyndi, not a wolf or the monkey she claimed to own, which were always mysteriously away with some unnamed friend whenever I came to visit. Someone with common sense gave this kitten to Cyndi. When this friendly ball of fur climbed up to nestle against my neck, my heart melted. Listening to Pocahontas purr, I didn't want to move.

At four months and five pounds, Pocahontas was as lithe as a ballerina. She hopped from my lap alighting like a butterfly. That's when I noticed she was missing half her tail. "What happened to her?"

"What do you mean?" Cyndi asked

"Her tail, did it get cut off?"

"Nothing happened. She's a Manx," Cyndi said. "That's just the way her tail is. She's extremely intelligent and valuable because she's a rare breed."

I'd never heard of that breed before. I just thought her tail looked funny and hoped nothing awful had happened to her. Cyndi told me how much money she spent on the cat's play tower and toys, and the electric self-cleaning litter box. She was aghast over the expense.

"Speaking of the litter box, would you mind doing me a favor?" she asked.

"What is it?"

"Could you get the pooper scooper from behind the door and clean out the litter box? My CNA refused to do it."

Though I thought it rude asking a guest to clean your cat's litter box, especially someone who was not a cat owner, I agreed to help. First, I needed to figure out how the self-cleaning litter box worked. I soon realized that the electronic scraper didn't actually remove the waste from the box as I imagined, but merely pushed it to the end where it was piled almost five inches high! I gagged at the stench. When I finished cleaning it, I told Cyndi I needed to get back to work and promised to come again soon.

Two weeks later when I returned, Cyndi was complaining of a fever.

"I'm sure I have a bladder infection," she said. "I'm never wrong."

Cyndi said she was waiting for a taxi to come and transport her to the emergency room. "Can you do me another favor?" she asked. "I know they'll admit me to the hospital. They always do. Can you take Pocahontas home with you?"

This request was totally unexpected. I was inclined to say no because my husband hated cats. At least that's what he always said. But then, Pocahontas was not a cat. She was a furry ball of joy with eyes and a purr that melted your heart, so I reconsidered.

"Okay, sure. I'll take her." What could a few days hurt? Surely, Jim wouldn't mind a little guest for a short time.

Along with the tiny cat came the cardboard carrier, food, toys, and litter box Cyndi had me gather for my journey home. I felt like a happy little kid bringing home her first pet, nervous as to what Jim would say.

I needn't have worried, though. When Pocahontas cuddled up to Jim as he worked on his laptop, he fell in love with her right away. We ended up keeping Pocahontas for four days, even though it turned out Cyndi was wrong. The doctors at the hospital emergency department determined she didn't have an infection and sent her back home.

This kind of error in judgment on Cyndi's part was not new to me. Thinking back on the stories her mother told me, I knew Cyndi's life had been a constant whirl of health problems stretching over her 40 years. Most of the family's life had revolved around Cyndi. In these last two years, without either of her parents, Cyndi now had me caught up in her whirlwind. She would call me at least once every week, and the more I learned about her, the more I realized her health problems were not only physical.

After her mother died, Cyndi told me she and her aide were moving in together, into a house they were building, complete with indoor spiraling wheelchair ramps. I thought it was a wishful dream. I knew a house with spiraling wheelchair ramps would have to be huge. It was no surprise when that house never materialized. After her aide ended up in legal trouble over drugs, Cyndi ended up in a nursing home.

I visited her a few times at the nursing home. Once, while her roommate slept, I sat on the end of Cyndi's bed in the dim light listening to her talk about her medicine man. This was the first I'd heard about him. Cyndi said he was 103 years old and traveled by bus. She said he was on his way to visit her from the Indian reservation in Oklahoma where he lived and was bringing her a wolf named Tuku.

"The medicine man picked her out," Cyndi said, her face sparkling with joy. "Tuku's spiritually divined especially for me."

Harriette had never mentioned Cyndi having a medicine man. I didn't know whether to believe Cyndi. I'd never heard of anyone these days having a medicine man, and the nursing home where she lived now was no place for a dog, let alone a wolf!

Cyndi insisted that she was getting out of the nursing home because she had "passed the test" and now she was a medicine woman. She'd started "healing" the other residents, though to continue her work she decided she had to move out. I had doubts about all this talk. I couldn't imagine where else she could go. She was severely disabled and had no family other than her brother. This wolf and her healing work were pure fantasy. I knew it, even if Cyndi didn't.

During that visit I told Cyndi I was having surgery soon and would be unable to see her for a couple of weeks. Later, while I was home recuperating, she called to say she was moving in with a friend and had to get all her stuff out of the nursing home right away. Oblivious to my post-surgical limitations she asked if I could come to help her move.

"Cyndi, I can't drive, or lift anything right now." I said, wanting to scream at her thoughtlessness.

A few days later, she reported she'd checked out of the nursing home and was now sleeping on her friend's couch. It didn't surprise me when she wound up with an infection and ended up in the hospital. Again.

After they discharged her from the hospital, instead of going back to the friend's house, Cyndi went to a motel. When she called me, she spoke with an air of confidence, like she knew exactly what she was doing. I knew she was lost.

I drove an hour that day in the July heat to bring her a sketch pad, drawing pencils, and erasers, so she'd have something to do at the motel. Her room, though clean and sunny, held only a foldout couch and a small refrigerator. She had little food. A motel didn't seem to me like a place to live. And after saying goodbye to her that day, I left with a sinking feeling.

I fully expected the next call from her would be to beg me to come and rescue her from the motel. Fortunately, that wasn't the case. Cyndi's brother, Jeff, whom she's always made out to be an adversary, had found the condo for her. Though she never gave Jeff any credit, when I heard this,

I came to believe that he was looking out for her. Shortly after she moved in, however, Cyndi called asking to borrow $120.

"The bank made a mistake on my account," she said. "There are withdrawals I didn't make!"

There was no way I was going to lend her the money. I knew I would never see it again. But I did want to help her. She was struggling. She'd never lived on her own before. She needed sound advice.

"Close your account immediately," I'd said.

"They won't let me, because I'm overdrawn."

I offered to meet her at the bank to help straighten this out, but when I asked for the address of her bank, she didn't know. Cyndi said she would find out and call me back. When she did, she said she'd found someone else to lend her the money.

After this I questioned everything Cyndi said. I didn't want to get involved in her troubles or feel guilty for not helping her out of her fixes. It didn't seem like she was learning from her mistakes, either. I also gave up trying to reason with her. Reason and logic don't work with someone who is not rational. And I stopped trying to have normal conversations with her. They were always one-sided. She talked about her nonsensical life while I listened.

Three weeks after I'd taken Pocahontas home for the weekend, Cyndi got an infection for real and was admitted to the hospital. On the tenth day, right before her discharge, I visited her and Cyndi brought up her money problems again.

"I can't believe what has happened," she said. "For the first time I'm having money problems. I'm overdrawn at the bank."

She must have forgotten that a month earlier she had called me about this. Now she asked me to lend her some money.

"I need it for food," she said.

The disarray of her life never ceased to amaze me. "Why do you need money for food?" I asked.

She didn't want to tell me. And she didn't want me to say anything to her brother either. I didn't want to lend money to Cyndi. I didn't trust her anymore. I'd given her things before and she'd lost them. I talked around the subject for a while, hoping she'd forget, and she didn't mention it again. However, before I left the hospital, I tracked down a social worker. I thought the hospital staff should know they were sending her home while she had no means of providing for herself. The social worker seemed genuinely concerned.

"I'll talk to her brother," she said.

* * *

Stepping out of my car in front of Cherokee House I saw Ernie hurrying up the street.

"Hey lady!" he called out. "Am I late?" He walked at a good pace despite his limp. "I have to get home. I can't be late!"

I waved, shaking my head. Ernie soon caught up to me and held out something in his hand. "Here, you can have this. I don't want it no more," he said.

It was a silver jewelry box, decorated with silver roses, and a red velvet interior. "This is beautiful, where — "

Ernie, kept walking, turning ahead of me onto the path alongside the house. Trailing behind, somewhat stunned, I asked, "Are you sure you don't want this?"

"Nah," he grunted.

Ernie made it into the house just under the wire. The men were waiting, seated on the couches, and Verna had her yellow pad and pen ready.

"Okay, you guys, what do you want for our Halloween party?"

I slinked down on a wooden chair, sliding my purse and the silver box underneath, and began interpreting for Carlos. Verna made a list of the food and candy they wanted her to buy. Then she asked which movies they wanted her to rent. The guys burst forth with titles of scary and funny movies they liked.

"*Edward Scissorhands,*" someone suggested.

I finger-spelled the title of the movie for Carlos and glanced at Nick, who I thought looked like Johnny Depp, the lead actor in that movie. Nick was bent forward running his fingers through his thick hair. He sat up with his hair spiked upward and looked straight at me with his Johnny Depp eyes. I wanted to tell him that he looked just like the actor, but I kept interpreting. Nick didn't look like he was paying attention to the conversation anyway.

Just then, I noticed Carlos wasn't wearing any shoes, just socks. Zach, sitting next to him, noticed Carlos' shoeless feet at the same time I did. "Tell him his socks look like inside-out combat boots," Zach said.

I interpreted, but Carlos didn't respond.

"Hey, it's a joke," Zach said.

Ronnie, at least, laughed at the joke. "He's cleaning the floor for us—with his socks."

I signed everything they said. Though he looked embarrassed, Carlos said nothing. I didn't know if he understood that they were teasing him, or if he was even paying attention.

Carlos simply signed, "I'm tired."

Verna ignored all of it. Before she wrapped up the community meeting, she asked each client for feedback. They were required to say something during the meeting or to give some kind of feedback at the end to get credit for participating. It was another house rule. They were not allowed to zone out or sleep through meetings. They had to remain focused and stay present. Verna told me this demonstrated that they're working on their goals toward reentering society. She didn't care what they said. She just wanted them to be mentally present and engaged. A couple of them commented that the party would be fun.

Out of turn, Ronnie blurted, "I'm looking forward to the party if Diane comes."

His comment, so unexpected, was funny to me. I was supposed to be invisible there, a nonparticipant, so it struck me when he suddenly inserted me into the conversation. I almost burst out laughing, but Verna kept on top of things.

She reminded him, "Ronnie, you know that's not appropriate talk for this meeting."

Still, he persisted, "Diane, are you coming to the party?"

No one had mentioned the party to me until now, so I didn't know if I would be coming. The guys were restless and stirring and no one seemed to be listening anymore.

That's when Verna announced, "Meeting's over."

I followed Ernie on my way outside, monitoring his uneven gait on the path. "Why are you limping?" I asked.

"My feet don't hurt no more," he said. "They used to, but they don't hurt no more." He told me he walked three miles a day and I believed him.

Driving home with the silver jewelry box sitting on the seat next to me, I wondered what the story was behind the box and whether I should have accepted it.

* * *

On Halloween, I went to Cherokee House, as usual, as it fell on my regularly scheduled day. Only Carlos and Casey were dressed in costumes as they had just returned from a party at the recreation center. Casey, of course, was dressed as a football player. Carlos, in a batman cape, wore a head mask over his glasses.

There was no community meeting on account of it being Halloween, so I sat at the far side of the room while Carlos and the guys ate candy and chips and watched movies they'd already seen. I was glad when it was time to leave.

November 2006

Indian summer had slid into fall and it was already pitch dark at 5:30 in the evening. An icy cold lingered from the snow that blew in two nights before. It seemed as though winter had arrived too soon. Huddled in the car in front of Cherokee House, I stared at the full moon hanging low in the sky. A sheer cloud covered it like a veil. I remembered the weather being warm when I first started coming to Cherokee House. For a person who didn't like to get stuck in one place too long, I'd hardly noticed the months flying by.

Emerging from the warmth of the car, I trod through the dark following the path along the side of the house. As soon as I reached the door Carlos greeted me with the latest news.

"Joel is getting kicked out," he signed, adding that it was for his messy room.

I reacted with half surprise and half distress showing on my face. Apparently, the clutter in Joel's room was stacked so high it had become a health and fire hazard. The room must have looked similar to Joel's van that was parked out in front, stuffed to the brim. I was curious about what Joel was going to do now and where he was going to sleep.

Joel was seldom around during the house meetings, though when he was there he was often complaining about the government or proclaiming he was reducing waste by never throwing away plastic silverware, even though the house rules dictated otherwise. Instead of discarding them, he put them in his van. Now, as he gathered up his belongings everyone could hear him hollering about his rich conservative brother who never talked to him, who was planning to come to Colorado to "kidnap" their mother and take her to Florida behind his back. This sounded a bit crazy. I wondered if Joel was off his meds.

* * *

On Thanksgiving Eve I met Ian, another substitute mental health worker. Ian talked to the guys that evening about the holidays, how they can be stressful, and cause worsening of depression or psychosis for persons with mental illness. Apparently, this was the case for Eli, who was refusing to participate in the meeting or the holiday plans. It was the same last week when he had sat through the meeting staring downward.

Verna had asked him, "Do you want turkey for Thanksgiving?"

"No," he replied.

"Stuffing?"

"No."

"Pie?"

He shook his head.

"Nothing?"

In a lighthearted manner she'd tried to pull him out of his slump, to no avail. Now Ian couldn't get Eli to say anything, either. For the clients who had nowhere to go for Thanksgiving, I saw sadness in their eyes.

Ian was trying to lift their mood. "We'll have a special meal tomorrow at lunch, with turkey, mashed potatoes, and dressing," he said.

No one seemed very interested. I sensed Ian purposefully keeping the conversation low key. Like Verna, perhaps, he didn't want to stir up these guys' emotions.

Verna had said, "Their hallucinations, or voices, might already be bothering them, and they could escalate to where they start seeing scary things coming out of light bulbs or through the windows. The voices that tell them to hurt themselves or hurt somebody else might become overwhelming. One additional stressor could push one of them into a full-blown episode."

Ian ended the meeting abruptly after ten minutes. I had another hour before it would be time for me to leave. Someone turned the basketball game on, and Carlos went upstairs to his room. Ronnie and Eli were still sitting on the couch when Ronnie said, "Hey, Diane, do you like the cold weather?"

"No, not really," I replied.

"It's the worst thing about not having a job—facing the monster."

"The monster?" I wondered.

Ronnie continued: "Yeah, we have to be out of the house all day. We're homeless for eight hours. It's freezing! The only way to get back at the monster is a nine to five job."

"Where do you go?"

"To the rec center or the Franciscan Friends of the Poor—just somewhere 'til we can come back here. Are you from around here?"

"Yeah, I grew up here."

"I'm from Nebraska," Ronnie said. "We used to have an auto body shop, but we lost it. I don't know where my parents are now."

I studied Ronnie as he spoke. His chest strained with every breath over his huge stomach. He seemed sad, yet somehow accepting of his situation.

Eli added to the conversation. "It's a two-hour drive to where my family lives."

He said he would not see them for Thanksgiving. It pained me hearing about their torn lives and families, knowing I'd be with my family for Thanksgiving.

Carlos came back down the stairs signing to me that he needed some scissors to cut up his credit card because he didn't have enough money to pay the bill. He didn't seem upset about it, but then, I'd never seen Carlos get upset over anything, including Thanksgiving. He didn't have anywhere to go either, but during the meeting he said he was looking forward to the dinner there.

I followed Carlos into the office where he asked Ian for a pair of scissors and proceeded to cut the credit card into tiny pieces over the trash can. When he finished, Ian asked me, "Can you interpret something?"

"Of course," I said.

Ian started in on Carlos. "I caught you today, smoking weed. I could smell it. And, you lied the other day when I asked if you had used."

Ian said he knew because Carlos' eyes were bloodshot and his pupils were large. Ian warned Carlos that he was very close to being kicked out of the house for good.

"You're fortunate, you know. There's a waiting list of 100 people, living on the streets right now, who are trying to get in here."

Carlos' eyes grew big and froze open for a minute. He slumped onto a chair as though filled with guilt and worry about being put out on the street, just like Joel. Leaning over his lap with his head bent down, his long, dark hair covered his face.

"Are you scared?" Ian asked.

I tapped Carlos on the shoulder. He looked up, peeking through his hair and I signed Ian's question.

"Yeah, a little," he replied.

I saw that Carlos did have feelings like everybody else. He just didn't show them the way most of us do.

3

Will You Stay In My Family's Life?

December 2006

Ninety days after her last admission, Cyndi was in the hospital again. I sat with her as she stretched out in a recliner next to the bed with its freshly laundered sheets. She said this new infection had truly knocked her down. She asked if she could borrow money again, confiding that the reason she needed it was because she spent all of hers on a plane ticket for her medicine man.

Though I listened, showing concern, I was mostly sad for her. She had fallen into a desperate state. So worried about her health, she considered it urgent that she see her medicine man and flew him out here. I didn't know where her money really went, and I didn't know how sick she was. I thought perhaps she was getting close to the end. Her mother always said that Cyndi wouldn't live long.

I hesitated to ask questions because most of the time the answers she gave were not answers. They were just more vagaries, leaving me with more questions that served only to annoy her and make me more confused. On this particular day, Cyndi was upset about a letter she'd gotten from her latest home care agency informing her that after the end of the week, they would no longer be providing care for her because they could not meet her needs.

Perhaps their withdrawal of care was the result of what happened recently in the middle of the night with her colostomy bag. When I visited her on the morning after the incident, she'd told me that she had called the agency asking for someone to come help her with an emergency, but no one came.

I hadn't even known Cyndi had a colostomy bag, but she proceeded to tell me that waste had leaked from the bag onto her skin and caused a burn. I was curious to see the burn, but she didn't offer to show me. Instead, she proffered a tired threat to sue the local home care agencies. She had gone through them all.

"There's no one left to take care of me," she complained. "I can't be alone! I need a live-in private nurse."

I suppressed the urge to tell Cyndi that her brother was right when he'd said that she should have stayed in the nursing home after her mom died. She changed the subject anyway, to why she was overdrawn on her bank account.

"I sold $2,500 worth of my art. I thought Jake put the money in the bank and I spent $700 on gifts for Christmas, but guess what? It was a bad bank! The money wasn't there. Now, I have to get the artwork back, because Jake didn't put the money in the bank."

Another confusing mess. I wasn't sure what the relationship was between Cyndi and Jake. The only time I'd met him was at the hospice center where I was visiting with Harriette. He had brought Cyndi to be with her mother. Besides all of his piercings, Jake wasn't a bad-looking young man, but now I was suspicious. I left the hospital wondering if Jake had taken Cyndi's money. Perhaps Cyndi hadn't realized it yet. And the artwork—what was she talking about? Cyndi hadn't produced anything new in months, and her older work, the framed pieces I'd seen on the walls of her parents' house, I thought they'd all been lost in her moves.

* * *

Snuggled on the couch just before dawn, I watched the lights blinking from our Christmas tree, and breathed in the scent of pine. One breath for life, one for family, another for health and home. I was reminded every day, you couldn't take any of it for granted. I relished the blissful moment, for it was soon gone, forgotten by the hustle to work and the noise of the day.

By 9:30 I was sitting with the "walk-ins" at the Social Security Administration with my deaf client. People without appointments sit for hours sometimes, waiting for their number to be called. Fortunately, my client had a scheduled appointment.

For two hours I interpreted myriad questions for the applicant. At last, the representative leaned back from her computer and said, "I'll send your application to Determination Services, and you should hear something within 30 to 90 days."

They had such an arduous process just to determine if a Deaf person was deaf. From there, I set off to a medical assignment, and later in the afternoon I was on my way to my third job of the day at Cherokee House.

Nearing the house from a block away, I could see Carlos standing out on the sidewalk. Typically, clients don't wait outside for me, but Carlos was like a kid waiting for Santa Claus. It must have been the break from his silent world that he looked forward to; to be with someone with whom he could communicate in his own language.

Most days Carlos had things he was eager to show me, like an invitation to an event or a science project he ordered from a catalog that arrived in the mail. Sometimes he would be out in stockinged feet or in short sleeves when the temperature was in single digits. One evening he snuck up to my car in the dark, scaring the wits out of me when he suddenly pointed a flashlight in my eyes, like a policeman stopping a traffic offender.

Today I figured Carlos was eager to see me because I'd been away recently at a conference. When I was about to turn onto his street, Carlos came out, waving his arms, motioning for me to go away, so I turned left at the corner instead of right. I drove the opposite direction from Cherokee House, giggling as I watched Carlos in the rearview mirror changing his signal, motioning for me to come back.

During the community meeting Verna asked each client what he would like for Christmas. The only stipulation was that it needed to be something inexpensive, as it was a gift from the house. The guys asked for practical things, like the long johns Randy requested. He often returned from the Community Mental Health Center red-nosed, bundled in a hat and puffy coat. Apparently, he needed more layers to guard against the cold while waiting for buses. The weather was just one more hurdle to these guys who were trying to rejoin society.

* * *

Two days before Christmas, I was pounding out the miles on our treadmill when the phone rang. It was Cyndi. No longer in the hospital, she asked, "Are you sitting down?"

"Why, are you going to tell me that you walked?"

I knew she'd been working with a physical therapist recently, trying to stand using leg braces. Her bones were so brittle. It was actually dangerous for her to stand, but she insisted upon it. She wanted to believe that she'd walk again.

"No, but I have exciting news! I'm going to have a one-woman art show at one of the most prestigious art galleries!"

"Really? Where?"

"Downtown, at Howard Lorton. Save the weekend of March 1st."

I thought Lorton's was a furniture store, but maybe they had an art gallery, too. I was unfamiliar with the art world, though I knew Cyndi was a talented artist. I'd seen portraits she'd drawn in pencil, and multimedia 2D paintings, but I knew of nothing that she'd done recently.

"Where is all your artwork now?"

"In my brother's shed. This is going to be in all the newspapers. This is how people become world-famous. I'm going to be famous!"

While I was skeptical, I told her that was great. "So…how'd this come about?"

"Jake. He knows someone."

Jake had been kind and helpful to Cyndi since she'd been on her own, though I was curious why he was hanging out with her so much. He was much younger than Cyndi and I thought he had a couple of girlfriends. I questioned his motives as much as I questioned this art show.

"So, why don't you take the Access-a-Ride, go downtown, and check out the place?" I asked.

"I don't need to use Access-a-Ride anymore. Jake bought me a van with hand controls."

I mustered a response: "That's nice of Jake."

"Yeah, and guess what else? I'm getting live-in help and my own private nurse!"

This all sounded outlandish to me. "Is Medicare paying for this?"

"No, I am. Well, Jake and my medicine man are—the Indian Tribal Community is."

Cyndi had told me she was part Indian and belonged to a tribe. This seemed odd, as her mother had never talked about this. I still hadn't met the medicine man and didn't even know if he existed. Yet, I tried to figure out the logistics of what Cyndi was telling me.

"Where does the tribe get the money from?"

She evaded the question, but I kept pressing. "Where is this organization? Are they national?"

"They're a special organization."

This all sounded crazy. Still, I was trying to make sense of it. "How long will they pay for the private nurse?"

"Forever. Well, they don't need to. We won the lottery."

"Who's we?"

"Me and Jake!"

That was it. All the talk, from the new house with spiraling indoor ramps, and the secret ranch she said she owned with horses and ponies, to the wolf and the monkey—it was all making sense now. I'd chalked it up to her naiveté and wishful thinking, having suddenly been left to find her own way after her mother had died, but now I saw it. She was either delusional or just plain lying.

I had nothing to say in response to her lottery winnings. I wanted to slam the phone down and run. Instead, I offered a polite goodbye: "Cyndi, I need to start packing. We're leaving for Breckenridge in the morning. I'll call you next week."

As I hung up, I knew I would not call her that soon. I hated talking to her now. The conversations were impossible. I didn't know who, or what, I was dealing with anymore.

By morning I was convinced Cyndi was suffering from either bipolar disorder or, worse, schizophrenia, and wondering if I was the only one who saw this. Clearly, she was sick and needed help.

I remembered Harriette looking at me during one of our last conversations when she was in hospice care. She asked, "After I'm gone, will you stay in my family's life?"

I promised I would. Now I thought, is this what Harriette had meant? That I needed to keep an eye on Cyndi and help her? If Harriette knew Cyndi was like this, why didn't she tell me? Or maybe Cyndi's craziness stemmed from the loss of her mother. Trauma can play a role in triggering mental illness. Or perhaps it was the long-term use of steroids for her asthma that was causing her mania and delusions.

I looked to the sky, hoping for a glimpse of Harriette's face through the clouds. *"Are you there? What do you want me to do?"*

I stared at the clouds for a while before deciding to call Jeff, knowing that he and Cyndi didn't get along. I rarely spoke to him and hated to disturb him so close to the holiday, but I had to ask if he knew that something was wrong with Cyndi.

4

Total Craziness

With Christmas over, the new issue at Cherokee House was bedbugs. The house was infested with them. This was the second time in a year and Verna, her face red and dripping in sweat, was fuming.

"The bugs are in Joel's old mattress. The exterminator's gonna have to come back and spray the whole place," she complained during the community meeting.

They'd discovered the bugs after his roommate woke up with an itchy trail of red dots running across his abdomen. I interpreted for Carlos as Verna shared information about bedbugs to the group: "The adult can live up to 550 days without food, and the females lay eggs that can hatch in 10 days…"

I had no idea how invincible the tiny bugs were. It sounded nearly impossible to win a battle against them. While my skin tingled at the thought, I prayed there were no bugs on the upholstered chair I was sitting on. I made a mental note not to touch anything in the house.

When the meeting was over, Carlos followed Verna into the office, with me trailing behind. The room was dimly lit, making it hard to see if there were any bugs in there. I avoided the chairs altogether, electing to stand.

Just then Miguel appeared, holding a paper cup. "I got a bug," he said.

We gathered around him with our heads bent over the cup, inspecting the tiny reddish-brown bug he'd found in the closet.

"Yep, it's a bedbug!" Verna declared.

Over her desk, she tried transferring the bug from Miguel's cup to a smaller one so she could show it to the guys. As she flicked the bug it missed her cup and fell off. In a rage of expletives she searched for it on her desk.

I suddenly remembered the flashlight Carlos had shined in my eyes the time he scared me while I was sitting in my car. "You have a flashlight?" I signed.

He nodded and rushed to get it. When Carlos returned, Verna was already using her own little flashlight to look for the bug, but it was still too dark in the room to see well. Carlos' flashlight helped some, but none of us could find the tiny bug.

"Oh fuck," Verna yelled. "Now the office is infested!"

"Maybe you could vacuum," I suggested.

Verna thought for a second then stormed across the hall to the utility closet and pulled out a dusty portable vacuum and dragged it into the office. She finished vacuuming just as Randy returned from the community center.

When Carlos told him about the bug, Randy just shrugged: "At least it's not roaches."

His comment didn't assuage Verna, however: "Maybe you don't mind them sucking your blood, but I sure do!"

Backing my way out of the contaminated room, I couldn't wait for my shift to be over so I could home. All I could think about was washing my clothes and taking a shower.

* * *

January 2007

Verna started the first meeting of the new year holding her yellow pad of paper up in the air.

"Okay guys, what topics do you want to talk about in our community meetings this year? You say you don't like to talk about drugs because then you just want to use them. So what kinds of things do you want to learn and talk about?"

"Let's talk about alcohol," someone suggested.

This idea immediately stirred up excitement, and I was soon interpreting a lively conversation. Demonde recalled a time he got wasted on Everclear mixed with Kool-Aid. Sean, a new client with huge muscular arms, piped in with a story about a pony keg.

"I laid on an air mattress and drank it straight from the hose. I drank the whole thing myself in three days!"

A couple of others offered their fallin'-down-drunk stories, too. The only responses to any of them were attempts to top the last one with a better story.

The subject quickly changed to cocaine. "How do you make crack?" someone asked.

"You mix cocaine with baking soda and water. Then you heat it 'til it's all creamy. Then the water evaporates and it gets hard," Zach proudly stated. "Then you smoke it."

I found it interesting that most of these guys never graduated from high school, yet they knew *everything* about this stuff. As I speculated whether Zach was correct, Randy added, "Yeah, but you don't want to get too much baking soda or it tastes bad."

Sean agreed, "Yeah, just something to cut it with."

Assuming Carlos was as naïve as me about drugs, I wanted to scold these guys. *You're teaching Carlos how to do this!* They all seemed to be experts on the subject. Randy mumbled something in a condescending manner, to which Zach took offense. "Hey, I've been smoking marijuana longer than you've been alive!"

"I'm 41," Randy snapped back.

Nick interrupted their feud by showing up late with a bag of Hershey kisses. He tossed the bag onto the couch where Sean was sitting and slid himself down on the other end. Sean helped himself to a handful of the chocolates while the others started in.

"Hey, toss it to me," Demonde yelled.

"Gimme some!" Eli whined.

I spoke up for Carlos when he signed, "I want some," but nobody paid attention to him. They just wanted their share.

"Toss me the bag," Eli shouted as Jesse helped himself to the candy.

"Don't give any to Eli," Demonde ordered.

Jesse tossed the bag to Miguel. In a game of keep away from Eli, they threw the bag back and forth. Nick was the last one holding the nearly empty bag.

"Can't I have some?" Eli asked, sounding hurt.

"After group," Nick said.

Eli wouldn't wait. Heaving himself from his spot on the couch, where it was permanently dented in his form, he lugged his large frame across the room, heading for the candy, and Nick gave in. Satisfied with two bits of chocolate, Eli trudged back to his seat.

With the diversion over, they went back to where they left off, telling stories that morphed from drunkenness into vomiting and other body fluid themes, with Demonde laughing himself silly over the images conjured up until Eli interrupted, "The interpreter has to sign everything you're saying."

While I attempted to sign everything I heard, Carlos wasn't even watching me at this point. His eyes were closed as if he were bored with it all. It seemed that candy, drugs, alcohol, cigarettes, and movies were the only topics that interested most of these guys.

Verna, finally put a stop to the chaos. "Enough," she called. "Time for meds."

* * *

When I returned the next week I saw that two new clients had moved in at Cherokee House. When one person left, it seemed there was always another to take his place. Verna said most of the time the clients came from jail or the hospitals. Families of these guys were reluctant to take them in. They couldn't cope with fists smashing through walls, or their threats to kill themselves or someone else. The families were too terrified, exhausted, or broken to deal with their loved one's irrational, unpredictable, or violent behavior.

The clients at Cherokee House were stable on medication. They were closely monitored, and their time was structured. They had chores and rules to follow. They were required to be out of the house during the day and to return by curfew. If they messed up, they were out. Usually, that meant they were back on the streets and would likely go off their medication from lack of money or disorganization, or because they decided they didn't need it anymore.

If someone with a mental illness goes off their medication, their disturbed thoughts and feelings will return. Some turn to illegal drugs to self-medicate. Others commit crimes to get money to buy drugs or to feed themselves. Sooner or later they get caught, arrested, and thrown back in jail, or they become so delusional that their erratic behavior gets them readmitted to the psychiatric hospital. It's the cycle known as "the revolving door." Those working in the system know it well. They see patients returning to the psych ward over and over again.

Both of the new clients at Cherokee House were African American. Tito, wearing a puffy parka inside the house, sat staring at me with beady eyes. He moved slowly, looking like he was about to say something, but the words were stuck in his throat. Rudy, a small thin man, came in wearing a red knit hat. Verna wanted the group to go over the house rules for the new members. So she asked each client to recite one.

"Be out of the house from 9:00 to 3:00," Ronnie stated.

Nick offered, "Show up for group."

"Clean your room," Demonde droned.

As they spat out the rules, one by one, it was clear the guys could all recite them, probably even in their sleep.

Later, Verna whispered to me in her office, "Going over the rules was for Tito, so he'll start following them. He won't get up in the morning." She told me that twice that week, she had to call his case manager to come and wake him up. "He makes me nervous," she said with a shudder. "There's something odd about him, but he's on his way out of here."

"You mean he's moving on, or getting kicked out?" Ordinarily, I didn't ask questions about the clients, but some happenings in this house affected me, too. I was part of the dynamic.

"Evicted," Verna replied.

As loud and tough as she appeared, even Verna had vulnerabilities. She admitted she got scared sometimes. If Verna was scared, then I was definitely scared. She was the only protection I had if any one of them suddenly decided to turn violent. I was confident the staff was trained on how to handle such situations, but no one had instructed me on what I should do in such an event. I thought about this on my drive home that evening, along with my husband's constant warning to me every time I left to go to work: "Be careful!"

True to Verna's word, Tito was gone from Cherokee House after the weekend. It was a relief to not have his eyes following me anymore. That day the issue at hand was broken objects in the house. The toilet on the main floor was the biggest problem, and the guys were complaining, "The bathroom stinks." There were burned-out light bulbs and other small things they brought up that needed fixing. As they spoke, Verna made a list of them. I was just glad the bedbug problem seemed to be resolved—at least no one was talking about it anymore.

Following the discussion about broken objects, Verna asked the guys, as usual, for their feedback. She kept track of who contributed and who didn't on her yellow legal pad. She started with Ronnie. "Do you have any feedback for the group?"

"Yeah. The interpreter turns me on."

"Ronnie, that's dirty!" Verna hollered.

Zach jumped out of his seat, starting toward Ronnie. "That's not appropriate!"

My signing hands froze mid-sentence as my brain whirled and spun. They had been talking about toilets and broken objects. Where did this come from? Clearly, Ronnie was not with the group, thinking of things that needed fixing. He was with another group—the voices in his head—and suddenly I was on the spot. Carlos was probably wondering what was going on for Zach to have jumped up so suddenly. I told him that Ronnie said something bad about the interpreter. I should have told him what Ronnie said, but I'd gotten knocked off course.

I drove home that evening wondering if perhaps I had become the distraction that Verna originally feared. Maybe she would decide not to have me come back. I questioned it myself, but I had grown to like this job. I didn't want to leave.

***

It was cold and dark when I finished work. I'd been in Denver without my cell phone all day. When I got home, I found my phone on the counter, exactly where I had left it in my rush that morning. There were six new messages, all from Cyndi. What could she want?

Ever since I talked to her brother, I felt I had an ally. The morning I called him right before Christmas, I was nervous about how he was going to react when I told him I thought something was wrong with his sister. Surprisingly, he was receptive and said that he, too, had been puzzled by her behavior and the things she said. Jeff admitted he had been struggling with Cyndi, too. We agreed to work together to figure out what to do.

Before I got my coat off, the phone rang. It was Cyndi again.

"I'm going to Oklahoma with Jake and my medicine man. We're leaving tonight and I need you to take Pocahontas." Cyndi was adamant that I come right away.

"What's going on? I just got home. Can't I come get her tomorrow?"

"No, we're leaving tonight."

"Why? Where are you going?"

"They're building a house for me on the reservation, and I have to be there to tell them what I need for my wheelchair, for the counters…"

I was baffled about this reservation and peeved by her urgency. "What time are you leaving?

"As soon as Jake gets here with the van."

I'd never seen the new van. As far as I knew, she hadn't either. I was still wondering if there really was a van, and why they were building a house for her, and where this reservation was.

"Where is the van?" I asked.

"They're fixing it. They'll be here as soon as they get it up and running. Can you come now to get the cat?"

"What's wrong with the van? Isn't it new?"

"Something was wrong with the new wheelchair lift."

It seemed odd that something could be wrong with a brand new van, with a brand new wheelchair lift, and brand new hand controls. For months Cyndi had been saying the van was in the shop, getting converted for her to drive it. I'd stopped believing this, but now she was insisting. This was madness.

"Cyndi, I just got home. It's a long drive back to Denver—more than an hour. Why are you leaving tonight? Are you going to drive through the night?"

"Yup."

"Why not leave in the morning? I can pick up the kitten then."

"No, we have to get there as soon as possible."

"Could I meet you halfway or something?"

"Wait…my CNA is just leaving…"

The CNA agreed to meet me halfway with the cat. An hour and a half later as the snow began to fall, I arrived back home with Pocahontas. Jim was delighted to see her again.

By morning the snowstorm had turned into a blizzard and my interpreting job was cancelled. I was relieved that I didn't have to drive anywhere, but looking around the house I couldn't find Pocahontas. I searched for her under beds and behind furniture, wondering whether Cyndi, Jake, and the medicine man had made it safely to Oklahoma. Pocahontas was not in any of the bedrooms, nor downstairs or in the living room. Finally, as the phone started ringing, I spotted her on the third shelf in the bathroom closet, sleeping on a pile of towels. I hadn't thought to look up high for her.

It was Cyndi on the phone.

"Are you in Oklahoma?"

"No," she said. "We didn't go. Can you bring Pokey back?"

This was unbelievable. I was furious: "Cyndi, we have three feet of snow! I'm not driving anywhere."

She knew she had no power to manipulate me into bringing the cat back right then. Though reluctant, she gave in. We ended up keeping the cat for four days. Jim and Pokey had become friends, and he'd grown attached to her. When it was time to take Pocahontas home, I had to pry her from Jim's arms.

"Why don't we just keep her?" he said. "You know Cyndi's going to ask you to take care of her again." While I knew he was probably right, I also knew what I had to do.

* * *

Cyndi was in her living room unpacking her doll collection and Indian figurines with her CNA when I arrived with Pocahontas in her cardboard carrier. Cyndi's hair was freshly braided and her cheeks were pink with fever from an infection that was still plaguing her. Before anyone said a word, Pocahontas jumped out of the cardboard box. Racing around the room, she ran from Cyndi in her wheelchair and leapt onto the dining room table, scattering various items onto the floor, provoking Cyndi.

"Pokey, get down," she hollered. "Did you learn some bad habits? You know you're not supposed to be on the table."

I felt Cyndi's scolding directed more at me than the cat for having kept her for so long—as if it were my fault. Jumping up on the table was something cats did. I didn't think it should merit this much anger, but it permeated the room. The house suddenly felt inhospitable, and I wanted to disappear. It was the first time I'd felt this tense around Cyndi. I politely excused myself and left.

I didn't expect to hear from Cyndi for a while after that, figuring she was pretty mad at me, but she called a few days later, acting as though nothing happened. She told me that her medicine man and Tuku were arrested on their way to her house. The medicine man was in jail and Tuku had been taken to the pound. The new live-in nurse, also from the reservation, was supposedly on her way to Cyndi's place as well, but now she was with the van.

"Where's the van?" I asked.

"At Three Wheels, where it's getting fixed. The nurse has to stay with the van because it's loaded with $12,000 worth of gifts. The gifts are for me from the tribe, because I am now the new, and the very first, woman chief. They're showering me with gifts!"

"How nice."

According to Cyndi, the medicine man and Tuku had been on a bus, bringing a "shitload of pot" for himself and for her. "We both have papers for it, for medical reasons," she said, "but he forgot the papers, so he got busted. It'll cost $500 to get him out of jail and $300 to get Tuku out of the pound."

This was total craziness, her grandiose fantasies, the inconsistencies, and contradictions. Tuku was a she, now he was a he. All the poor decisions, her spending problems, her anger, her denial and irritability. Adding them all up, they could only mean one thing: Cyndi was mentally ill.

* * *

As I sat next to Cyndi's bed while she rested one afternoon, she told me about Tuku, who, not surprisingly, was not there. Tuku was being trained to become a service dog for Cyndi. "She'll be here in a week or so," she said. "Well, she's not really a wolf. She's part Shepherd and part Husky…"

My sporadic involvement with Cyndi made it difficult to know which things in her day-to-day life were true and which were part of her illness or imagination. I didn't know how to react to her. Should I go along with her stories, or confront her with the irrationality? Neither choice seemed right. Mostly, I listened and nodded, hoping the next time I saw her, I would have figured out whether something she told me was true, or she would have forgotten it and we wouldn't have to talk about it anymore. But too often, she'd bring up the crazy idea again with a new twist or curve. She never seemed to forget these ideas. Instead, she would build upon them until they became more and more elaborate.

I was disappointed to hear Cyndi keep saying she was getting the wolf. She hadn't had good outcomes with her previous *real* dogs. After her mother passed away she couldn't take care of the two she had and had to give them away. "You're really getting a Husky?" I asked. "They're sled dogs. They need to run. Jim and I raised three Huskies. They need a lot of exercise," I said, remembering how ours hated being penned up and frequently dug under or chewed through our wooden slat fence to escape. I couldn't imagine how Cyndi thought she could keep one in her tiny home with no yard. I kept trying to convince her that it was not a good idea. "Huskies are very independent. They need a lot of room, and they need a big yard!"

Cyndi was unfazed. "This dog will be fine," she said, with a confident smile.

5

Textbook Schizophrenia

Carlos may as well have been appointed supervisor at Cherokee House, the way he would watch over everyone and how he'd await me out on the street and then escort me to the office where Verna was usually preoccupied with one thing or another. I'd stand behind him while he'd tap on his wrist, signaling to her that it was time for group. One evening he had a manila folder wedged under his arm, lending him an air of importance. He pulled a stapled bunch of papers from the folder and handed them to me.

"It's your copy," he signed.

A glance at the papers showed me they were about the transit system—new TVs on the light rail and buses. I assumed he planned to share this information with the group.

"Do you ride the light rail?" I asked, signing and speaking aloud.

Verna answered for him. "No. It's too expensive. It costs $1.75."

"Are there TVs on your buses?" I asked Carlos.

"No, too expensive," he signed.

"What are the TVs for?'

"For the police, to watch out for fights," he answered looking concerned.

I gathered they were video cameras. There wasn't time to read the information before Verna yelled up the stairs, rousing the stragglers from their rooms. The guys on the couches were unfazed by her thunder call, though I still found it unnerving. Ernie, per usual, was the last one to emerge. We all waited as he limped down the stairs.

This meeting was nothing more than Verna announcing, "All chores must be finished by 4:00, except for the kitchen."

She announced this as though it were something new, a change in the rules, even though I'd heard it many times since I'd been coming here.

With no further discussion, she went straight to asking for feedback. She called on Jesse, who everyone knows never says a word. Slumped down in his customary way with his head supported by the back of the couch, his belly was just round enough to make him look healthy. Jesse smiled, like he was honestly going to say something this time. My hands were up, ready to interpret, but nothing came except for tremors from his hand, a side effect of long-term use of antipsychotic medications. Verna spoke for him, as though she were reading his mind and counted it as his feedback. I could tell she cared about her boys.

She then called on Carlos, who slouched next to Jesse, exhibited the same poor posture. With the manila folder pressed against his chest, his signs were lazy, too sloppy for me to decipher what he was saying. I voiced something about Office Max and Zach talking to someone. The guys tried to figure out what Carlos was talking about.

"I'm lost," Verna said.

Carlos sat up straight. Sliding the folder to his lap he repeated what he said before, making his signs more precise. He said he went to Office Max, and he saw Zach talking to someone in front of the coffee shop where the guys go sometimes.

"You mean Starbucks?" someone asked.

"Yeah."

He didn't mention the information he printed about the video surveillance cameras. I guess he had other plans for the papers in the folder. After the meeting, Carlos was first in line for meds. I sat at Verna's desk, keeping a lookout for small bugs that might be crawling over her desk or on the grungy carpet, while she pulled the medicine containers from the closet. She handed one to Carlos. He poured himself some water from a pitcher and swallowed a handful of pills with one gulp. He then hovered over the next guy and the others, watching while they each took their meds. I was hoping that Carlos could have a job someday, doing something where he could use his supervisory skills.

Ronnie sat at the other side of Verna's desk staring at me while he waited his turn. I did my best to ignore him, but he spoke to me anyway.

"My voices said that I am God, and I invented the word *suicide*. That's why I to have to carry it out."

He waited for my reaction. I knew I should not respond at all, but I found myself asking, "The voices told you that?"

"Yeah."

"Recently?"

"Uh-huh," he nodded.

Sliding the last med container back onto the shelf, Vera took the heat off of me, once again. "Ronnie, she's not a therapist."

"I'm a re-creation of my left nut," he added.

My worry as to where this conversation was going was nipped in the bud when Zach jumped in. "That's not appropriate, Ronnie."

"It's rude," Verna scolded.

"I'm not trying to be rude. I'm serious," Ronnie said. "I'm a re-creation of my left nut!"

I glanced at the clock. It was seven. Carlos, "the supervisor," knew it, too, and alerted me as if I hadn't been watching the time myself.

"Verna, Carlos is saying it's time for me to take off."

Nodding, she slid the last box onto the shelf and locked the cabinet. "Yeah, he's keeping us all in line."

Carlos walked me out to the street. As we moved along I replayed in my mind what just happened in the office. Zach had intervened once again, protecting me. Despite their own issues, the guys were looking out for me.

* * *

The bugs were back. It had been two months since the last outbreak, and Verna was in a rage over this new one. The inspector had come and picked one off of her shirt. She suspected that the two new clients who had been in homeless shelters recently had brought in the bugs.

She told the guys, "I don't know if the landlord wants to spray the whole house or just the rooms where we found the bugs. We may have to move all the furniture out of the rooms and lean the mattresses up against the walls, just like we did before. Or if you guys are getting stuff out of dumpsters and bringing it home, it could have bugs."

I noticed her looking specifically at Ernie, known for his dumpster diving, who was asleep on the couch with his head pressed against Ronnie's shoulder.

As I sat on a metal folding chair interpreting for Carlos, I convinced myself that bugs didn't like metal. When the meeting finished, I stood for the remaining hour, remembering my vow to not touch anything or sit in one of the upholstered chairs. At home, I decided not to mention the bedbugs. I was afraid if I did, Jim would demand that I stop working at Cherokee House. And I wasn't ready to do that.

* * *

Cyndi was back in the hospital with an infection. I visited her each day I could. She told me she hadn't been sleeping. "Why not?" I asked.

"I've been working, healing people. We have a list of 100 people. We've raised a million dollars!"

She went on saying that she and the medicine man were healing them and that she had stayed awake all night waving her sage stick while chanting healing songs for the sick people on her list. She didn't mention what the million dollars was being raised for.

I didn't believe any of it, though I didn't doubt that she had been awake all night. I left the hospital thinking maybe it was time to contact her brother again, to see what he thought about getting her a psychological evaluation. I planned to call Jeff after work, but I started feeling ill.

At first, the pain was just a glimmer in my abdomen. When it started coming in waves I figured I should get home and called in sick for my last assignment. I was nervous starting the drive, worried that I'd suddenly need a bathroom at an inconvenient spot. Snow had begun falling and the road was covered in white. Halfway to Conifer, with the snow coming down thick and heavy, the pain intensified and I started feeling faint. At a turnoff, with no others in sight, I got out of the car and squatted behind it in the blowing snow.

The diarrhea lasted three straight days. I missed work and lost nine pounds. Days later, when I was feeling better, I was reaching for my vitamins and fish oil in the pantry, when it dawned on me. The fish oil, the pure stuff the doctor recommended, which I had to drive all over town searching for, is what made me sick. I'd been taking it for less than two weeks. I gathered the bottles of the expensive supplement and threw them in the trash. I went back to work, adding another vow to my list: quit trying so hard to be healthy. It was then I remembered, I never called Jeff.

* * *

Getting in touch with Cyndi's brother slipped my mind, as interpreting assignments piled onto my schedule. A last-minute request came late one afternoon from a medical clinic. They had forgotten to arrange for an interpreter for a patient's eye exam, and they needed someone as soon as possible. I'd just finished a job and told them I could get there in 15 minutes.

Serena, the deaf patient, was in the waiting room. With her long blond hair pulled back into a clasp, I recognized her from past assignments, recalling how confrontational she'd been, not to me but toward the person she was meeting with. She'd acted irrationally. Now, after waiting over an hour for an interpreter, Serena was visibly upset.

"I know it's frustrating," I signed. "I'm here now; it's okay."

"It's not okay," she replied. "I need you to tell the woman to write what happened and sign her name."

We approached the reception desk and Serena had me interpret her demand to the young receptionist.

"I don't understand. What does she want me to write?" the woman asked. I signed her question to Serena.

"No, not you," Serena signed. "The other woman who was here before. I want to speak to her again." She pointed to the hallway, indicating where the previous receptionist had gone. I didn't know what transpired before I arrived that had Serena so upset.

"Well, she's busy with another patient right now," the receptionist said.

Serena didn't believe her. "What patient?" she demanded, looking around the empty waiting room. "I haven't seen any other patients."

The same edgy feeling I'd felt before while interpreting for Serena crept in.

"I'm sorry," the woman insisted. "She's with another patient. You can have a seat until she becomes available."

Reluctantly, Serena acquiesced.

While we waited, Serena complained to me about the clinic, saying the staff was in a conspiracy against her. Fortunately, we didn't have to wait long. When the receptionist that Serena wanted to speak with appeared, Serena handed her a piece of paper and, with me interpreting, demanded that she write a statement.

"What do you want me to write?" the woman snapped.

"Explain what happened and sign your name," Serena signed.

With a sigh, the woman gave us a disgusted look, turned around, and disappeared down the hall. I was starting to bemoan racing over here, only to jump into this unpleasant situation, when a man in a suit with a pained look on his face and mussed hair approached.

"What seems to be the problem?" he asked.

When he suggested that we move to a more private area to talk, Serena refused.

"I have nothing to hide" she signed emphatically. "We can talk right here in the waiting area."

"I'll tell you what," the man said. "Why don't we go ahead with your eye exam? We can deal with this later."

It seemed like a reasonable idea to me. We followed him down the hall to where they had the machine that shoots a puff of air into your eyes to check for glaucoma, but things didn't go smoothly there, either.

Pointing to the machine, Serena signed, "What's that?" She stepped back as if the machine were dangerous. "Who are you?" She asked the technician.

Before the technician could answer, Serena decided she didn't want this person to test her eyes. She demanded to have someone else, the person she had before, but that person had already left for the day. The man in the suit was still with us.

He looked at me and said, "We can skip the preliminary exam."

Everyone seemed to be walking on eggshells around Serena, including the doctor. From the examination chair Serena handed him a pair of glasses.

"These are not right," she signed.

Apparently, this doctor had seen her recently. After he reexamined her eyes, he told her that the glasses were fine, that she indeed had the right prescription.

"No," Serena said, "something is wrong with them, I don't want them."

The doctor's kind demeanor faded as he shook his head. "That's all I can do for you. If you are still unhappy, you can see another doctor."

It was not until that evening while I was cooking dinner that an explanation for Serena's behavior came to me: *paranoid schizophrenia*. Could that be what was going on with her? The times before when I had interpreted for her, she had also made assertions of people conspiring against her. She'd stated that the government was spying on her, but she said she was on to them and wasn't going to let them manipulate her.

I recalled the nervous, uncomfortable reactions of the people she had met with. I remembered thinking while I was interpreting, *this is craziness*, but the word *schizophrenia* hadn't occurred to me. I had believed that people with schizophrenia were homeless, disheveled souls, who talked to themselves while pushing shopping carts full of dirty blankets and such along 16th Street. But I had just realized this wasn't always so.

The revelation took me back to an experience I had early in my career when a well-educated Deaf man told me that he had been drugged by the DEA. I figured the DEA was some government agency and thought this sounded odd. "What is the DEA?" I asked him.

"The Drug Enforcement Administration," he said.

I couldn't imagine how, or why, these people would drug him and wasn't sure if I believed it. I nodded politely while imagining men dressed in black, clandestinely operating on his head.

"Why did they do that?" I asked.

"It's a long story," he said. "No one believes me, but I know it really happened."

I'd learned in college that delusional thinking was a symptom of schizophrenia. Often it's a belief that a computer chip or something has been implanted into their brain, or body, against their will, or that the government is plotting against them. This man's belief that the DEA had drugged him was textbook schizophrenia, yet he looked and behaved like a normal person.

I was a young, unseasoned interpreter working in the community, and even though schizophrenia was staring me in the face, I didn't see it. I interpreted for this man a few more times and eventually realized he had a mental illness.

The last time I saw him he told me he was getting his life together and going back to school. Shortly after, I learned that he had killed himself. I was shocked. The fact is that suicide is not uncommon in individuals suffering from schizophrenia. Sadly, it often happens when they are getting better, when their mind becomes clear enough that they can carry it out.

As for Serena, she unveiled a truth to me: People struggling with mental illness are not just the homeless ones downtown, pushing overstuffed shopping carts along streets.

6

Matters of Importance

Carlos was standing in the street between ridges of ice leftover from last week's snowstorm when I pulled up for work. There was little traffic in front of Cherokee House, yet it was dark and hard for motorists to see him. It wasn't exactly a safe place for him to be waiting.

After I parked and stepped out of the car, I noticed Carlos' glasses were broken. With one of the arms missing, they sat crooked on his face, as if his way of seeing the world wasn't distorted enough. He said nothing about his glasses. Instead, he asked if anyone had called me the week before to cancel.

"Yeah, they called me."

Then he told me why my assignment had been cancelled. "I got kicked out—for smoking weed."

He looked remorseful, though I sensed that he was not that sorry because this was not the first time it had happened. He knew the rules and what would happen if you broke them: You got to spend the night on the street, or in a homeless shelter if you were lucky.

In group Carlos watched me interpret peering through a paper with two eyeholes cut out of it. The paper was an advertisement for clear or transition lenses that changed to dark when you went outside. His antics were amusing, though I didn't encourage him. I proceeded to interpret to the paper face, while the group discussed the ghosts in the house. Ronnie said he'd seen the shadows and others said they heard them.

"I hear them talking," Sean said, with a wide smile as if he were bragging. With his broad shoulders and muscular arms, maybe he was not afraid of ghosts. "They repeat what I'm thinking," he added.

Rather than trying to dissuade them from believing that the house had ghosts, Verna assured them, "The ghosts here aren't evil."

It was a way to lessen the chance of someone getting anxious or riled up. It was the same during Halloween when she didn't allow scary costumes or masks. "It's not good for these guys," she'd told me when others were not around.

Zach changed the subject from the ghosts when he turned to Carlos. "What'd you get kicked out for yesterday?"

"Using."

"Using what? Crack?"

The guys threw out several guesses: "Weed? Rubbing alcohol? Cough medicine? Glue?" "Did the pillow get stuck to your face?" They busted up laughing. "Maybe it was paint thinner," another one teased. "That'll kill your brain real fast."

I was uncomfortable interpreting their poking fun at Carlos. In true Carlos form, he just nodded his head, like yeah, yeah, I've heard this before.

At the end of my shift, Verna called for Zach and asked him to walk me outside and watch me till I got in the car. She didn't say why, but then she had mentioned earlier there had been some recent violence in the neighborhood involving parolees.

That night I drove home with myriad thoughts. It was always good when Verna and I could debrief after meetings. It helped me understand the guys better and process what went on, like what Ronnie had said a week ago.

I'd asked Verna, "For some—do their meds not really work?"

"The meds help, but not totally," she said.

She told me that Ronnie took eight medications, twice a day, but he still heard voices.

"Miguel seems practically catatonic," I'd said.

Agreeing, Verna added, "We've got a real assortment: Catatonics, stalkers, bipolar huffers and puffers, a mainliner, a dumpster digger, a trash-food eater, and a re-creation of a left nut!"

Verna could always make me laugh.

* * *

Damien was back. He'd been in an inpatient program for a while. When I first noticed him, I did a double-take. He'd dyed his hair blond. He'd been kicked out of Cherokee House for using. I thought the rule was that you didn't get to come back after you'd been kicked out. But here he was. Carlos had gotten to come back, too.

"Damien was smoking rock tonight," the guys reported. Two of them said he invited them to smoke, too. Another client, Derrick, had been threatening Ernie because Ernie used his bathroom without permission and urinated on the floor, so Verna issued a warning, "Don't be threatening anybody or you could find yourself getting dragged to the hospital!"

I couldn't help but notice the dichotomy between this microcosmic social environment and the rest of society. Here, matters of importance surrounded learning how to be a responsible member of the house. Meanwhile, the rest of the world was focused on the Winter Olympics, on athletes who had worked and trained for years, striving for top physical and mental excellence, hoping to win a gold medal.

I was not without my own issues. My adult daughter was threatening to quit her job at a preschool. "I can't stand my classroom aide," she said. "If I quit, I'll have to move back home."

I couldn't solve her problems for her, so I just listened. I was up in the air on my own decisions, anyway. Should I register for the national interpreter conference in San Francisco? Should I propose to teach a workshop? Should I call my mother-in-law and offer to take her to lunch instead of cleaning my house? I ended up doing none of these things and ran errands for my husband instead.

* * *

On the phone with my sister one day, she told me about her friend, Susan, whose adult son has schizophrenia. He lives with his mother, and she is afraid of him. He paints violent images and writes frightful messages on the wall in their house. Susan called the police on him once, but they said, "Without sufficient evidence that he is in imminent danger to himself or others, there is nothing we can do."

Susan worried about what her son might do next. She was angry and frustrated with the system. Since her son was an adult, she had no power to make decisions for him. She could urge him to get treatment, but under our current laws he had the right to refuse.

"He doesn't want treatment," Susan said, "because he doesn't think there is anything wrong with him."

I heard the concern in my sister's voice, wishing I had something helpful to say, but I had nothing to offer.

When I saw my sister some weeks later, I asked about Susan and her son. She said he'd recently started a fire in their basement. Susan was at her wits' end. She changed the locks on all the doors because she didn't know what else to do. Since then Susan hadn't heard from her son and didn't know where he was, but she worried constantly that he was going to come back and hurt her.

As a mother, I can't imagine how devastating it must be, to be so afraid of your own son, that you have to lock him out, and then worry because you don't know where he is, or if he's even alive.

7

A Call From Denny's

Spring 2007

A social worker walked me to a patient's room on one of Denver's filled-to-capacity hospital psychiatric wards. "This hall has rooms with video cameras, so we can monitor the patients on suicide watch 24/7," she explained. "Olivia is here because she stopped taking her medicine and has been suicidal."

We found Olivia asleep on the bed. The social worker tapped her on the shoulder and Olivia opened her eyes.

"Would you like to get up?" the social worker asked. "The interpreter is here. I can show you around the unit."

When I signed to Olivia, she rose from the bed. Disheveled in green hospital scrubs, she willingly followed us. With her flawless skin, Olivia could have been in her thirties, yet her mature body shape belied that age, so I really couldn't tell how old she was. The social worker showed us the community room and where to get snacks. She introduced us to the process group, where Olivia and I slipped in, joining the circle of patients discussing how they might think and live differently, once they got out of the hospital. Interpreting for group therapy was nothing new to me. I enjoyed the work because I believe we can always get better, even at the lowest points in our lives.

Unlike Olivia, the other patients were in street clothes. While articulate, their conversation was slow, and they seemed sad and unmotivated. A few admitted to feeling hopeless. Two, nearing discharge, read their safety plans aloud with the actions they promised to carry out if they felt suicidal again.

Olivia stared at me as I signed. Her foot jittered against the floor, causing her knee to vibrate up and down. The muscle twitching, a side effect of medication I assumed, didn't seem to bother her. Olivia sat quietly during the group session.

The following day when I returned to the ward, Olivia was no longer in the process group with the depressives. They'd moved her to another group where we gathered around a big table, which hid her foot and leg jitters, but there was a new distraction. A patient with abnormal eye blinking and mouth movements, kept me thinking she was about to say something. My hands came up automatically, ready to interpret, but she did not speak. I soon realized her twitches were involuntary and stopped reacting to them.

The pace of this group was much slower than the one yesterday. Olivia watched me with heavy eyes. A few times she started to nod off in her chair, but fought it off and stayed with me, taking part in the activity. It seemed this group was a better fit for her than the process group.

On my fourth day, It surprised me to hear that things had gone downhill after I left the day before. I found Olivia, wrapped in a blanket, curled up in a chair in front of the nurse's station where she'd been all night. The staff said Olivia was put there last evening after burning her forearm with a cigarette during a smoke break. I interpreted as Olivia told the staff she did it because she wanted to kill herself.

"I want to be D-E-A-D," she fingerspelled.

The chair she'd been sleeping in looked horribly uncomfortable for that purpose, but Olivia didn't look any worse than she had for the last few days. She still hadn't bathed and was wearing the same set of hospital scrubs. Olivia's mood was as scruffy as her short hair, flattened on one side and sticking straight up on the other.

"I want to hit that man," she signed, mad at the person who told her yesterday she couldn't have any more cigarettes.

As if they'd already dealt with the issue long enough, no one reacted to her comments. Instead, one of the staff ushered us off to a group, where the therapist was handing out paper and pencils. To get everyone's mind off their troubles, she asked them to write three things they were grateful for. When the therapist noticed everyone writing except Olivia she asked her, "What makes you happy?"

I signed and Olivia replied with a question, "Swimming?"

"Yes, you can write that," the therapist said.

A few read their list aloud, and the therapist told the other patients to raise their hand if they heard the same word that they had written. The severely depressed patients and those who were hallucinating or hearing voices had a hard time focusing. For them, this task was difficult. Most were in the hospital getting regulated on their medications, which made them sleepy. Some barely paid attention.

"I want to go home," Olivia signed.

"Try to keep positive. Think of things you're grateful for," the therapist reminded her.

It was the same theme with Olivia every day for the next two weeks. She wanted to go home. Twice, she tried to escape. One of the times I watched her crawl along the floor beneath the counter of the nurse's station, toward the exit. Crouched below, she waited, I assume, for someone to open the exit door so she could fly out before anyone caught her.

The staff seemed more put off by Olivia's behavior than worried about her escaping. These acts only got her put into seclusion in her room with everything taken away, except for a pillow and bedsheets. But even those were gone after she wound one of the sheets around her neck.

Having no other options in her eyes, Olivia threatened to stop taking her mediation, and with her last ounce of power, informed them, "I won't eat."

It saddened me to see a person in such a state and to hear words, I would never say, come out of my mouth as I interpreted for her.

Chatting with some of the staff during a lunch break one day, I learned that most of the patients came to the locked unit from the hospital emergency room. I asked, "What kinds of things bring them initially into the ER?"

"They get a call from Denny's," someone behind me replied.

"Yeah," another person interjected, "the police bring them in after they're found loitering somewhere, talking to themselves. Or sometimes they call 911 on their own, after they've thrown their TV out the window, because the people on the set were talking to them, giving them messages."

Through the staff's candor I learned the ropes of the mental health system. In less than two weeks I'd eased into working there and almost wished it weren't a temporary assignment. The staff showed me respect, and I was used to the other patients, like Carlotta, who dressed in snow pants and a down parka every day while it was pushing 60 degrees outside. Carlotta wore her hair in pigtails with big white sunglasses perched on top of her head. She carried a huge satchel. I watched her pull out a tube of dark pink lipstick and smear it over her lips as she talked to the other patients about her kids.

"I make them waffles every morning," she said," with Karo syrup."

She insisted that it had to be Karo. Carlotta was kind and mothered the other patients. I pictured her family at home, her kids, who have a mother who thinks it's normal to wear snow clothes indoors on a warm day.

I thought about the others as well. Though I was not privy to any patient information, I learned things about them while interpreting in the groups. The staff, however, told me, "Olivia does so much better when you're here. There are no emotional outbursts or behavioral upsets."

That is my role. Like electricity, to a deaf person, interpreters bring light and meaning into the room.

* * *

On the fourteenth day of her hospitalization, Olivia stood at the counter of the nurse's station. I interpreted as she asked for a shower, her first since she'd been on the ward. A mental health problem can affect a person's ability and motivation for caring for themselves, and poor hygiene is often a red flag for depression. A lot of the newly admitted patients were unkempt.

Everyone took this as a good sign. Olivia returned from her shower in clean scrubs with wet, uncombed hair. A nurse ushered us into the morning group. For the activity that day, the patients were to interview each other, to encourage getting out of their own heads by engaging in conversation.

Half of the patients were nodding off. One, with her elbow on the chair's armrest, held her head up with her hand. Another rested his head on his folded arms on the table. He startled us when he suddenly looked up and yelled, "Stop talking you guys, Goddamn it."

Nobody responded to him. It took me a second to realize it was not the other patients he was talking to, but to the voices in his head.

Olivia's partner for the exercise was a petite Korean woman. Listening to her pleasing accent reminded me that mental illness affects people from all walks of life, in every country. For a second I lamented that Olivia had no way to appreciate interesting foreign accents. I was sure she had other thoughts on her mind anyway. Unlike the other day when she sat quiet and had a hard time thinking of something to write, Olivia was alert, observing the other patients. I called it progress. Considering how uncommunicative she had been, I was curious how Olivia would manage this "talking" game.

She surprised me by coming up with several questions for her partner: "How old are you? Where do you live? Do you have a cat?"

Her Korean partner, however, was not quite up to the task. She couldn't think of anything to ask Olivia. She said her family was all gone. "Every one of them has gone to heaven and I am the only one left."

"What happened?" Olivia asked.

"Something bad. I was a very bad girl."

Olivia accepted this answer with no further question, leaving me wondering what terrible things happened to this unfortunate woman. Was it the trauma of losing her family that brought her into the hospital? Or was it psychosis telling her that her family members were gone when they were actually fine? I will never know, but I'll always remember this petite woman with the sweet accent.

There was joy in Olivia's eyes on the day of her release from the hospital. She was going to a group home run by the state mental health system until they could find her a permanent place to live. Moving to a group home is not something most people would relish, nevertheless, Olivia was all smiles that day. While I was happy for her, a part of me was sad that my job there was ending.

8

A Step Up

For patients, leaving a psychiatric hospital and moving to a group home is a step up. From my perspective, Cherokee House was more than just one step up from the locked ward. In a group home, clients have supervision, but they are also allowed to go independently into the community. This is huge. Being locked up takes away a person's dignity. In the group home they pay rent and are responsible to cook, and clean. They're encouraged to work or engage in activity outside of Cherokee House, and out they go, even if the temperature is freezing.

One evening at the start of my shift Carlos had just come in from the cold wearing coveralls over his clothes. I gathered he'd picked them up at one of the mental health center's clothes banks. The guys were teasing him for wearing them, calling him Dick.

Ronnie called out, "Hey Diane, have you met Dick?"

It had been a while since Ronnie acknowledged me, since the day he embarrassed himself with "the interpreter turns me on" comment.

"Yeah, Dickie's our new client," Demonde quipped.

The guys laughed and someone yelled, "How about calling Carlos *Dick Head*?"

"Yeah, how do you sign that one?" another called out.

I was put off by the tasteless joking and thankful that Carlos was no longer paying attention, so I didn't have to interpret their last comments.

I glanced over and caught Nick watching me as if he understood the uncomfortable situation I was in. Nick had not participated in the teasing. We gave each other a look that said we were the prudent ones here.

It was not until the end of my shift that I realized where the teasing was coming from. On the front pocket of Carlos' coveralls was the brand name Dickies®.

* * *

Another difference between a psychiatric hospital and a group home is when you are in the hospital, you are a *mental patient*, and your stay is usually as short as possible. Whereas, in the group home, you are a resident with a mental illness, and your stay is longer. It can be as long as two years.

Carlos was near that halfway point at Cherokee House. Today, I noticed he had fixed his glasses. They weren't crooked anymore. Between the dark strands of his long hair I could see the temple piece reattached with tightly wound bright red yarn.

Before the meeting began, Carlos said he wanted to show me something and ran up the stairs to get it. When he came back, I saw it was another yarn project. He had a small screen and a sponge along with a purple skein of yarn. As he began unraveling the skein, I asked him what the sponge was for, but then the meeting started.

The group discussion was about bugs again. The exterminator was coming the next day to spray a couple of rooms. I no longer had the same level of anxiety regarding the bedbugs now. If the exterminator was spraying only two bedrooms out of the five, then the bug problem didn't seem as egregious to me as it did before, nor as disgusting. As with Pine-Sol, the longer you're exposed to something, the more you get used to it.

Verna put the topic of bedbugs aside to announce it was time for the pillow exchange and sent the guys to their rooms. They came back with stained and dirty pillows, some exuding wafts of mold. In solemn procession, they dropped their pillows into plastic bags to be disposed of. When the bags were full and tied shut, Verna handed each resident a new white fluffy pillow. I saw it as another step upward.

Remembering the purple yarn project on my way home, for the life of me, I couldn't figure out how the yarn and the screen were to go together, and the sponge. What the heck was the sponge for?

* * *

Smoking was the topic of the next house meeting. Nearly all the guys at Cherokee House smoked. As Verna read to us about all the cancer-causing chemicals in cigarettes, we also learned that among individuals with schizophrenia, 90% are addicted to cigarettes and there are various theories as to why. Some say smoking reduces depression or tremors caused by antipsychotic medications, and others say that nicotine temporarily reduces fear, confusion, and delusions. While scientists are still studying the effects of nicotine on the schizophrenic brain, they have determined that frequent use of marijuana before the age of 18, when the brain is still developing, puts an individual at particular risk for developing schizophrenia.

While I thought this was fascinating information, the guys had little to say about it. And after the meeting and their evening meds, a few of them still went out to smoke. I left with the vision of Eli in my mind, smoking with his head against the brick of the house, cushioned by his forearm.

When I returned the next week, Eli was sitting in his usual place on the couch. While we waited for the stragglers to show up, he told me he was leaving the group home.

"I'm moving to a place. I just wanted to tell you I think you're real nice," he said.

I was surprised to hear this and was a little sad, too. He seemed to be one of the permanents.

"Thank you, Eli. I wish you well with your move," I said.

Nick had also been looking for a place. "I'm close to getting out," he said, joining the conversation.

Though he'd said nothing about moving on, Carlos seemed to be more on track these days. He wasn't showing me useless stuff he ordered from catalogs anymore. Instead, he would bring out things like a map of his home state of

California to show me where he was from and the school he attended. Still, I couldn't picture Carlos living on his own yet.

When I started working at Cherokee House, I was told the assignment would be ongoing. No one said how long it might be, but I didn't anticipate it being more than a few weeks or months. I still didn't know how much longer I would be here. The funny thing was, I'd settled in. But when Carlos left, I would have to as well.

9

Who Was Keeping Tabs?

I was at home doing laundry when Cyndi called. She was in the hospital again. She said they rushed her in because it was an emergency.

"I have internal bleeding," she said, "and I'm freezing because I'm losing so much blood."

She was talking fast, all in a flutter over the IVs and problems with the veins in both of her arms. I never found out where her bleeding was coming from before she hung up.

Her health problems and hospitalizations were happening so frequently, I couldn't keep up. I didn't know what to do, so I did nothing. Several days passed and Cyndi called again, just as I was entering the post office.

"They're goin' in," she said,

"What do you mean, goin' in?"

"I just had another procedure, a scope," she explained, with no further details.

Not knowing what else to say, I asked, "Do you want a visitor?"

"Yes, sure, but they're screening my visitors. I don't want my aide to come, because I just fired her because she lied to me."

I held the phone away as I sighed. I didn't want to hear about the aide. I wanted to steer clear of Cyndi's troubles. I only wanted to be supportive while she was in the hospital. So, after mailing my package, I headed down the mountain to the hospital. When I got to her room, Cyndi handed me a photo of her insides, which they'd taken during the scope.

"What is this?" I asked.

"It's my intestines. They found the reason for the bleeding. It's a benign tumor," She stated it as though she was a trained radiologist.

"How do you know it's benign?"

"We don't, but I'm convincing myself that it is."

Curious, I asked, "Did they do a biopsy?"

Cyndi shook her head. "They can't. They don't know where to cut me open."

Before I could respond, she changed the subject going back to the clash she had with the aide—something about her stealing Jake's car.

"She was my favorite aide. She tried to rectify the situation, but I can't forgive her."

I didn't ask what the lie was. I knew my questions would only lead to more confusion. To avoid going down another rabbit hole with her, I commented simply, "It sounds hairy." I don't know if it was my comment that led her to drop the subject, but she skipped onto another.

"Guess what?" she asked, smiling. "My medicine man worked on my arms. They're healed, and now the IVs go in. And guess what else? Jake bought me a monkey!"

I'd been hearing about this monkey for months. It was curious that she was bringing this up now. Had she forgotten that she'd already told me about it, including how small and cute it was? And how she was going to buy doll clothes for it to wear? I couldn't even fake a smile. I didn't believe what she was saying about the medicine man or the monkey. But if Jake had bought her a monkey, it would just show how completely foolish they both were. Cyndi was too sick to care for herself, how could she possibly handle a monkey?

Deciding it best to leave before I got pulled into the next drama, I stood and asked Cyndi to call me as soon as she heard something about a surgery.

The next day I was shopping when she called me in tears.

"It doesn't look good. They found a spot on my pancreas. It means it's metastasized!"

"You said they didn't do a biopsy. Did you have a CT scan today?"

"Yeah. They found the spot. I can't believe it."

"But—"

She interrupted me with more talk. None of it was making any sense. So, I told her I had to go to work but I would visit her tomorrow.

When I arrived at the hospital the next morning, the first thing Cyndi said to me was, "I'm not stupid. I know what it is. I'm sure I'll be talking to an oncologist soon."

She acted like she knew everything about cancer, probably because she'd been around it so much with her mother. I wasn't convinced she had cancer, but I listened because I knew she needed someone to talk to. When she asked me to French braid her hair, I finally felt useful. That was, something I could do for her.

* * *

The doctors determined Cyndi's tumor wasn't cancer and soon released her from the hospital. While her cancer scare was over, her crazy phone calls about the dog, the medicine man, Jake, the van, the monkey, and her money problems kept coming. After so many months of dealing with Cyndi, I'd worn my family out with my unending talk and worry about her, as I tried to unravel the mysteries surrounding her stories and behavior. My husband and daughter were at a loss and no longer wished to hear about Cyndi. Respectfully, I stopped sharing the details about her, realizing the burden I'd put on them, though I didn't stop looking for a way to address Cyndi's mental health and to decipher her relationship with Jake.

To understand her I needed to know, was he the one filling her mind with stories of the house on the Indian reservation and promises of a van, a dog, and a monkey? Was he telling her these lies, and she believed him? And why would he even do that? Was he preying on her vulnerability? Was he stealing from her? Or were these fantasies coming straight from Cyndi's imagination? My instincts told me if I pressed her with questions or voiced my concerns, she would get angry and shut me out. She had so few people in her life. I felt bad for her. Without her mother, who could help her and protect her from being taken advantage of? Who could oversee her social, financial, and legal decisions? And who was keeping tabs on her mental state?

I figured Cyndi had a caseworker since she received disability checks. If I knew the worker's name, I would have called her to report my concerns. But asking Cyndi straight out what her caseworker's name was, she would want to know why I was asking. I didn't want to stir up trouble between us. Besides, Cyndi was good at evading questions she didn't want to answer.

I mulled this idea over for weeks, hoping Cyndi might drop her case manager's name into a conversation, giving me another piece to the puzzle. Too often though, the conversations went in wild, unexpected directions and I was the one caught off guard.

During one visit after she returned from the hospital, I sat on the end of her bed with the afternoon sun lighting the room. A glare on the TV hovered over another rerun of *Dr. Quinn, Medicine Woman*, while Pocahontas slept on the bed next to Cyndi. As we talked over the television Cyndi turned the focus from herself for a change.

"You've had breast cancer. I have something for you. Can you get that box for me?" she asked, pointing toward a high shelf in the closet.

I reached up for the wooden box, curious what it held for me. Maybe a bracelet or a pink breast cancer lapel pin. I brought it to Cyndi and she opened the lid. It wasn't filled with jewelry, but tiny bottles organized in rows and columns.

"This is my medicine woman box," she said, studying the vials. She picked one out, handed it to me, then changed her mind. She put it back and selected another one instead.

"Here, you can take this. It's for breast cancer."

I looked over the small vial in the palm of my hand containing minuscule, pink, waxy balls all stuck together.

"What is this?"

Cyndi shrugged. "I forgot, but it's for breast cancer."

With no intention of using the potion, I simply said, "Thank you" and helped by returning the box to its shelf.

10

What Are We Doing Wrong?

A flyer announcing an interpreter conference, including a workshop on interpreting religious music, arrived with the mail. It sounded like a fun and uplifting way to spend a Sunday afternoon. Translating songs into sign language is a creative and artistic endeavor. Since recovering from breast cancer, I had vowed to spend my energy on positive things and music is therapeutic. This workshop would nurture my soul and enrich my skills. I decided to go. Unfortunately, I didn't stay long enough to get to any of that.

The workshop began with a panel of Deaf parishioners expressing their opinions of the interpreters at their churches.

"She signs so big; it's embarrassing."

"Ours signs too small; she's boring."

"Our interpreter is skilled, but he's not a believer."

"My interpreter's a believer, but she has poor skills."

Watching them make these comments made my heart pound and my skin turned clammy. I thought religious people were loving and understanding, full of peace and happiness. So why were they airing public all these grievances? And when would the music start, so we could begin being creative? To my dismay, the complaints continued.

"… Our interpreter decides for all, even the signs we must use for the songs…" another parishioner said.

Twenty minutes into this, I decided this workshop was not going to nurture me. Instead, it was starting to wear on me, so I gathered my bag and headed for the door at the back of the room. In the hallway I ran into the workshop organizer who was on her way in.

"Where are you going?" she asked.

"To another workshop, down the hall," I stated.

"If you leave, you won't get the Continuing Education credit."

"Yeah, I know."

I felt liberated walking out of that workshop, as though I'd just been released from prison. Except for the organizer, I doubted anyone else noticed or cared that I left. Though a few days later, I bumped into another interpreter who had also been at the workshop. She had noticed my departure.

She asked, "Did you leave because they said that some interpreters were non-believers?"

"No," I replied. "I left because they were bashing interpreters instead of encouraging and teaching us."

* * *

The negative feeling stayed with me for two whole days. I couldn't shake thoughts of being lured in by the bait of creating with music in ASL, only to be ripped apart for our skills. Interpreters work hard learning to perform in a language that, for many of us, is not our first language. We push ourselves to improve and beat ourselves up enough as it is for being imperfect. Perhaps they hadn't intended to come across so disparaging of us, and I should have been more patient, but one thing I've noticed about cancer survivors, we sense that time is short, and we don't want to waste it on negativity.

A few days later at work I finally felt my mood shift. After being away for two weeks, it felt good to be back at the house with the guys. A substitute worker began the meeting with some new rules, apparently because there'd been some recent problems in the house. It wasn't a bug problem this time, but rather another kind of filth. It was about bad attitudes, bad language, and bad behaviors. Disrespectful talk about, and toward, others—ironically, the same stuff I'd been stewing over the past three days.

In a firm voice the substitute emphasized, "From now on, any time someone is caught swearing, using bad language, or making negative comments about others, you will be kicked out of the house for two hours. And if a second person joins in, they will also be kicked out for two hours. And if there is a third, then everyone will be kicked out, all day Saturday and Sunday, with only dinners served!"

With that ultimatum he asked the guys to each say something positive about another resident. Their affirmations to each other had a calming effect on everyone. Interpreting this benefitted me as much as it was supposed to benefit them. The guys started by saying kind things about Sean and Zach, whom they all seemed to get along with and respect. Sean had spent time in prison and his arms were covered in tattoos. He was the most mature, knowledgeable, and considerate among them.

After the meeting it was just me and Sean in the community room. He opened up saying, "I've been in prison the longest—for a total of 18 years for assault and attempted murder."

Attempted murder? When I heard this I could see my husband pacing nervously, knowing I was only a couple of arm lengths from a potentially dangerous and violent criminal. Sean then told me he got shot in the head when he was nine years old, right in the Italian neighborhood where he lived with Mafia gangs roaming the streets. I didn't know of any neighborhood around Denver where Mafia gangs controlled the streets, so I figured Sean wasn't from around here. But just in case, I was curious to know where this dangerous neighborhood was, so I'd be sure not to go there.

"Where are you from?" I asked.

"Oklahoma."

"The Italian Mafia is in Oklahoma?"

"No, in California."

Sean listed the various state prisons and jails where he'd been incarcerated. I was more interested in his schizophrenia. Was it the cause of all his legal problems and incarcerations, or was it the legal troubles and prison life that brought on his mental illness? Though I was curious, I didn't ask these questions. It was not my place to be talking to the guys about their illnesses. Sean, however, offered information on his own.

"I've always had problems since I was shot in the head."

I nodded, as I listened, wondering if he was, truly, shot or if this idea was delusional thinking.

"When people talk, whatever they're saying, I think it's something real in the present, and I react. I get paranoid and then I fight. That's why I was moved to so many different prisons—for fighting."

I couldn't resist asking, "Were you on medication in prison?"

"No, I stopped taking it. Medicine didn't work. I didn't want to stand in lines out in the snow."

"For your meds, you mean?"

"Yeah."

I was interested in hearing more of his story, but we were interrupted. It was time for everyone's meds. Randy, standing in line, mentioned my two-week absence. "When you were gone, the other interpreter managed to find this place."

"Yeah, and he interprets cuss words and you don't," Eli, said. "They signed to Carlos when we were cussing him out. You don't do that."

"That's because you guys don't swear in front of me," I retorted, smiling.

"He was a good interpreter," Randy added.

"So, I'm replaceable?"

"Nah, we want you."

The substitute approached me on my way out. "Thanks so much for your help. Especially tonight; it was really important."

"Sure," I said.

I didn't know if people understood that I did this work because I enjoyed it and because I learned a lot in the process, but it was nice to hear that I was making a difference for others, too.

April 16, 2007

Breaking news came on the radio as I pulled into the parking lot of a west-side medical clinic: *"A shooting at 7:15 this morning occurred in a dorm on the campus of the Virginia Tech University. One person is dead. Police are looking for the shooter."*

I paused to think if there was anyone I knew who lived in Virginia. No one came to mind, so I turned off the motor and headed into the building. Two hours later, when I returned to my car after my assignment, the news was still focused on the shooting. Chaos and horror of monumental proportions had struck the campus. By late afternoon, the broadcast from Blacksburg, Virginia, was calling it a massacre—"*The worst single event mass shooting in American history.*"

The evening news revealed that two people were shot and killed in the dormitory. Two and a half hours after that, the shooter opened fire again in the engineering building. Videos showed emergency vehicles with sirens blaring, people running, and police with assault rifles swarming buildings. Thirty-three people were dead, including the gunman who was still unidentified. By morning we had learned more disturbing details and the name of the gunman. Seung-Hui Cho, 23 years old. He was a student at the university. The associate vice president of the university described Cho as a loner.

I sat in front of the TV, stunned that such terror and carnage could happen again. Flashing back to the bloodshed and emotional pain suffered at Columbine, the depth of this tragedy left us with many of the same questions. *What was wrong with Seung-Hui Cho, and why did he do this?* Another question I heard no one asking was, What are *we* doing wrong?

* * *

The media was still talking the next day about Seung-Hui Cho and what he did at Virginia Tech. I was still feeling troubled by it when I got to Cherokee House, though no one there mentioned it. It was business as usual, giving me a chance to distract myself from dwelling on the massacre.

After a non-eventful house meeting, Sean, garrulous once again, asked me, "Do you exercise a lot?"

I interpreted the question for Carlos before I answered, even though I knew Sean was speaking to me, "Yeah, some."

"I need to lose some of this weight," Sean said, patting his belly. "I've been busy walking all over the place, trying to get my social security supplemental insurance check. I haven't been receiving any money since I was released from jail seven months ago."

As Sean spoke, Carlos became interested in the conversation. "Do you pay rent here?" he asked.

"No, I have to get my social security. When I get my money, I'm moving."

Carlos asked him if he had social security disability insurance.

Sean shook his head. "No, I get SSI."

"Did you have a job before?" I interpreted Carlos' questions, realizing that I had not experienced him engaging like this before, with any of the residents.

Sean smiled and answered, "No. I'm a criminal."

I finger-spelled the word for Carlos.

"What do you mean?" he asked.

"I'm a criminal. That's all I know."

Carlos didn't respond. I didn't know if he was taken aback or if he didn't know what the word *criminal* meant.

"I think I'll buy a tattoo gun," Sean said, breaking the silence. "I used to give tattoos to all the gang members in the slammer."

Carlos' interest in the conversation had waned.

"Come on," he signed to me and headed toward the office. It seemed he'd rather hang out with Verna than talk to these guys. Still, I could hear Sean talking in the other room.

"...it was the cops' fault."

"The cops' fault?"

"Yeah, they busted down my door. The voices were telling me they were the Mafia. I was fighting them, so I got arrested."

Aha. I had my answer and thought, *you need to take your medicine, Sean.*

* * *

Carlos had been volunteering to do extra chores at Cherokee House. He was competing for "Client of the Week," hoping to receive the five-dollar award. He seldom got in trouble anymore. He also smiled more often and had finally gotten new glasses. It took three months for the government to approve them. It was nice seeing him move forward in such a positive way.

Demonde seemed motivated, too. When Verna queried the group on what they wanted to do, he was the first to speak.

"Can we discuss our issues? We should talk about those."

This sparked my interest as something constructive, but Verna didn't respond.

"I need to lose weight," Sean said, with Demonde echoing, "Me, too."

A thin gray-haired older man, new to the group, didn't need to lose weight, so he suggested music. "Do you like classical? Vivaldi? Four Seasons is beautiful!"

Their suggestions impressed me. People, who are in a bad way, can turn their lives around with some guidance and tools, and here was their opportunity. If I had been running the group, I would have said, "These are splendid ideas!" I might also have suggested games, exercise, and art therapy. Unfortunately, Vera seemed distracted and their talk soon faded into their usual feedback, like how dinner was and what their plans were for the rest of the week.

There was no Vivaldi playing in the background at the next house meeting. The talk was of bedbugs once again. They were found in two of the bedrooms. No one was riled over the bugs anymore. Not even Verna.

"The exterminator is scheduled for the end of the week," she said, as if it were their regularly scheduled shipment of Cheerios.

The only excitement was about Ronnie, who had gone AWOL. In his absence, Ernie had taken over Ronnie's spot on the couch.

"He has some money saved up," Ernie said. "The last I seen him was at 3:00 this afternoon."

Ronnie had not returned to the house by 4:00 p.m., to do chores, so now he was reported as missing.

"He'll be back," Ernie promised.

"He does this sometimes," Randy added. "Now and then he goes off on one of his adventures."

Verna admonished another resident who had been missing yesterday. "You are a stay-in tomorrow," she told him, "and you are responsible for doing everyone's chores!"

Though I was curious, no one mentioned where this client had been while he was out, missing. Zach announced that he would be leaving the group home soon. Then Randy asked me to tell Carlos his good news.

"I got Section 8 Housing!"

"Where are you moving to?" Carlos asked.

"I don't know yet. I have to look at some places."

Carlos showed no hint of how he was feeling about these guys leaving, though, later, when we were in the office with Verna, I could tell it was bothering him when told Verna he might be moving, too.

"Where're you goin'?" she asked.

"Maybe somewhere out of state."

Verna ignored him. She was focused on an incident that happened earlier that day at another house in the neighborhood where some parolees lived.

"One of them barricaded himself in his room," she told me after Carlos left the office. "When he started cutting his arms, the staff called the police who came with sirens blaring, along with the paramedics."

Verna shared it was not uncommon for parolees to end up back in jail or in the hospital before they managed to move out of group homes or into an apartment.

"Once in a while there's a success story," she added. "If they're motivated, they can do something with their life. It makes it all worth it."

It was heartening to hear this about our government rehabilitation system. Yet, I was left to wonder about Carlos. Was his comment about moving out of state realistic or just wishful thinking?

11

Wreaking Havoc

Bubbles coming from the kitchen at Cherokee House were oozing into the living room through the crack beneath the door. Verna was irate.

"Whose job was it to do the dishes?"

"Ernie's," Carlos signed.

Verna directed a cutting gaze at Ernie, who was sitting on the couch. "Then why didn't you do it?"

Ernie shrugged.

"It was your job," she scolded.

Someone used the wrong soap, putting dish soap into the dishwasher. Miguel was still in the kitchen mopping up the mess. Ernie got off the hook when Sean changed the subject. Looking at Ronnie, who was back, Sean asked him where he'd been.

"In jail," Ronnie said.

Demonde perked up when he heard this, instantly engaging in the conversation. "Jail? What were you in jail for?"

"I stole something."

"Jeez, man. What'd you steal?"

Before Ronnie could answer, Sean interrupted. "How did you like it in jail?" he asked, grinning as though they were sharing old high school stories.

"It was too noisy. They were shouting."

"Who was shouting?" Verna asked. "The other inmates, or the voices in your head?"

"The voices in my head."

I thought Ronnie looked sad, or scared, or maybe he was just tired.

Sean and Demonde shared their experiences with the legal system with Ronnie, along with their opinions on the possible fine he'd have to pay. "Maybe you'll get community service," Sean offered.

For many, this is how it goes. To jail, then to court, and from there to the mental hospital to get stabilized with medication. Next, comes probation and counseling, which usually leads to improved behavior. But often after being released to the community, they stop taking their meds and the cycle repeats, starting with weird behavior and then a trip back to jail. Unfortunately, this is the reality for many who struggle with mental illness.

August 2007

Along with the summer heat, I needed to vent my increasing frustration. Since I stopped discussing Cyndi with my family, I'd had no one to confide in, except Jeff, and it wasn't often that we communicated. I felt lost in trying to find someone who could help me, help Cyndi.

Lately, Cyndi had been talking about her parents' gravestones and complications getting them done. She was worried that they wouldn't be completed in time for the unveiling ceremony. I was unfamiliar with Jewish traditions, but from the way Cyndi was talking, it sounded like another disorganized mess. It had been almost three years since her mother died, and a little less since her father passed. I had no experience in these affairs to be of any help to Cyndi. I could only wish her well.

To her credit, she pulled it together. I received an invitation to my first unveiling ceremony. It was blistering hot the morning we gathered at Rose Hill Cemetery. Cyndi, in her wheelchair, looked lovely in a navy blue flowered dress. I bent down to hug her and noticed she was soaking wet with perspiration. Everyone was perspiring. With visible beads of sweat on his forehead, the rabbi prayed aloud while standing next to the double-sized headstone covered with a sheer cloth. Gazing at the gatherers I recognized Emily, a petite young woman with soft brown hair, I had met a couple of years earlier at a birthday party for Cyndi. I knew few of the others.

At the end of the prayer the rabbi asked a woman to lift the veil from the dark granite headstone. She read to us the words engraved on the stone as we paid our respects to both Harriette and Stanley Grober. When friends and family members stepped forward and began placing small stones atop the headstone I helped someone push Cyndi in her wheelchair across the grass to place her stone.

An hour later we were sitting in Jeff's small living room eating from paper plates on our laps, listening to Cyndi impress a group of older ladies circled around her with the details of her upcoming one-woman art exhibit.

"It's at a gallery downtown and there will be a champagne reception afterward," she told them.

"Oh, you don't say," said one woman with sparkling eyes.

"How lovely that is," said another.

"Wonderful!" the others agreed.

Right, I thought, the same show that was supposed to be held at Howard Lorton Gallery five months ago. As I sat wondering if I was the only one who knew this was total fantasy, Emily, sitting next to me, whispered, "So many things, that never seem to happen." Unsure if she was talking to me or to herself, I whispered back, "Do you think she's delusional?"

"No. I don't think so. It's just that these things she talks about never seem to come about."

"That's my point."

Eager to discuss my concerns, I asked Emily if we could step into the side room where we could talk privately. Sharing details of the many things Cyndi had been telling each of us, Emily shared my concerns. She admitted she felt confused and had the same reservations I did about Jake. Yet, she was not convinced Cyndi was delusional or mentally ill. After 20 minutes of comparing notes, Emily's opinion swayed closer to mine.

"Well, maybe, she is."

"Would it be all right if I call you sometime and we can talk more?"

She nodded, "Definitely."

September 2007

I avoided calling Cyndi and dreaded her calls to me. Listening to her latest grandiose scheme or reports on the daily fixes she got into agitated me. But she left me a phone message one day, asking for a mutual friend's phone number, so I called her, intending to keep it short.

"Oh, I have something to tell you," she said. "I'm a mother. I just found out I have a one-and-a-half-year-old daughter!"

I sat in my car, thinking, *this is going to be a good one.*

Cyndi was fired up. "I've been keeping it a secret, but now it's going to happen. I'm adopting. They're bringing her this weekend. Don't tell anyone! Ever since I got home from the hospital I've been babysitting different kids, and they've been watching me. They had hidden cameras all over and I passed! I have my own daughter, and—another thing—Jake bought me a pony!"

As usual, I didn't know what to say. She was telling me that she was suddenly going to be a mother, and a second later, she was excited about a pony? I couldn't get past a gut-wrenching feeling over the baby. What kind of adoption agency would allow this to happen? Cyndi couldn't walk, nor get herself in and out of bed. How could she take care of a baby? And, as if this were not enough, she threw in a pony? This was pure madness.

I didn't bother to ask about the one-and-a-half-year-old. Instead, I asked, "Where are you going to keep the pony?"

"At the ranch," she asserted. "And, I have a question to ask you. Will you help me write my autobiography?"

A baby, a pony, and a book. I hesitated, as always, fumbling for words. She spoke with absolute confidence, and I, reluctant to go along with her magnanimous ideas, came across as a blithering idiot. "Autobiography? That means you write it yourself."

"I have all these vignettes."

"That's a great start. Keep writing."

When we hung up I immediately called Emily, getting her voicemail. After I left her a message I discovered she had left one for me, too.

"Holy Cow!" she said, "Have you talked to Cyndi today? I'm really scared." At the end of her message, Emily added, "I'm becoming convinced. I agree with you. Cyndi is delusional."

* * *

Emily eventually reached me, and we agreed our friend was in trouble. Emily originally got involved with Cyndi as a volunteer through a service organization and had been helping Cyndi with various things for a few years now. We started phoning regularly, consulting each other on every new twist and turn with Cyndi. When Emily would ask her where the baby was, she would get varying answers like, "She's in Colorado Springs getting her shots," or "They were bringing her and their car broke down." Then, it was a snowstorm, and they couldn't make it to Denver. Another time Cyndi said they had to take the baby for her naming ceremony. As with the van and the medicine man, the baby was always "on the way," but never arrived.

Emily and I tried to figure out if Jake was taking advantage of Cyndi by promising her things he knew she wanted, like the art show and now the baby, or if Cyndi was just living in her made-up fantasy world. Was she truly mentally ill, or just a pain in our sides? And was she in legal trouble with Jake? We didn't know. But Emily and I didn't trust Jake. On one call we debated whether it was our responsibility to alert the authorities of our suspicion that Cyndi might be in danger, or whether we should stop meddling altogether.

* * *

Checking my phone as I always did after interpreting assignments, I found another message from Cyndi asking me to call her. Dreading what she might have to say, I put off returning her call until after dinner. When all the dishes were clean and put away, I dialed her number.

"Are you going to the Race for the Cure?" she wanted to know.

The race was in three days and I'd already decided not to participate this year. "No, I have too much going on. Are you going?"

"Yeah, there's a group of us, and I made bracelets for you and some other breast cancer survivors."

Cyndi sounded disappointed. I knew that she'd been planning this for a while, but after seven years of involvement with breast cancer groups, I was ready to move on.

To soften the spurn, I added, "I'm sorry, I can't, but I'll be thinking of you."

"Well, I have a secret to share with everyone after the race," she said.

"A secret?"

"Yeah, Jake is having a huge mural painted for me in my new apartment."

She claimed that the apartment was in the new complex adjacent to the Denver Art Museum.

"Ten people are working on the mural because it's so intricate. The mural is the story of my life!"

"What are they painting?"

"I don't know. It's a surprise, but it's huge!"

I didn't believe any of this, but to avoid confrontation I told her I couldn't wait to see it and even found myself adding, "We should have a party to celebrate when it's finished."

* * *

Stopping at the library on my way home from work, I dropped a stack of books into the return slot and went inside to look for more. *The Dinosaur Man, Tales of Madness & Enchantment from the Back Ward* was in the stack I brought home, and that evening I started reading about delusions. The author, Susan Bauer, said they serve a purpose for the person experiencing them. Fantasies fill them with self-worth. Self-aggrandizing is how they make themselves feel important and needed, and their delusions are often intertwined with reality.

So *this* is what made it so difficult listening to a self-aggrandizer. It was exhausting trying to decipher what was true and what was part of their psychotic beliefs. Susan Bauer might as well have been describing Cyndi.

Baur wrote, "Delusions cannot function as a protective shield unless they remain impenetrable."

I understood now why I could not break down Cyndi's falsehoods. Not me, not anyone, could take her delusions away.

As this became more clear to Emily and me, we decided to let Cyndi have her delusions. Still, we worried that Jake was taking advantage of her, stealing her money and medications, and we both felt it would be terrible if we ignored this. We agreed we should start by speaking to Cyndi's brother. It turned out Jeff had heard the same stories we had. He, too, wondered if any were true. The three of us agreed Cyndi needed professional intervention, but without her cooperation, we had a problem. If we called Adult Protective Services, what would we tell them? We had no proof of harm being done. And calling the police would be futile. If they paid her a visit, they'd just find her watching *Dr. Quinn: Medicine Woman* and determine her to be in no imminent danger. They would not arrest her or take her to a hospital. But maybe they would talk to her. If we told them about Jake would they ask her about him?

For weeks we grappled with these questions. Emily did call Adult Protective Services for advice, and I called the director of a community mental health center. The director sympathized when I told him about my friend, who was showing symptoms of some sort of psychiatric illness.

When I asked, "How do people get into the system?" He told me what I already knew: "They come in through various ways, but if you believe she's a danger to herself or a danger to others, you should call the police. Another option is to see if she's willing to go for a psychological evaluation. If she's not and refuses, you could present your case to a judge and ask him to order an evaluation to be done on her."

Cyndi was severely disabled and not capable of hurting others except verbally in how she manipulated us into getting involved in her chaos and how insensitive she was to what we might have going on in our own lives. But perhaps she *was* a danger to herself. Could poor decisions that got her into trouble medically, financially, and legally be considered such? If she spent all her money and couldn't afford to buy food, wouldn't that be considered a danger to herself?

But knowing what needed to be done and actually doing it were two different things. Maybe the psychiatric evaluation was best left up to her brother.

Maybe he should be the one to decide whether he wanted to ask her to submit to one or petition the court to order it. Picturing the possible outcomes of our options, I was stuck in limbo.

One evening, however, I called the local National Alliance on Mental Illness (NAMI) affiliate and spoke with the president. She was kind and friendly and listened while I described my delusional friend. She heard me in a way my family never had, understanding precisely what I was talking about. I asked her how to seek help for someone in the throes of mental illness, who was wreaking havoc not only in her own life but also in mine. I told her I was afraid Cyndi would get angry if I suggested that she get a psychological evaluation.

"Oh yes, she will get angry," the woman said. "They usually do. They don't think there is anything wrong with them. But when their lives are a mess and they've lost grasp of reality, it starts affecting other people, like it has you."

I felt so relieved speaking with the NAMI president. Perhaps Emily and I were on the right track. Still, after all these calls, we felt we'd come up short.

Disheartened, Emily stated the obvious: "Our hands are tied."

12

The Psych Ward

Fall 2007

Peering through the window of a heavy steel door, I pushed the buzzer to an intercom next to it. A female voice answered. "Can I help you?"

"Yes, I'm the sign language interpreter assigned here for this afternoon."

"I'll be right there."

In a minute she was unlocking the door letting me onto Unit 6, the psych ward of another Denver Hospital. "Dallas is on the computer," she said, pointing across the room with no further instructions.

Wearing a baseball cap backward over her shoulder-length blond hair, Dallas was absorbed in a video game and didn't notice me at first. Finally, she looked up.

"Are you the interpreter?" she signed.

I nodded "Yes" with my fist.

"I can't sign good with this," she said, pointing to a cast on her arm.

"What happened?"

"Surgery. I had an infection."

"I see."

"A piece of metal was stuck in there, in the bone."

Puzzled at how a piece of metal could get in her forearm, and against my gut telling me it was not appropriate to inquire about patients' health information unless it was imperative for the assignment, I asked, "What kind of metal?"

"A razor blade," she replied with such nonchalance as if this sort of thing happened all the time.

"Did you do that to yourself?"

"Yeah."

I was aware that people with severe emotional problems sometimes injure themselves, though it seemed ghastly to me at that moment how someone could dig into their arm like that with a razor blade. I also knew it was wise not to show any reaction. I simply nodded.

Dallas shrugged, then added, "I was mad at my husband."

Mental health professionals called individuals who purposefully injure themselves in this way "cutters." A person might think someone who does this is seeking attention, but for some people with emotional disorders, cutting themselves and seeing blood flow brings relief from an unbearable torment that's plaguing them. Other individuals might bang their heads, pull out their hair, or punch things instead, trying to release anger, fear, or frustration. Some self-injure to punish themselves or to feel a sense of control.

As Dallas resumed playing her video game, I sat observing the other patients in the dayroom. An older man with a hunched back, gray beard, and shaking hands stared at me. I assumed his shakiness was tardive dyskinesia, a side effect of psychotropic medications. Aside from his hands shaking, he seemed to be frozen in place. I smiled at him and, unexpectedly, he returned one, attached to a string of drool. He never spoke. Neither did the thin woman with uncombed hair who approached me with a stern look.

I suddenly wondered if I'd committed a faux pas: "Oh, did I take your seat?"

She didn't answer. Instead, she went to a couch on the other side of the room and sat staring down at the floor.

Another woman sat at a table with her lunch tray, though it was long past lunchtime. She peered over the top of her glasses at the food on her tray. Her brown hair, matted in the back, hung in tousled strands over her face. Her lips silently mouthed words as she spoke to the voices in her head while picking at a salad in a Styrofoam bowl. I watched as she brought a piece of lettuce to her mouth with a plastic fork, but before it touched her lips, she set it back down on the plate. I empathized with the difficulty she had completing a task as simple as eating a piece of lettuce with so much interference from the relentless conversation going on inside her head.

The woman stood and shuffled to the water fountain. Bending over, she took a long drink while a baked potato and roasted meat turned cold on her plate. She started to return to the table, but then, as if the fountain itself was pulling her back, she spun around and returned to the fountain. She finished her second drink and began to head back to the table, only to be interrupted once more by a thought more compelling than eating, and returned to the water fountain. She did this five or six times. Wishing she would just eat her food, I couldn't stop watching her. No one seemed to be paying attention to her except me.

While I'd found the woman's behavior amusing at first, it became sadly troubling. I'd heard of people dying from drinking too much water. As I contemplated alerting the staff, a social worker interrupted me.

"Can you interpret for me while I meet with Dallas?"

"Yes, of course," I said.

We moved to a private room to talk. When we returned to the dayroom, less than 15 minutes later, I looked for the woman who was trying to eat her lunch, but she was gone and so was her tray. To the staff that woman was probably just another patient. To me, she was a person with serious mental illness. As I drove home I thought about her and wondered what caused her illness. I wanted to know why so many people like her have to suffer.

* * *

When I got home I called Cyndi to find out how the Race for the Cure went. She said her group raised over 1,000 dollars. Then she told me her mural was finished.

"Have you seen it?" I asked.

"I saw it on TV."

"On the news?"

"Yeah. It's attached to the new art museum. There are two rooms built out above the lawn. One is my bedroom and the other is my studio. It has bulletproof glass and shades that go down. My art studio is over the parking lot and has windows that look out over the mountains. The other wall is one huge mirror, like what you see in a dancing school. It has a porch, too, where I can let the dogs out. And I don't have to worry about picking up the poop. A man will come and do that. After my monkey has her baby, I'll have two monkeys and two dogs." Cyndi laughed, delighted at the thought of it all.

I didn't remind her that she told me a month ago that the monkey was pregnant and was to give birth any day. Now Cyndi was telling me the capuchin monkey would give birth at the end of the month, the same time she would be moving into the new apartment.

When we hung up I looked up the gestation period for capuchin monkeys and learned that it is six months. I'm pretty sure Cyndi's monkey had been pregnant for at least a year. As for the new apartments, I found a website announcing the *Grand Opening of spacious new apartments adjacent to the newly renovated art museum.*

I called Emily to tell her the apartments Cyndi had been talking about were real. "They're ready to rent," I said. "Now, we just have to find out if Cyndi owns one, or if she just believes that one belongs to her."

As for the mural, I didn't bother to bring it up. We already knew the answer to that one.

13

A New Suitcase

My job at Cherokee house ended once Carlos moved out. He'd since enrolled in a vocational preparation class for persons with disabilities, and I started going there to interpret for him. One morning before class, Carlos showed me a test tube from a science kit he'd ordered from a catalog. I thought he'd moved past such things, but I guess I was wrong. A colored liquid filled the tube halfway, and Carlos had me watch as he poured another liquid from a jar into the test tube. Together, the liquids fizzed and overflowed onto the table before dripping onto the floor. Looking embarrassed, Carlos scrambled to clean up the mess before the instructor showed up.

His experiment reminded me of the kinds of experiments I did with friends when we were in the fourth grade. When our mothers weren't around, we'd scrounge the kitchen cupboards for things like baking soda, food coloring, spices, and whatever else looked interesting and stirred up concoctions that expanded and overflowed their containers. We made all kinds of messes, then hurried to clean them up before we got caught. By fifth grade I'd outgrown that kind of experimenting. As for Carlos, I never did learn what kinds of liquids he had in the test tube.

The class instructor arrived. He began asking the students how their job search was going and what they were working on in preparation. Calling on one student he asked, "How are things going for you, John?"

"My fish are doing good," John said.

He'd said the same thing last week. I'd picked up that John used to be a computer technician for a major corporation, but started having mental problems and difficulties on the job, so he had to leave. He hadn't held a job since. His fish seemed to be his job now, and they weren't doing well. John mumbled something about the power filter and then admitted to not cleaning the tank often enough and that maybe he was feeding them too much.

John said he was in the process of looking for a job, but it seemed he never got further than working on the cover letter for his resume. In class he preferred talking about inventions he was creating at home using guitar strings and radios. He didn't explain enough for us to understand what he was talking about. Mostly, the students talked over him like he wasn't even there.

The other students shared issues they were having with their job or in finding a job. Carlos rarely participated in these discussions, though he attended class faithfully, bringing half of his belongings with him in a shopping cart. He always seemed to have problems with the cart overflowing: Water bottles, coats, gloves, or notebooks often fell out onto the floor. A large jug would sometimes teeter on top. Getting the cumbersome cart through doorways and other tight spaces was always awkward, but he managed to do it showing little frustration, which impressed me.

Sometimes the issues students brought up were completely unrelated to employment. One time a student sitting next to me, named Carol, was upset because the place where she was living had bedbugs, and her landlord was blaming *her* for the problem. That was the second time someone in the class had complained about having bedbugs. It seemed I couldn't escape them. Carol complained that she had a cough from the fumigation of her building. While I sympathized with her, I tried inching away from her as I was signing. I had avoided bringing bedbugs home from Cherokee House and wished to avoid doing so again.

Carlos had to leave class early that day to catch the bus. As I stood waiting for him to gather his belongings, Carol asked me why I had to leave.

"I'm always a little upset when he leaves and you have to go, too. I want you to stay longer," she said.

"Yes, I'm disappointed too," I replied, "but, I'm not allowed to stay since I'm not a student."

"I know," she said, downhearted.

I think Carol was unhappy because she hadn't had her turn yet to speak about her job search. Over the years I've come to realize that sometimes people just want to be listened to.

* * *

The following week in the vocational prep class John didn't mention his fish or the problems he was having with the tank. He had something different on his mind.

"I turned down a job supervising five people in manufacturing components for aerospace and semiconductors," he said, surprising everyone.

"Recently?" someone asked.

"No, in 1978, because military school damaged my ability to lead. They did experiments on me at the school. I thought it was pus, but it was mayonnaise they rubbed on my temples."

I was fascinated, listening to John speak, but Carlos wasn't paying attention to my interpreting. He was picking up papers and packing his cart. We had to leave, and I was disappointed. I wanted to hear more about John's military school and what made him think they were doing experiments on him.

* * *

Sifting through my husband's shirts, I picked out the ones he never wore, including some fleece, flannels, and a winter jacket. I folded the shirts into a stack and placed them into a plastic trash bag. I planned to take them with me to the vocational prep class and give them to Carlos. Jim would never miss them, and Carlos could use them more. Carlos' clothes looked old and worn. He had no one to fuss at him over his abysmal attire, so I thought I could help.

I arrived early for class that day and told Carlos I had clothes for him in the car. "Do you want to come with me to get them?" I signed.

His eyes brightened, and he nodded. He followed me to the car, and I opened the tailgate showing him the bag full of shirts, and the jackets.

"You can look through them and take whatever you want."

"All," he signed and swooped up the entire load. As we walked back into the building, I wondered how he would carry the load of clothes home on the bus. Carlos, however, did not seem worried about it. I suppose he was used to managing loads of stuff on the bus.

Winter 2008

One morning I noticed Carlos sporting a new suitcase. Well, it wasn't exactly new. It was a bit tattered and had a torn front pocket, but it seemed suitable enough as the new replacement for the shopping cart he'd been using. The suitcase had wheels and rolled along behind him on the way to class. Since the rash of snowstorms we'd had lately, and the bitter cold, I figured his suitcase was full of warm clothing and a jacket for the waits at the bus stops. When we reached the classroom, Carlos spun the suitcase around, parking it next to his seat.

Pointing to the bag, I asked, "Is that new?"

"Yeah," he nodded.

"What's in it?"

"Tea."

"Tea? What for?" With that much tea, he must have a new job as a distributor, I mused.

"It's to drink. They're different flavors."

"I see. Do you have other things in there, too?"

"Yeah."

He bent down to unzip the top section of the bag, but before he could reveal its contents, the instructor interrupted by starting class. I began interpreting and forgot about the suitcase. I was just thinking how nice it was that Carlos was living independently and hoped he'd be able to handle his new freedom. So far, he was being resourceful. He told me he washed his clothes in the sink because he had no money for the laundromat.

While I signed, Carlos fiddled with his thermos and pulled papers from the suitcase, glancing upward at me now and then. His lack of attention made me believe, despite his progress, he still had a way to go before he could land a job and make it on his own in the world.

By noon sunshine had replaced the morning clouds, warming the layers of snow blanketing the grass and the thick bumpy ice on the streets. I slipped through slush and puddles on the way to my car, recalling past winters like this one. I remembered the "ice rinks" my dad had created for us in our small backyard when we were kids. He would run the water from the hose over the grass and let it freeze overnight. Repeating this over several evenings, the ice would build up, thick enough for us to skate on. My sister and I would go out in the dark, skating over ruts and bumps wearing knitted hats our neighbor had made for us, mine with jingle bells sewn on the side. My sister's had a long ponytail made from yellow yarn. I loved those hats and the ice skating, and the fact that Dad had created those winter memories for us.

My reverie faded by the time I got to the car. As I drove away I remembered Carlos's suitcase. He was just about to show me what it had inside when class began. I never did find out what treasures he had that were so important he had to lug them everywhere.

14

I'm Sorry. Its the Privacy Laws

The first time Cyndi mentioned Jane Seymour to me was more than a year ago. I was cooking dinner when she called full of excitement because she had seen Jane Seymour on *Dancing with the Stars*.

"Jane is my cousin, and the show is coming to town, and I have tickets," Cyndi exclaimed. "Do you want to go with me? They're $1,000 tickets!"

I asked a few questions just to delay answering. I wasn't going to commit to scheduling myself for another one of Cyndi's wild fantasies. It wasn't the ticket price, it was her stating that Jane was her *cousin* that had me doubting the entire event. I told her I would check my calendar and get back to her.

Neither of us spoke again about the show, but now she was calling Jane her best friend. "Jane is selling her five homes in California and coming here to live with me. We're going to live on her ranch in Colorado Springs," Cyndi bragged one day.

"Where in Colorado Springs?" I asked.

"I'm not allowed to say. But we have so much in common. We're both medicine women, and we both have ranches. She's a fabulous artist, and I want her here to work on my mask with me for the contest."

I wasn't familiar with the mask contest. Cyndi said she'd won it last year. When I inquired about it, she brushed me off by changing the subject.

"I haven't been in the hospital since last May. Nine months. It's a record! Except now I might have colon cancer again."

I wondered why Cyndi was saying this. She never had colon cancer. The tumor she had last year was benign. Did she forget?

"I have to have a biopsy. I'm so scared to go to the appointment alone."

Suddenly, I saw an opening, to slip in the question I'd been dying to ask for some time: "What about your caseworker? Don't you have one? Maybe she could go with you."

"Yeah, I have one."

"What's her name?"

"I don't want her to go with me. Jane is going with me...."

My scheme didn't work. Cyndi either sensed my trick, or she was so practiced at avoiding answering questions, she skillfully dodged them. I knew I couldn't press her.

She kept on talking at a manic pace.

"I want to start dating... and my daughter had her rebirthing... will be one year old on March 10th."

"Isn't that your birthday?"

"Yes, she was born on my birthday."

What a coincidence. "Where is she, anyway?"

"In Strasburg, with a nanny, because I've been sick and I would feel terrible if I gave her anything. I have cancer on my hand, or maybe it's MRSA, but it's healed now..."

Cyndi jumped from one subject to the next. It was pointless to even try to comment on anything she was saying.

"In two hours they're going to be here. I'm finally getting my daughter! I can't believe it's real. Jane is bringing me a whole bunch of clothes because she lost a lot of weight from doing *Dancing with the Stars*..."

I didn't want to hear this nonsense anymore. I felt guilty because I didn't want to listen and irritated that I was wasting my time attending to her fake business, while not attending to my own real business. I hung up feeling cold and sweaty, my heart racing with anger.

Did she think I was so stupid and gullible that I'd fall for her lies? I was weary and torn with nowhere to dump all the crap she loaded onto me. My husband refused to let me talk about her anymore. I could simply tell her not to call me anymore. I could just walk away. No one was forcing me to be nice to her, or even pay her any attention, so why was I putting my mental health at risk, trying to deal with her?

I asked the question already knowing the answer. In my mind I saw her so clearly. Harriette, lying in bed in hospice wearing nothing but a hospital gown and the necklace with the gold bike charm I'd given her for her birthday. The week before she had been riding her bike and walking in the Race for the Cure. Now with the cancer in her lungs she was too weak to stand or walk. Her voice had faded to a whisper. I leaned in close so I could hear her.

"Do you know how much you mean to me?" she asked.

I'd been holding back tears, but now they spilled down my face. My throat grew tight and I could barely speak. My words came out whispered, too. "Yes," I said, grasping her hand."

"I'm worse," she said.

"I know."

At this I broke down, aware that neither Harriette nor I had ever seen each other cry. She always said she never cried, and she didn't cry now, but I was sobbing and unable to speak at all.

Over the last two years of her life, Harriette and I had developed a close friendship. She'd always been open with me about every aspect of her cancer. We never tiptoed around it or avoided talking about death. We both knew she was going to die, someday, and here it was.

"I'm crossing over to the other side," she said.

While I sat smearing my eye makeup with tissues and tears, Harriette was still being Harriette, the athlete who had breast cancer. She asked, as if we were going to a wedding, "What size are you?"

"Six," I replied.

"Good, because I want you to have my clothes. I don't want them thrown away, they're new."

Forever practical, she was the responsible one who looked after Cyndi, ordered her medicines, and dealt with her hospitalizations. Harriette took care of everything in her family's roller-coaster life.

Enduring the painful effort it took, she rolled toward me and gave me a hug.

"You're my sister," she said. "I never had a sister."

Harriette's comment touched me deeply, as I'd never taken time with so much going on with her to think about how much she meant to me, too.

"I still have the bike necklace," she'd said, her fingers stroking the gold charm.

"Don't take it off," I said.

"No, I won't," she promised.

The next day Jeff and I stood on each side of her bed, watching her chest straining with each breath. I noticed the necklace was gone from her neck. Before I could ask, she told me she'd given it to Jeff. It hurt me at first, as I wanted something to remember her by, but when I looked at his face, so proud to be wearing it, although tight around his neck, it made sense. She always rode with him.

"I knew you'd understand," she said.

I thought once again of her last words to me." Will you stay in my family's life?"

Harriette lingered for a couple more days in hospice, but I didn't go back. I had believed I was strong. I thought I'd been strong through the two years I'd spent with her, journaling her life with cancer. I'd believed I could handle her death, as we'd been preparing for it for a long time. I had envisioned that I'd be with her until her last breath. But I couldn't do it. I was too broken, shattered really.

Now, nearly four years since she'd passed, I was still grappling over what my responsibility should be toward Cyndi.

***

The next time Cyndi called it was from the hospital. It had been a year since she'd had the surgery on her colon. I hated to admit that I'd been *waiting* for this day. Waiting an entire year for Cyndi to go into the hospital again, where I knew there would be a social worker I could speak to. The final straw convincing me that Cyndi was in serious trouble was Cyndi's recent call to Emily, asking if she had any narcotics. Cyndi said her best friend, Jane, had breast cancer and needed them for pain.

There was no more time for hesitating or speculating on Cyndi's mental state or what Jake was up to. I was done making calls to NAMI, to the mental health center, or anyone else. Now, bolstered with courage, I was on my way to the hospital to speak to a social worker. I was prepared to do this the last time Cyndi was hospitalized, but she was so sick then. I honestly thought she might die. Since that recovery, she'd had one of her healthiest years, physically. Her mental state, however, was a different story.

With only an hour before work, I was in a race to track down a social worker, a doctor, or a nurse. Avoiding the slow elevators, I hustled to the stairwell. Pushing against the spiraling steps, I reached the second floor with ease. Feeling my thighs tightening by the third floor, I forced myself up one more flight, arriving out of breath, not only from the climb but from nerves. There was no time to stop to catch my breath.

Through gasps of air, I spoke to the first person I saw at the nurse's station. "I need to speak to ... a caseworker ... or someone ... about concerns we have about Cyndi, one of your patients."

"What is it?" the woman asked.

I could hardly hear her through the pounding of my heart. "Her brother and I have concerns about her mental health and some bizarre things she's been telling us."

"She told me about her daughter."

"You heard? You've heard her stories?"

"Yes, is it true? Does she really have a daughter? I was wondering how she could take care of a baby."

"No. Well, uh, we don't know. We, or I, don't believe that she does. Her brother and I, and one other friend, we'd like to meet with a social worker."

It turned out this woman was Cyndi's nurse. To my delight she was now an eyewitness for having heard straight from Cyndi about the baby.

"The social worker is not available now," she said. "I'll have to take your name and number. I'll have her call you."

All that rushing, panting, and nervousness just to leave a note. I waited all that afternoon for the call, which didn't come.

After 24 hours of not hearing anything, I feared the social worker might never call. I couldn't wait a second longer. I got dressed and drove to Denver, stopping by the hospital again on my way to work.

This time I was lucky. When I asked at the nurses' station for a social worker, a young dark-haired woman sitting with her back to me turned around.

"I'm the social worker. I got your note."

"Do you have 10 minutes? May I speak to you privately?"

She hesitated at first, then led me to a small conference room and closed the door behind us.

"I need to speak to you about Cyndi," I said. "Her brother and I, and another friend, would like to meet with you tomorrow, maybe at 3:15?"

I had the meeting visualized, how the three of us would present our evidence of Cyndi's erratic behavior, and the social worker would listen and then immediately step into action. I was certain we would finally get Cyndi the professional intervention she needed.

But right away, there was a glitch.

"I can't speak with you without her permission," the social worker said, "and Cyndi has already denied me permission to speak with her brother."

This can't be. My heart sank.

"I'm sorry. It's the privacy laws," she said.

I had to think quickly. I knew about the privacy laws. There was no point in arguing with her about them. If Jeff was now out of the picture, then it was up to me and Emily. But Cyndi might deny permission for the social worker to speak to me, too, if asked. If I didn't speak now, there might not be another opportunity.

"All right, I understand you are not permitted to speak to me, but you are allowed to listen, correct?"

She nodded, though her body language told me she was not that eager.

"I only have 30 minutes until I have to go to work, so I'll try to tell you this as best as I can."

I sped through the last two-and-a-half years, telling her what Cyndi had told us, about the pets, about Jake, about the $12,000 worth of gifts from the Indian reservation, and the medicine man who always on his way but never appeared. I included the 60' x 60' mural, of which 10 people worked on around the clock for one month, depicting Cyndi's life. I told her about Jane Seymour, whom Cyndi idolized and believed to be her best friend, and how she thought they were going to live together on a ranch. Then I shared how Cyndi had asked Emily for narcotics, for Jane, and told her about the baby that Cyndi now claimed to be adopting.

I was speaking so quickly, jumping from one subject to another, that I was half afraid the social worker would think I was the one who was manic or delusional.

"I know I'm talking fast, but there is so much to tell you and I don't have much time."

The social worker's aloofness had softened. Her eyes engaged with mine, yet she remained quiet. I knew this was my only chance to make my point, so I just blurted it out.

"I believe Cyndi is a danger to herself. She has no food and no money. I told her brother, and he says he doesn't understand how that can be. He says she should have plenty of money from their parents' will."

The social worker hadn't uttered a word or moved an inch, so I kept on talking as long as she allowed me: "... and this guy she's involved with, I think he's shady. We fear he's stealing from her, taking her money, and maybe her prescription medications. And maybe he is bringing her a baby from the reservation. We just don't know."

Finally, the dark-haired woman broke her silence.

"Have you seen the child?"

"No. I don't believe there is a child. I think Cyndi's delusional. But if I'm wrong, and if there is a child, this child is in danger. Cyndi can't take care of *herself*, how is she going to take care of a baby? I think she needs a psychological evaluation. But if all you ask her is, what year is it, and who is the president, you're not going to find out anything."

With her dark brows furrowed, she nodded and stood. "I'll look into it," she said, reaching for the door.

I walked to the elevator, shaken and spent. As the doors opened I stepped in only to discover the birthday card I'd brought for Cyndi was still in my purse. I darted out before the doors closed and headed back to the nurses' station, catching a glimpse of the social worker proceeding down the hall. She turned into Cyndi's room. Feeling like a stunned bird who'd just flown into a window, I left the card, addressed to Cyndi, on the counter and my feathers on the ground.

Soon after, I told Jeff and Emily about my meeting with the social worker. Jeff called me the next day to let me know he'd heard from Cyndi's home health agency.

"They went to her home to investigate," he said. "They checked her refrigerator, and it was empty."

"Wow," was all I could say. After months of getting nowhere, this felt shocking. In truth, it was months ago when I was helping to feed her hungry cat, that I'd looked inside her refrigerator and noticed it was empty. I was glad they didn't find me to be a liar.

"My sister was mad at me," Jeff said. "She thought I was the one who called the hospital."

Yet Cyndi admitted to him that Jake had stolen $15,000 from her. I wanted to hear more about this, but Jeff went back to relaying what the agency had told him.

"They're quitting taking care of her. She's been through eight home health agencies in one year. *Nobody* wants to care for her anymore. They say it's 'behavior issues.'"

"Well, she's going to be mad at me, too, when she finds out I was the one who reported my concerns."

"She doesn't know who it was."

I hoped that was the case, but I doubted it.

When the call came, my heart jumped and started pounding as I recognized Cyndi's number on my phone. I considered not answering, then decided to just get it over with. She didn't waste time with wild stories like usual. She went straight to accusing me.

"Why did you call the hospital?"

The birthday card flashed through my mind. Left there on the same day the social worker confronted her. It wouldn't have been difficult to make the connection that it was me who ratted on her, even for someone delusional. I saw no value in denying it.

"I was concerned."

"Then why didn't you come to me?" Cyndi, however, didn't wait for a response. "They think I'm loony. They're going to take my daughter away! Friends don't do this to friends. You are *not* my friend."

Her outrage was no surprise, nor was her hanging up on me. Still, I felt the sting. No one had ever hung up on me before. So friends really *don't* do this for friends? How else was I supposed to help her? Cyndi may have had the right to be as crazy as she wanted, but did that mean I should look away and allow her illness to grow worse? How humane would that be?

15

It's the Law

An assignment on another psych ward came in for me. It was easier now for me to recognize the symptoms of psychiatric disorders—depression, bipolar disorder, borderline personality disorder, and schizophrenia. I'd gotten used to seeing patients sit for long periods of time without moving or speaking, while others paced and spoke aloud to people who were not there. The highly agitated, newly admitted, practically flew from room to room, yelling at one person or another. Some would shout into the community telephone about how they'd been "kidnapped" or locked up against their will and demand to speak to their lawyer.

Simone, the patient I was interpreting for, was arguing with a nurse over her medication, refusing to take it because she said it was the wrong one.

The nurse didn't push it. She simply said, "I'll let the doctor know."

I saw how going without medication was affecting Simone. She stood in front of a couch in the dayroom signing to someone invisible. I tried to read her signs, but they were too disorganized to follow.

I interrupted her when someone announced, "It's time for group."

After the announcement, we walked with the others to the conference room. The group discussion was about using alcohol or other substances to mask symptoms of anger or anxiety.

The woman leading the group session said, "Many people with mental illness use street drugs or alcohol to help them feel better or to calm their agitation. Once they become addicted to these substances, they're considered to have a dual diagnosis."

Simone was attentive. "I don't use alcohol," she signed.

I voiced her comment but no one, not even the group facilitator, responded to her. Soon her eyes glazed over as if a sheer curtain had been drawn between us. I continued signing, though she was no longer focused on my interpreting, but on something in front of her, off to the side. She reached out for it, but there was nothing there. She gestured to the object, then stood and motioned for me to follow her. No one stopped her or bothered to ask where we were going when we left. Perhaps the group leader was used to this kind of behavior from patients, or at least from this patient. But it felt awkward to me. I didn't know what had compelled Simone to suddenly decide she had somewhere else to be.

As we headed up the hallway toward the nurses' station, I figured Simone needed to speak to someone. However, when one of the mental health workers called out, "Courtyard time," we were soon stepping outside with the others.

While some patients sat and smoked and others played volleyball, my client walked barefoot around the perimeter of the fenced yard. She studied the dirt near the brick wall of the building for several minutes. Then she came and told me that Princess Diana was buried there. I looked around for a staff person, thinking I should interpret this to them, but no one was accessible. A few minutes later we were all being escorted back inside.

The next day Simone was still refusing her prescribed medications. I overheard the nurse talking to the doctor, and his response was, "We can only hold her for 72 hours against her will. After that, if she refuses to take her medication, we have to let her go."

I couldn't believe what I was hearing. It sounded ridiculous. This patient was totally psychotic! Didn't she come to the hospital because she needed help? I was appalled that they would release someone as mentally sick as her out into the community, alone.

After the doctor left I asked the nurse, "Is it true, what he said?"

"Yes, she replied, sensing my concern, "it's the law."

***

It was funny how I'd grown to care about Carlos. I never saw him mad, angry, whining, or upset. He made it easy to like him. I'd seen him worried, though, usually about the weather. Yesterday, he greeted me with serious concern about an impending tornado. He'd seen a weather alert of possible severe weather and tornados in Northeast Colorado. I'd just come from outside where the skies were clearing. I didn't like seeing him filled with fear. I wanted to reassure him.

"The tornados are out east," I signed.

"I live east," he asserted, leading me to a computer in the building's lobby, where he showed me the weather map on the screen.

"Yes, but the tornado, it's far away, close to the next state, not here."

Carlos didn't seem convinced. "We'll see," he signed, turning off the computer.

Back to using his unwieldy shopping cart, he spun it around and pulled it toward the elevator. I followed, thinking about his conversations. There usually wasn't much depth to them. A few facts exchanged seemed to be enough for him. His shopping cart had more depth and weight to it than his conversations. Stuffed to overflowing, the cart banged into walls and tables as he tried to maneuver its unbalanced weight.

On this particular day the students in the class were enjoying a free lunch provided by the vocational education program. They ate while talking about their job searches or their forever-changing vocational goals. I continued signing the group's conversation, though I knew Carlos was not paying attention. He was busy sawing kernels off a piece of corn on the cob with a knife. He cleaned the cob of all its kernels and pushed them into one pile on the plate, then scooped them up with his fingers and crammed the fistful into his mouth. A couple of kernels stuck to his face and a few others fell back to the plate. For a second I was stunned by his poor manners, but then, the others were eating their corn on the cob with their fingers, too.

After the momentary distraction of the corn kernels I brought my attention back to the other students. When one began describing the life skills class he'd just come from, I immediately thought about Cyndi, wishing she could be in a program like that one. She would benefit from a life skills class.

Spring 2008

A month had gone by since I'd last seen Carlos. With other jobs taking up my attention, I hadn't noticed the lapse in time, but one day I ran into a student from the vocational prep class at a convenience store.

The student recognized me first. "Hey, weren't you the interpreter for Carlos?" he asked.

I then recognized him. "Yes, that's right. How is he? I haven't seen him in a while."

"Carlos moved to California."

"I've been wondering what happened to him."

"I guess he couldn't find a job here."

I was surprised to hear that Carlos had moved. It wasn't uncommon for clients to disappear, and we never learned what happened to them. At least I knew now what happened to Carlos. It's easier to move forward when you have closure on the past. Without it, you're left guessing.

It had been months, too, since I'd heard from Cyndi or Jeff. With no word on any progress or updates on her situation, I decided to check in with Jeff and inquire about Cyndi.

"How is she?"

"She's been talking about her friend, uh… what's her name?"

"Jane Seymour?"

"Yeah, her. She says Jane has cancer. She said she didn't have time to talk to me, because it was her turn to do some healing work on Jane, who was sleeping in her bed. She said there was a team of people doing the work because it's so exhausting. My sister is as crazy as ever," Jeff said, with a hint of laughter. "I don't know what to do about her," he added.

"Yeah, me neither. We saw how well my last idea worked." We both forced a laugh.

I didn't think to ask Jeff before we hung up, who was taking care of Cyndi.

Summer 2008

Cyndi was no longer speaking to me. She still spoke to Emily though, and periodically Emily would call me when she needed help sorting out stuff. Emily told me that Cyndi admitted to getting confused with her own thoughts sometimes, where she couldn't tell what was real and what wasn't. At one point Emily just needed a break from Cyndi and stepped back. But today she called with her voice full of excitement.

"Guess what? I've got good news!"

"What?"

"Jake's in jail! He's in for something unrelated to Cyndi, but she has come clean! She admitted there's no apartment downtown, there's no ranch, no horses, and the child she imagined to be adopting was the little girl down the street."

"Really?"

"It was all Jake's lies. He's been lying to Cyndi."

"You mean Cyndi was talking to you rationally?"

"Totally."

It felt good to hear this, yet I wasn't convinced that Cyndi had changed. Emily told me how mad Cyndi had been at me for "calling" the hospital.

"I asked Cyndi what she thought about what you did, and she said, 'I didn't like Diane putting herself in my business, but she knew what was going on with Jake.' I told her, 'We all did, but Diane was the only one with the courage to do something about it.' Then I asked her, 'What kind of friend is that?' Cyndi answered, 'A good one?' and I agreed."

Emily divulged that Jake was in jail for not paying child support to the mother of his child. I thought it would have been for something criminal, since we suspected he had a trail of wrongdoings, including stealing money from Cyndi, but maybe there would be more to come on this.

Though I never expected to hear from Cyndi again, she called me one day to apologize.

"I was so mad at you," she said, "but I had to hit rock bottom before I could see it."

This clarity of mind and rational talk was something I had not heard from Cyndi in three years. She spoke of Jane Seymour, but this time it was truthful things that Cyndi had read about her. We had a normal, amicable conversation, the kind we had when Harriette first introduced me to her daughter. Still, I was guarded.

Was Cyndi now trying to save face from being caught in her delusions by trying to blame everything on Jake's lies?

When I mentioned my reservation to Emily, she sighed.

"I don't know. My goal now is to help Cyndi straighten out her financial mess and get into counseling."

I was truly appreciative of Emily. She's that angel that appears in times of trouble. Cyndi, who had alienated so many, was lucky to have Emily in her life, as was I. I couldn't have dealt with Cyndi this long without her. Emily helped me keep my sanity, and for that, I will always be grateful to her.

Part 2

16

The Revolving Door

As a freelance interpreter I'm never privy to information about a company or the people in the places where I work, though spending time in one place I can observe and draw my own conclusions. The easy part for me, working on a psych ward, is I don't have to wonder or figure out on my own if my client or another patient has a mental illness. Someone else has already done that work for me.

Camille was one such patient. With gray-streaked hair draped over her face, she would sit in the dayroom on Unit 6 wrapped in a green or white hospital blanket. It didn't matter if it was hot or cold outside. Sunny, windy, or snowing, she'd have a blanket wrapped around her shoulders or her waist. She'd sit by herself, rarely speaking unless someone spoke to her first.

hile other patients attended groups or participated in activities, Camille sat in the dayroom wrapped in a blanket. Sometimes she'd mumble or shout obscenities at other patients. The only consequence for being verbally assaultive was being sent to her room. No other consequences were available, because Camille had nothing for the staff to take away. She had no hobbies or activities that she engaged in, nor did she watch TV. She did not converse with the other patients or ever have visitors. She didn't own a thing. All she had was a government bed in her government-controlled life.

One afternoon, while Dallas watched TV, I had little to do and was sitting at the staff desk when Camille hobbled over with her blanket pulled tight around her legs. She came near enough so I could hear her, but stood back as if she was afraid to come any closer.

"Could you help me find my husband?" she asked.

There was only one way to respond. "I'm, sorry. I'm not able to do that," I said, "but would you like to talk to staff?"

"No. They're no help," she grumbled, turning and hobbling away.

I looked to Tony, one of the mental health technicians, standing across the room, who was giving me an upward nod with his chin. He'd seen Camille talking to me but hadn't heard over the noise in the milieu what she'd said. I half-heard him and half-read his lips. "Anything relevant?" he asked.

I shook my head. I'd heard Twyla, another technician, remind Camille enough times when she got in these moods, stating quite frankly, "You don't have a husband, Camille."

Ordinarily, hospital staff would never ask an interpreter if something a patient said was relevant. However, after working at the hospital for several weeks, the staff treated me as though I were one of them, making me feel like part of the team.

Besides, Unit 6 was like a family of sorts, as some patients, like Camille, stayed there for long stretches of time only because there was nowhere else for them to go. I'd heard that no group home or nursing home would take her. Trenton was another one who had no other place to go. Like Camille, I never observed Trenton participating in anything. Mostly, he sat in the dayroom with his arms folded and a baseball cap pulled down over his long hair, its brim hiding his eyes. He often fell asleep like this, as he was now, sitting on one of the pink plastic couches arranged around the TV.

Dallas was postured on the other pink couch, directly in front of the TV. While she was absorbed in *The Price is Right*, I watched Trenton as he woke up and stood. He took slow careful steps on account of his poor vision. Sometimes people offered him verbal directions, but no one ever offered him an arm for guidance. It seemed insensitive to me, though as I thought about it, I figured it had something to do with the rules about no physical contact with others. Trenton took a few more steps, then stopped. If he'd taken just one more, he would have stumbled right onto Dallas.

Twyla called out, "Trenton, turn to your left. There's someone sitting in front of you."

Twyla told Trenton to follow her voice, and he turned away from Dallas.

Watching this reminded me of an incident the previous week when the staff almost left Trenton in the parking lot. We had just returned from a group trip to a medical clinic. We had all climbed out of the van and were headed into the hospital when someone happened to look back and saw him standing by himself.

"Oh Trenton," Twyla cried.

She ran back and shepherded him into the building. I wondered how long he might have stood there had no one noticed. I doubted Trenton was a run risk, anyway, like some others on the unit.

The more I worked at the hospital, the more familiar I became with the patients' personalities and behaviors. For some, it was not their first hospitalization. "It's the revolving door," Twyla said. "It happens to a lot of these people. They come and get better. Then they get released. But when they get on the outside, they stop taking their meds and end up right back here."

She said it as casually as a restaurateur would say, "We get a lot of repeat customers."

I found this terribly disconcerting. If professionals knew it was likely a patient would be readmitted sometime after they'd been released, why wasn't something in place to prevent that? It would seem that greater monitoring or supervision of patients after they are released would help reduce the possibility if they are at risk of readmission.

The "revolving door" problem gnawed at me just as much as our law that prohibited someone from being held in a psychiatric facility longer than 72 hours without their consent did. I was appalled when I first heard that. I thought it was ridiculous to expect someone in the throes of psychosis to consent to hospitalization and treatment. I'd thought immediately of their families, imagining the turmoil they must go through trying to get their loved one into treatment. Family members have little power if the ill person is of legal age to make decisions for themself. I didn't think this law could be good for those who were too far indisposed to recognize their own illness, nor was it good for society to have psychotic people roaming the streets. For a moment I envisioned riders on white horses galloping into the hospital calling on us to join them on a crusade to the capitol to protest our broken mental health system. If they'd had an extra horse I would have mounted and ridden away with them.

When this image faded, I saw the reality. No one was marching with signs at the capitol. And though the state recognized that some individuals needed to be hospitalized and would be even without their consent if a judge decreed it, many with severe and persistent mental illnesses were being released from their 72-hour holds with no treatment plan and no one to monitor their well-being. And for those who were released only to be readmitted later, and repeatedly, this lack of stability certainly was not healthy. Nor did it seem an efficient or cost-effective way to utilize our mental health system. Yet, instead of resolving this problem, it had been given a name: The Revolving Door!

17

Repercussions of Deinstitutionalization

With my work increasingly focused in mental health, I was gradually delving into its politics. Looking back, however, my interest may have been sparked long before this time, by what happened at Columbine High School.

I was at home that morning, on April 20, 1999, working on last-minute travel arrangements for my son's competitive soccer team. The boys were preparing to fly to Cincinnati to play in a college showcase tournament. Around noon I got a frantic call from our coach. "Have you heard what's going on at Columbine?" he asked.

"No, what?" I replied.

"Turn on your TV," he said. "There's shooting and pipe bombs going off!"

Several of our players attended Columbine. I spent the rest of that day in front of the television, frightened and nervous, watching students with their hands raised above their heads streaming out of the building as SWAT teams and emergency vehicles surrounded the school.

My son was not a student at Columbine, so I knew he was safe, but throughout that day, I talked to the anxious parents of our players who attended the school, as we tried to identify the whereabouts of each of the boys. We didn't know if any had been injured, or where they might have gone, as students had scattered through the Columbine neighborhood as they fled the campus.

By late afternoon all of our players had been located, and we had some solace finding that none were hurt. Still, a sickening heartache permeated the community as we began finding out the extent of the bloodshed. Ten students had been shot and killed in the school library and 12 others were injured. The final count at the end of the day was 15 dead, including the two who were responsible for the killings, Eric Harris and Dylan Klebold. Twenty-one others had been wounded.

The question left on our minds was, why? Why did those boys do this? Many people, like me, wanted to know what had been wrong with these two teenagers. Police investigations came up with few answers to our questions, so theories as to what caused these two teens to commit these acts ran rampant, from violent video games to neglectful parents, to mental illness.

There had been signs that these two boys were troubled. They'd had previous run-ins with the law. They'd made violent, hateful writings and drawings. They'd accumulated a stash of weapons and bombs. This behavior, even without the shooting rampage and their ultimate suicides, suggested mental illness at its root. The question then became, were these boys born antisocial, or did they become antisocial by some influence along the way? Was their behavior the result of playing violent video games? Or was it something within their brain chemistry that changed, as it does in depression or schizophrenia?

After the Columbine tragedy, I began reading about mental disorders trying to learn what causes a person's brain "to break." I wanted to know what effect mental disorders had on people's lives. I needed a better understanding of our mental health laws: how and why they came about and how were they were affecting families who were dealing with mental illness. I thought if crazy people could walk into schools with pipe bombs and guns and start killing students and teachers, then we've got a big problem, and we can no longer ignore mental illness in our society.

My research taught me the sad history of psychiatric treatment in our country and about deinstitutionalization, which began in 1954 when the antipsychotic medication, Thorazine, became available. Thorazine worked to quell hallucinations and calm agitation in many mentally ill patients, which meant they could be released from the hospitals and go back to living in the community. The idea that more patients could be safely treated outside of hospitals spread.

The concept grew more powerful during the 1960s, after journalists, like Geraldo Rivera, exposed the deplorable conditions of filth, overcrowding, and inadequate care found in some of our mental institutions. These revelations and findings of women who were not mentally ill, but who had been unjustly committed by their husbands, reinforced the belief that mental patients deserved to have more rights and freedom. This led not only to a string of lawsuits but ultimately to the Community Mental Health Centers Act, signed by President Kennedy in 1963. The intention of this Act was for individual states to replace their inpatient psychiatric hospitals with community treatment facilities.

Four years after the Community Mental Health Centers Act, the state of California passed the Lanterman-Petris-Short Act, which made it illegal to commit someone to a mental institution against their will unless there is compelling evidence that the person is a danger to himself or others. Other states followed suit and soon there were waves of patients being released from the state mental hospitals into the communities. From 1955 to 1994 nearly half a million patients were released in the United States, and eventually, thousands of state mental hospitals closed.

The repercussions of deinstitutionalization were disastrous. The money previously allocated to the state hospitals did not end up going to build community mental health centers as envisioned. States spent the money on other things, and the assumption that released patients would go live with their families also turned out to be naïve. Many patients had no home or family to go back to. Some patients were sent to nursing homes or boarding houses. A large number became homeless. Over time, halfway houses or group homes opened, but to this day there is not enough housing or supervision for people with severe and persistent mental illnesses.

Nearly one in five adults in the United States experience mental illness each year. The National Institute on Mental Health estimates that 2.4 million American adults have schizophrenia, and another 5.7 million have Bipolar disorder. Millions more struggle with anxiety and depression. Without housing, jobs, or other support services, many of these people wind up on the streets, or in emergency rooms, jails, or prisons. With over three hundred thousand mentally ill people incarcerated, our prisons have become mental institutions. Our laws, created with noble intentions of preventing wrongfully committed people from being locked up against their will, have inadvertently resulted in many seriously ill people being moved from one locked-up place to another where there is little to no treatment available.

Learning the history of how we came to be in the dismal place we are in serving persons with mental illness helped me understand the macro picture of mental illness in our country, however, it did not answer for me two lingering questions: What causes mental illness, and what had been wrong with Eric Harris and Dylan Klebold? If we knew the answers to these questions, perhaps we could do more to prevent more "Columbines" from happening. It had been nine long years since I first asked myself these questions. After more digging around on the internet, I found an article that finally answered one for me.

David Cullen, the author of *The Depressive and the Psychopath*, wrote of the summit that was held after the Columbine massacre where a team of psychiatrists and psychologists—including Dr. Frank Ochberg of Michigan State University and Supervisory Special Agent Dwayne Fuselier, a clinical psychologist and the FBI's lead Columbine investigator—analyzed the personalities of Dylan Klebold and Eric Harris. Their conclusion at the end of the summit was that Klebold was a suicidal depressive and Harris was a psychopath. Nothing pointed to violent video games as contributing to their violent behavior.

This article confirmed my suspicion that these boys were suffering from mental disorders. The second question remained, however. If it wasn't violent video games that caused their sociopathic behavior, what did?

As our community gradually began healing after the Columbine shooting, our attention turned to other things, until it happened again, on September 27, 2006, at Platte Canyon High School, not far from where I live. A mentally deranged man entered the school, took six girls hostage, sexually assaulted them, and then shot and killed 16-year-old Emily Scott Keys. Her family and our entire community were in turmoil.

Less than a year later, on April 16, 2007, Seung-Hui Cho, a young man with a documented mental illness, slaughtered 32 people on the campus of Virginia Polytechnic Institute. Not only was the state of Virginia wrapped in turmoil, but the entire country was thrust into mourning.

Reeling from these tragedies, it was abundantly clear that our laws governing mental health were terribly inadequate. They were enabling, rather than preventing, these horrific occurrences. Yet, few were talking about this, and we seemed to be doing nothing about the obvious issue. It's impossible to prevent all such tragedies, but surely, we could do better. School shootings were not new in our history, but these jabbed me like a spur to the ribs. I could no longer be complacent.

18

It's Not Just Racing Thoughts and Spending Sprees

With a five-month reprieve from Cyndi's delusions and anger, I could feel my entire body back on an even keel. While I hadn't heard if anything positive resulted from my meeting with the social worker, I wanted to believe that Cyndi was at least getting some supervision, if not psychiatric intervention. I was curious how she was doing, but reluctant to call her. I didn't think Cyndi would ever call me again, but then she did. Jim and I were watching a movie when the phone rang.

Straight away she stirred up the fight. "What you did was uncalled for!"

My heart leapt into a sprint. I felt heat rising from my neck to my forehead. "So, you didn't mean that apology you made to me on the phone?"

A volley of yelling and scolding spilled into my ears, along with a blast of legal threats for violating her patient rights by talking to the social worker. A surge of anger rose from my belly to the tip of my tongue. I was ready to strike with a barrage of my own, but I held back, refusing to give her the verbal battle she wanted, a fight she would make sure to win. Instead, I gave her what she was not expecting.

"Cyndi, I'm sorry that you're considering that."

Before we got off the phone, she threw one more dart.

"You didn't even apologize."

Unwilling to take the bait, I simply said, "I'm not going to argue with you, Cyndi. You can have your lawyer call me."

I hung up and called her brother to let him know that Cyndi was threatening to call her lawyer about me. I doubted I'd done anything illegal, but the chill of her rancor had me shaken.

Jeff said she was threatening him with her lawyer, too, regarding their ongoing battle over the family photo albums she was demanding from him.

"The only reason I'm holding onto them is I'm afraid that if I give them to her, they will be lost or destroyed."

I understood his position. Cyndi had lost things I'd given her, too, and even had the gall to ask me to replace them.

"Yes, that's her track record, unfortunately."

Talking with Jeff put me at ease. The more people Cyndi threatened with lawyers, the less likely she was to follow through with her threats. Still, her phone call bothered me.

"My lawyer is a very good one," she'd emphasized, the same way she'd talked about her contractor, the "very good contractor" who was going to build the condo for her with the spiraling indoor ramps. Maybe her lawyer was another delusion, like the medicine man, the wolf, and the ranch she had with Jane Seymour.

It made me angry that Cyndi thought she could intimidate me, though, more than once, I imagined standing in court defending myself against her, the crazy lady. I hated that I'd lost patience with her and was even thinking such things. How I wished to tame this anxiety, speak to her with calm, and put an end to this drama, but I was afraid any attempt I made would be a dreadful failure.

Cyndi called on several more occasions, harassing me with the same threats. Each time I told her to have her lawyer call me. The last time, I shouted and told her to stop calling me before I slammed down the phone. I felt horrible, like I was actually guilty of something. I couldn't eat or sleep. I was losing weight, waiting for a letter or a phone call from her lawyer.

Disquieted, I searched for information to help me sort out the puzzle of Cyndi. Though I'd long suspected that her behavior was symptomatic of bipolar disorder, or even schizophrenia, I was curious if the steroids she'd been on for so many years for her asthma could be bringing on the psychiatric symptoms.

What I found out about bipolar disorder is that it's not just about racing thoughts and spending sprees, as I had believed. It causes extreme mood swings, changing from manic to depressive, with episodes lasting anywhere from a few days to a few months. Along with the mania and depression, a person with this disorder can experience psychotic symptoms, such as hallucinations or delusions. These contribute to them having unrealistic ideas, grandiose and distorted beliefs, and to making poor decisions. The results are damaged relationships and one messed up life. Classic Cyndi.

I also learned that corticosteroid drugs could indeed bring on a range of psychiatric symptoms. Reading this made me feel vindicated, at the very least, that I'd made the right decision when I alerted the social worker about Cyndi.

* * *

Throughout lunchtime on Unit 6 we listened to Earl preach, "Lord God Almighty, Heaven, and Earth. Christ Jesus, Jacob, Emanuel, Lord Almighty."

On and on he went, pausing now and then to take a bite of his food that was getting cold in front of him. He wore a long bib to catch the bits that were shaken from his spoon by his tremors. I'd been told that Earl had been living in hospitals since he was a teenager.

"He used to be bouncing off the walls, he was so psychotic. He was a real handful," staff said.

Now, decades later, Earl moved like a snail shuffling from his bedroom to the dayroom and back. I never heard him speak, except when he was praying during meals. His blessings lasted well after the others had eaten and the trays were gone. It's why his meals were delivered in Styrofoam boxes instead of on plates.

Earl was the one who had stared at me on my first day on the unit, drooling when he smiled. It hadn't seemed like much was going on behind his eyes, but now I saw how Patty, one of the technicians, could bring Earl out of his shell. Patty had long wavy hair and wore cowboy boots to work. She really "got" these patients. Patty would ask each one during the community meetings how they were feeling and what their goal was for the day. Once while I was interpreting for Dallas, Patty suggested at the end of the meeting, "How about we all sing 'God Bless America?'"

Dallas scowled and rolled her eyes. With a sweep of her hand, she brushed us off and stomped away. I could have left, too, since I no longer had anyone to interpret for, but I stayed. I saw Earl for the first time sit up straight. His eyes sparkled as he sang like a choirboy with Patty. At the end of the song the patients scattered and only Earl, Patty, and I remained.

Patty asked Earl, "Would you like to sing 'America the Beautiful now?'"

He nodded and the three of us sang the entire song. For a few moments Earl was not a mental patient. He was someone loving life.

After we sang Patty picked up her clipboard and went on to her other tasks. Earl went back to sitting and drooling, and I went with a nurse who wanted to meet with Dallas.

I sat with the nurse and a social worker across the table from Dallas in the conference room. We were on the easy escape side closest to the door.

"So what happened last night?" the social worker asked?

Dallas signed and I spoke for her, "Nothing, I was just helping Mala braid her hair."

"The night nurse said you were touching her."

"We were just braiding our hair."

"But you argued with the nurse when she asked you to stop."

"Because, she said I was touching Mala, but I wasn't."

"You know the rules. There's no touching other patients. You broke the rules so you are going to have to isolate in your room for 24 hours."

"NOoooo," Dallas cried, dropping her head onto her arms on the table. I wasn't sure if her sobbing was real or merely a show.

"Dallas," the social worker called, trying to get her attention, but Dallas was still crying with her head down. The social worker and the nurse stood, ready to leave, so I stood too. When we filed out of the room, Dallas stopped crying and followed us. No one said a word as we proceeded to the dayroom, though I saw other staff members, all with their eyes on us as though they knew something was about to happen.

As if in slow motion, Dallas picked up a chair from a table. Sensing nothing good was about to happen with this chair, I got myself to the far side of the room. Oddly, no other patients were in the dayroom and most of the staff had moved into the office. Dallas lifted the chair higher and heaved it toward the windows. In my mind I saw the glass shatter when the chair hit, but the window held firm. Of course, the windows on a psych ward would be made of unbreakable glass.

With surging anger, Dallas lifted a second chair and heaved again. This time the chair hit the window and broke into pieces. Parts shot off in different directions, sliding across the floor. No one spoke, and no one tried to stop her. Except for the crashing of chairs, an eerie silence hung in the air.

I was the only one in the dayroom besides Dallas, but I wasn't afraid. I was not her target. She then moved to a third chair and lifted it upward. Two uniformed men appeared as it hurled through the air, barely missing them.

The officers mobilized, one on each side of Dallas, and seized her. She barely put up a fight. As they escorted her to the seclusion room, staff members began flowing back onto the unit. Though I'd seen the fear on their faces, the staff was well practiced at dealing with violent outbursts like this, and they handled this one perfectly.

When my adrenalin settled, I felt the tension slowly release from my body. I guess I'd been more afraid than I'd realized. Still, I marveled at how it was that every time there was a flare-up on the unit, the uniformed officers magically appeared, and like an extinguisher to a fire, they put out the flames.

19

Psych Ward Distractions

November 2008

Saturday mornings were quiet at the hospital. With no appointments on weekends, the patients slept in, but this morning a line of them were at the staff desk when I arrived, each one asking for something. A couple of new admits in hospital scrubs milled about. Trenton was sleeping upright on the couch while Earl sat staring at people, drooling onto his shirt. Leola, the patient who approached me with the stern look on that first day, was sharing the couch with Trenton. Leola was drooling, too, and picking her nose. Finally, I spotted Dallas at a table reading a newspaper and sauntered over to ask what was on her schedule today.

She looked up from her newspaper. "Good Morning," I signed, suddenly aware of movement behind me. I turned to see Leola. A second ago she was on the couch. Now she was within inches of my face, mumbling. I looked at her lone front tooth while trying to decipher what she was saying. Leola reached out and instinctively I stepped back.

"Leola, watch your boundaries," someone called out.

"Move, Leola," Dallas yelled in her deaf voice.

Leola backed away, and I was saved, narrowly escaping her clutch.

Dallas told me she was going to her room to take a nap, so I had nothing to do but settle into a chair at the desk and watch Philomena, a large-boned woman in heavy eye make-up, pace back and forth. Philomena looked like she was ready to go somewhere, nervously waiting for her ride to show up.

For several weeks, I had thought Philomena was from another country by her exotic looks and silent pacing. I thought maybe she didn't speak English. Eventually, she started speaking, and it was English. In fact, she spoke quite loud, at times. Sweet and friendly to one person, Philomena could turn on a dime and fly into a rage over some perceived slight, hollering a barrage of insults. The hair on my arms rose whenever she got into screaming matches with other patients. I couldn't guess what Philomena's problem was, but when she was pacing, she was quiet.

A lot of patients would pace, for hours it seemed. The restlessness or agitation was either part of their psychiatric illness or a side effect of their medication. Ivy was another one who paced. Unlike Philomena, Ivy was petite, and she talked to herself as she walked. I saw Ivy coming up the hall from her room wearing a flowered skirt and T-shirt, walking with determination. She came close, then stopped and stared at me with big, round eyes. I smiled and Ivy smiled back. She turned and walked away, then spun around and came back toward me, as if she'd just remembered what she wanted to say, except she didn't say anything. She stood for a few seconds before turning and heading back to her room.

Something intrigued me about Ivy. Perhaps it was her dark eyes. They were like those of a fawn you'd stumble upon in the woods and wonder if you should rescue it, or leave the fawn to its own.

To make myself less conspicuous while I hung out in the dayroom, I went to look for a magazine. An old copy of *ELLE* magazine with Madonna on the cover was the best I could come up with. With all the distractions on a psych ward, it was too difficult to concentrate, anyway. So, reading anything of substance was out.

Soon, Ivy came up the hall again, wearing jeans with a printed shirt. Over the next two hours, I noticed a change in her clothing at least three times. When I mentioned this to Patty, she said, "Yeah, a lot of patients do that when they're manic."

After lunch had been served and cleaned up, Dallas appeared with tousled hair from her nap. She pulled a baseball cap on over it and slid onto a couch, only to get up a second later when Twyla called out, "Courtyard time." Then we all filed out.

It used to be that courtyard time in psychiatric hospitals was for patients who wanted to smoke. I remember working at a few of them. Cigarette smoke lingered in those yards from earlier smoke breaks, and each time we went out nearly every patient would light up, adding more smoke to the thick air. I'm not a smoker and would cough whenever we stepped outside, but smoking was soothing for the patients. The nicotine affected them in a way that gave them respite from the nagging voices in their heads. Inside those psych units, the old furniture smelled stale from all the years when people were allowed to smoke indoors. Smoking is no longer allowed around most facilities, though I still notice that rank odor sometimes lingering in old buildings.

These days courtyard time serves to break up the monotony of spending the day locked up, and the air outside is indeed fresh. This rooftop courtyard had planters with flowers and a small basketball court for active patients. Despite the surrounding fencing with barbed wire swirled along the top, being outside seemed to normalize everyone. We were no longer patients and staff. We were people enjoying the glorious fall weather. As I interpreted for Dallas, however, I was aware of Ivy off to the side conversing with her reflection in the window's glass. She spoke and laughed, fully animated with her entire body, as though she were joking around with a group of high school friends. I longed to know what she found so funny, but she was the only one who could hear the voices in her head.

Twyla brought us back to reality when she called out, "Time to go in, everybody," and we all marched inside, resuming our roles as patients and staff.

Dallas was working on a craft project with beads and colored strings when a new patient with unruly long hair approached her, signing. He was not using real signs. He was mocking her, or just acting like he knew sign language. Dallas rolled her eyes at him and turned her attention back to her beads. I was watching this and listening to another new patient argue with the staff about getting a razor. He wanted to shave and was getting agitated, raising his voice louder and louder.

"You can't talk to us that way," Tony told him. "We're being respectful to you and you need to be respectful to us."

Tony's admonition, however, had no effect. The patient escalated to yelling and stomping his feet. Sensing a brawl about to break out in the dayroom, I felt the hairs on my arms rising, waiting for me to act. Just then the omniscient "angels" arrived.

I assumed these uniformed officers were here to calm the agitated man, but they walked right past him. Crossing the room, they approached Trenton, who was slumped forward on the couch. The officers huddled in front of him, too far away for me to hear their conversation, until Trenton raised his normally soft voice and yelled, "I don't want gonorrhea!"

Oblivious to all the commotion happening behind her, Dallas was focused on the intricate set of knots she was tying between beads. I stood ready to alert her to the chaos, though soon, the staff stepped in clearing patients from the dayroom because of Trenton's problem. They knew when one patient had an issue it could have a domino effect on the others. To avoid this, they sent everyone to their room—everyone except for Dallas. Before I could wonder why, a doctor I'd never seen here before approached her.

"Please go to your room," he said. She looked to me to interpret.

I signed what he said and Dallas looked perplexed, then perturbed. "Noooooo," she yelled.

"Please help us," the doctor said. "Another patient is having a hard time."

Dallas rebelled: "No, I won't go to my room. I'm tired of this!"

Perhaps, to prevent a further outburst from Dallas, the staff decided she could stay as long as she moved to a safer spot. So, Dallas moved next to the window and looked out. The new patient who had mocked her was standing alone in the courtyard. Seeing her at the window, he feigned signing again. When Dallas flipped her middle finger at him, I sensed more trouble was about to erupt. Fortunately, since Trenton had settled down, the staff informed Dallas she could return to her beading and her attention fell away from the mocker. I sat down at the table with her and watched the officers move away from Trenton. They walked past us on their way out to the courtyard.

With a flick of her head in their direction, Dallas asked, "What's going on?"

We both knew the uniformed officers rarely went out there.

"I don't know," I signed.

We saw them talking to the mocker, and soon they were escorting him back inside. Acting loudly agitated, he leaned in toward Dallas as they passed by us, waving wiggling fingers in her face. I was surprised when she kept her cool, merely flashing him a look of disgust before going back to her beads and colored strings.

Despite the officers flanking him, the man spat out an ugly insult at Dallas, shouting behind her back, "Do you have any idea how STUPID you are?"

I cringed at his cutting remark. My job is to interpret everything I hear that's relevant to my client, but in that moment I hesitated. Should I get her attention and tell her what he said, allowing her the right to respond how she wishes, or let it go? I chose the latter. Watching the officers lead him away, I pictured what might have happened had I chosen differently: Dallas leaping out of her chair and throwing punches at his face. It was just how the day seemed to be going.

* * *

Sunday mornings were even quieter than Saturday mornings at the hospital. Few patients were in the dayroom besides Ivy, who was pacing through the room and the halls talking to herself. Lately she'd been hiding behind heavy eye make-up and overgrown bangs. As she passed by I tried to imagine what path had brought this pale-looking waif to a locked psychiatric ward. There was a mystery to unlock with Ivy. The way she looked at me, while other patients avoided eye contact, made me think her story was one the world ought to know—a story of how a lost orphan became trapped in a shell with her voices. The first time I'd said hello to her, she replied in a soft voice. Since then the staff had warned me, "Be careful, she can be violent."

I never witnessed violence from Ivy. She kept to herself, mostly, and rarely took part in group activities. I never even saw her leave the unit. Aside from pacing, her main activity seemed to revolve around her wardrobe. On this day, Ivy was wearing pink tennis shoes with neon pink polish on her fingernails. Her hair, sectioned and clasped with pink barrettes, looked as though a child had fashioned it. She passed by me several times before stopping, and then she looked straight into my eyes.

"Hi, Ivy."

"Hi," she replied.

I noticed her eyelids, heavy, like from exhaustion. Ivy turned, took a few steps, and came back. She did this several times, then took a chair, sitting near me. I don't think I'd ever seen Ivy sit, except to eat. She was too restless to stay in one place for any length of time. As I pondered the reason for her heavy eyelids, she looked at me and smiled.

"You have a pretty smile."

"Thank you," she said.

Her eyes stayed on me until I broke the silence. "So, what do you like to do?"

Ivy stared back at me with a blank expression.

"Do you like to dance and sing?"

I knew she did. I'd seen her dancing in the hallways and singing in the dayroom while watching her reflection on the blank TV screen.

"Yeah, I like to dance. I like clothes, too. I want to get some clothes at the clothes bank, but they say I can't go."

"Is the clothes bank here?"

"Yeah, but they say I have too many clothes already."

A social worker walked past and Ivy said, "I like her sweater. I want a black one like that to wear at home, all cozy over my teddy."

"Your teddy?"

"Yeah, with a glass of Zinfandel and some caviar."

I was unsure what to say next with the conversation going in this unexpected direction, but then Ivy fell into a trance. She was no longer with me. She'd gone somewhere in her mind with her gaze on someone in front of her who was invisible to me.

"Hey, come 'ere," she said, beckoning the person with her finger. She winked and added, "I've got somethin' for ya."

Seeing Ivy slip into her world, it dawned on me. Was that the mystery of Ivy that just unfolded?

20

Golden Brook

Jim kissed my cheek and left for work while I sat in my bathrobe eating a bowl of wheat flakes with bananas. Food was going down easier now, as time had passed without me hearing from Cyndi or her lawyer. I was looking forward to having the day to myself. I could stay in my pajamas and write all day, get a haircut, or even a massage. I was halfway through the bowl of flakes when the phone rang.

It was a rehabilitation care center. Another interpreter had given them my name. "We have a deaf resident who is having psychiatric symptoms. Are you by any chance available at 10:00 for a few hours?"

"Yes, possibly. Where is the assignment?"

"We're in Golden."

I glanced at the clock. "Yes, I can get there by 10:00."

I swallowed another spoonful of cereal, dropped the bowl in the sink, and headed to the shower. So much for a day off.

At Golden Brook Rehabilitation Care Center a woman, wearing her hair in a graceful gather of cornrow braids, introduced herself.

"Hi, I'm Lashay, the floor nurse. You're going to be working with Mr. Rousseau. He's deaf-blind."

No one had mentioned this to me. Fortunately, I had experience working with persons with this dual sensory loss. Not all interpreters did. It might have been useful information for them to include on the phone. It had me wondering though how they'd been communicating with him until now.

"Mr. Rousseau has been here a week, but it's my first day with him," Lashay explained. "He's having hallucinations, and he's really agitated. He's been aggressive, brandishing his cane at the staff."

Picturing this, I was curious if he was truly brandishing his cane, or just trying to communicate. I knew of instances where police arrived on a scene where a deaf person was involved and they mistook the individual's excited verbal noises and arm gesturing as violent, threatening behavior. The police responded with undue force when the deaf person was merely trying to communicate. Maybe Mr. Rousseau was trying to communicate and got frustrated. Maybe he *was* brandishing his cane—feeling confused and scared, like a growling dog cornered by a stranger.

"I'll take you to his room," Lashay said.

Scenarios of how I would communicate with Mr. Rousseau began sifting through my mind. My method would depend on whether he was fully blind, or if he had low vision or tunnel vision. I was about to ask Lashay if he used tactile communication, but we were almost to his room. I would know soon enough.

The room was dark with shut blinds and the lights off. Mr. Rousseau was in the bed near the window and a roommate slept in the other.

"How do I wake him?" Lashay asked.

"Just tap his arm."

Reacting to her touch, Mr. Rousseau sat up. He pulled a folded cane from under the covers and unfolded it. There was no brandishing, but he did appear on edge, a bit overly wary. As his dark eyes glared straight at us, I assumed he had some vision, though limited.

"Ask him if he's hungry," Lashay said.

He interrupted as I was signing: "I can't see you. I don't understand you," he signed. He slid his legs over the edge of the bed, where his feet touched the floor. I moved closer and repeated the question, but got the same agitated response. Thinking his vision must be worse than my first guess, I slipped my hand under his and tried tactile signs. People who are used to communicating this way welcome this touch. It's the door opening them to the human race. But Mr. Rousseau jerked his hand away. Recoiling, he clutched his white cane tight to his body as if he were afraid we'd take it away.

I sensed this deaf man had slipped into blindness with no preparation or assistance with transitioning to living and communicating without hearing or sight. Such isolation would be a blow to anyone. I took in a deep breath, determined to be helpful.

Lashay found a yellow legal pad sitting on the windowsill.

"Here," she said, "It looks like he's been writing notes with the night aide."

I read the top page: *Are you hungry?* And the answer: *yes*. It was the same question I'd been trying to ask for the last few minutes, and last night it was accomplished with a few strokes of a marker on a piece of paper. Lashay wrote her question on a new page and handed it to Mr. Rousseau.

He carried the legal pad over to the window where a sliver of light peeked through the blinds. He moved the pad from side to side under a ray of light, searching for the words on the paper, but soon gave up and pushed the pad back onto the sill. Despite the sleeping roommate, Lashay turned on the ceiling light.

"Ask him if he wants to go eat," she said.

* * *

In the lighted room Mr. Rousseau could see better to read my signing.

"No, I can't eat," he signed. "The woman said 'no breakfast, no lunch, and no dinner.' I can only drink water or orange juice."

"Who told you that?" Lashay asked.

"A woman. Her face was all distorted."

Lashay told me to ask him if he thought the woman might be part of his hallucinations. Mr. Rousseau nodded. He agreed that the woman could have been that. Nonetheless, he said, "I don't like her."

Sensitive to his issues, Lashay, simply said, "Tell him he'll feel better if he eats something."

Mr. Rousseau balked when I relayed this, shaking his head. He refused to go with her to the dining room. With nothing more to do, we left Mr. Rousseau to himself.

As Lashay and I walked back to the common room she shared something with me.

"Because he recognizes that he's having hallucinations, we don't believe Mr. Rousseau has a psychiatric illness. Someone truly psychotic is not able to distinguish hallucinations from reality."

Having been through the experience with Cyndi, of trying to decipher whether she had a psychiatric illness, I could appreciate the challenge they had here with Mr. Rousseau. Adding the complexities of deafness and blindness to the mix with hallucinations, I envisioned the multiple layers they had to tease through, to figure out what was going on with him.

By noon Mr. Rousseau's hunger had, apparently, overcome his fear because he allowed an aide to walk him to the resident dining area. He ate heartily and asked if he could go outside afterward.

"Let's ask someone," I signed.

We found an aide who agreed to escort us, and he took Mr. Rousseau by the hand. Awkward together, they wobbled along and despite his cane extended in front of him, Mr. Rousseau bumped into a table and chairs.

"Watch where you're going," he signed, scolding the aide.

I spoke his words to the aide. As they started through the door, I gritted my teeth expecting a collision with the doorjamb. Sure enough, Mr. Rousseau hit it with his shoulder. With flying fingers and a gruff sound from his throat, he signed to the aide, "I told you to watch out!"

Outside, Mr. Rousseau stood with his cane, unshaven in a white T-shirt and green cotton institutional pants, holding onto the aide's arm. With graying hair, I guessed him to be in his fifties. Underneath the fear and anger I saw a sweet and kind man. As I studied him, I shared an observation with the aide.

"He seems to have some vision, but not peripherally. That's why he banged into the table and chairs when you two were walking, and then into the doorjamb. He didn't see them. I can show you an easier way to walk with him if you'd like, so he doesn't bang into things."

"Okay," he said.

Taking Mr. Rousseau's hand, I guided it onto the aide's forearm. "Instead of pulling him by the hand, let him hold your arm at the elbow. With him closer to you, you're more in control. You lead with him just a step behind you.

When you walk, give yourselves plenty of room on both sides so neither of you will bang into things."

These sound like obvious considerations, however, when you are guiding someone for the first time, your brain needs time to adjust to you suddenly becoming double in width. Following my suggestions the two of them were more steady trudging along in the fresh air. Soon, Mr. Rousseau said he'd had enough, complaining of scary figures darting into his path and the sun hurting his eyes.

I suspected that Mr. Rousseau had Usher syndrome because of the way he could not see in the dim light of his room and how the bright sun outside bothered him. Both are symptoms of retinitis pigmentosa, the eye condition involved with Usher syndrome. It affects the rods and cones, the light receptors of the eye, causing initial night blindness and tunnel vision. The degeneration of the retinas is progressive and can lead to partial or full blindness.

Throughout the day Mr. Rousseau communicated minimally and only with staff. It gave me plenty of time to think and, with little information about him, my mind teemed with questions. Was he truly psychotic, and how did he come to be here? I saw a rough road ahead of him and the staff in the next few weeks. But I was up for the challenge if they hired me.

Four days later I was back at Golden Brook, finding Mr. Rousseau in the residents' dining room eating on a blueberry muffin. I hated to interrupt him, but I wanted him to know I was there. He startled when I tapped his arm. Backing away from his muffin, he glared at me with his dark eyes.

"I'm sorry, I didn't mean to scare you," I signed. "I'm your interpreter."

With the morning sun brightening the room he seemed to recognize me, yet he said nothing, returning instead to his muffin. I noticed he still hadn't bathed, given his greasy hair that was stuck to the sides of his head and the sour odor I smelled. Apparently, I wasn't the only one who noticed this. An aide circling by our table introduced himself.

"Hi, I'm Jerry. Maybe Mr. Rousseau will feel better if he gets cleaned up today. When he's finished eating, can you ask him if he'd like a shower or a bath?"

"Sure," I said.

Mr. Rousseau stuffed the last bite of muffin into his mouth, pushed his chair back from the table, and unfolded his cane. He stood and took my arm, ready for me to lead him from the dining room. I tapped his arm, letting him know I first had something to say, and he stepped back, getting me in his line of sight.

"Jerry, the aide, wants to know if you want a shower or a bath," I signed.

Mr. Rousseau didn't respond. I didn't know if he was ignoring me or if he couldn't see my signs. I signed Jerry's question again, but Mr. Rousseau just motioned for us to keep moving.

We were halfway to Mr. Rousseau's room when I saw Jerry coming toward us. I knew he was expecting an answer.

"Is he ready for a shower now?" he asked.

Mr. Rousseau was still ignoring my signing. I didn't have an answer, but Jerry assumed the affirmative, so I turned us around and we followed Jerry to the shower room. Jerry unlocked the door and I peered into the tiny room, and signed to Mr. Rousseau, "Do you want—"

"I know!" he signed, with an angry tap at his forehead. "You keep signing it over and over."

It was clear now. Mr. Rousseau *could* see in the lighted hallways and *yes*, he *did* understand me. Jerry stepped inside the shower room, which was barely bigger than an outhouse, and gently pulled Mr. Rousseau inside where he banged his shin into a chair crammed in front of the shower. His cane tangled in the legs of the chair as he couldn't see a thing in the dark room.

"I don't want a shower," he signed, sweeping the back of his hand through the air while struggling to free his cane.

"It's OK," Jerry said, turning Mr. Rousseau around toward the hall. "It's too much for him right now. I know how he feels. My father-in-law is visually impaired."

I felt an instant affinity with this big burly guy. He just made my job easier. I didn't have to explain deaf-blindness to Jerry as I did with others.

"Yeah, Mr. Rousseau doesn't belong here," Jerry said. "He needs rehabilitation to learn skills for his blindness. He needs to be in a place that helps blind people."

I agreed with Jerry, though I knew our state was lacking in support services for deaf-blind people. Over the years I'd seen many people with Usher syndrome leave Colorado and move to other states that provided better services. I was glad, at least, that Mr. Rousseau had someone here on his side.

The next day, I discovered Mr. Rousseau had been moved to a single room. When I arrived, there was a woman sitting outside his door.

"Hi, are you the interpetator?" she asked, mispronouncing the word.

"Yes, I am."

"I'm Glory; his sitter."

No one mentioned a sitter coming for Mr. Rousseau. I didn't know why she would be here, except I knew that sitters were sometimes assigned to people who were suicidal and needed someone to watch them. I peeked into Mr. Rousseau's room and saw him stretched out on the bed.

I introduced myself to Glory and took a chair next to her. With Mr. Rousseau resting, I figured we had time to kill. Glory didn't explain why she was there. She only talked about herself, where she was from, her family, and even her religion.

"I have a way with people and me and Mr. Rousseau get along," she said. "He suffers from allusions. But he and I have the chemistry, and I got him to take a shower and we walked for 20 minutes."

"Wonderful!"

"Yeah, ya gotta exercise. Look what I brought with me."

Glory bent forward, unzipping the pocket of a rolling backpack on the floor. My eyes widened as she pulled out a stretchy rope.

"See, I work nights and I use this to get me some exercise. Only I can't use it here because some of these residents are mentally ill or suicidal."

Noticing Glory's arms, which were double the size of mine, I commented pointing to her biceps, "You have some good muscles there."

"I need them for lifting people in my job. Mostly, I sit. I'm a 'sitter,' but it's important to keep movin' and eatin' right."

As I was thinking of what to say, Mr. Rousseau stirred from his bed. Glory and I peered into his room. Cleaned up, he looked like a new person, different from the man I saw last week. Mr. Rousseau looked back at us standing in the hall.

"Good morning," I signed. "I'm your interpreter. You look nice today."

"I didn't have a shower for a month before today," he signed.

Mr. Rousseau no longer seemed scared and angry as he was in his previous room which was dark all the time. This room was light and fresh looking. Mr. Rousseau seemed more clear-headed and focused.

"Ask him if he wants to go have lunch," Glory suggested.

Mr. Rousseau nodded when I signed, and she led him to the dining room.

Glory decided to take a break while Mr. Rousseau ate. A few times over his turkey and mashed potatoes I saw him distracted by hallucinations, conversing with someone invisible to me.

"No, you get out of here," he signed. Looking over at me he explained, "You can't see her, but I see that mean woman out of the corner of my eye."

"I understand," I signed, flicking my index finger upward from my temple. I tried not to stare at Mr. Rousseau while he was eating, but it was difficult to ignore the gravy spilling from his plate as he tried to slice the meat with plastic utensils as it slid from side to side. Soon the sleeves of his wrinkled white shirt were smeared with brown grease. I think more gravy went onto the table and his shirt than into his mouth.

After his meal Mr. Rousseau asked, "What do we do now?"

"I don't know," I signed. "They have a TV here."

I didn't know if Mr. Rousseau could see well enough to watch TV, but while we waited for Glory to return, I led him across the room to an area with a large-screen TV.

"The TV has captions, and they have a computer here, too." Mr. Rousseau seemed interested, but then said, "I can't see TV or the computer anymore."

I heard Glory calling out behind us, "Hey, girl. You're workin' overtime."

It was time for me to leave, so I let Mr. Rousseau know.

"No, you can't go home yet," he signed, smiling for the first time.

Having a moment to appreciate that smile would have been nice, but Glory moved in between us just then and led him away. Before I could warn them,

Mr. Rousseau banged his shin on a coffee table in front of the TV. With his fingers flying, he scolded Glory for not watching where they were going.

21

Relentless Torment

I woke at 5:00 a.m., an hour earlier than I needed to, feeling unrested. Pushing my feet against the floor, my body sorely reminded me I was half a century old. I was fighting a cold, the second one in one month, or maybe I hadn't fully recovered from the first one. All I knew is I was feeling run down. Pouring myself a cup of coffee I thought maybe I was working too much and fulfilling too many obligations to family, friends, and projects. I'd been writing, too. As writers would say, "I had flow." While the thoughts were flowing, I had to write them before I forgot, lest a phrase so brilliant be forever lost.

Stirring cream into my coffee I stared at the white swirls. Like a churn that swirls cream and sugar into ice cream, my brain churned out words. As I brought the steaming cup to my lips, the words came spilling forth and I reached for my spiral notebook. Just as artists have to paint and climbers have to climb, for no other reason than because the rocks are there, writers have to write. Writing brings clarity to thoughts that were muddy before I wrote them. Clarity brings me peace, and I like heading to work that way.

At the hospital, a different kind of peace hovered in the dayroom. With only a few patients milling around, there wasn't the usual energy of a weekday, and someone new was supervising the floor.

I went to introduce myself. "Hello. I haven't seen you here before."

He spoke in a whisper. "I'm just here because of what happened last night."

Puzzled, I leaned in closer. "What happened?"

"They lost a patient. They found her lifeless in bed and everyone's in shock. This rarely happens here."

He told me who it was, and I remembered the patient as kind and friendly, one everyone seemed to like and have hope for. We all thought she would get well. Thinking about the harsh side effects of some of the medications patients take, I asked, "Was it from the medicine? Did she have a heart attack?"

"We don't know what happened. They informed the other patients this morning."

The atmosphere was eerily somber. No one else was talking about what happened. In fact, nobody seemed to be talking at all. Dallas was nowhere in sight and I felt awkward, as if I wasn't supposed to be there that day.

Ivy came stomping up the hall with her hair combed over the top of her head, fluffed out to one side, and her eyes and lips outlined in black. My mother would have called someone with that look, a floozy. Despite her new hairstyle and made-up face, Ivy didn't look happy. She paced in heavy, angry steps. She was upset, but not about the same thing everyone else was upset about.

"I need my social worker," she called out. "I need my money..."

Well, maybe it was a typical day.

* * *

There was a memorial service a few days later for the patient who died. I found out at the last minute that I would be interpreting the service. Typically, I prepared for such occasions, by studying the scripts or learning lyrics to the songs, but now the patients attending the service were already gathered at the door. I had no time to fret or worry whether I could handle interpreting an emotionally charged memorial service.

We walked across campus to a chapel. Dallas sat in the front row with a few social workers and staff. She told me she was wearing black today to honor her dead friend. During the service, people came to the podium behind me to speak. It was difficult for each of them. I translated their broken sentences, their unfinished thoughts, silences, and quiet thank-yous.

The psychiatrist had the toughest time of all, choking up between words, "In 17 years we have come such a long way with this disease, and... there is more... so much more we could... do. We try and we try..."

I saw tears streaming down the faces of nurses, social workers, and patients, as he struggled to continue.

"We tried everything—we never stopped searching—me—racking my brain to help these people put an end to their torment."

If anyone thought that mental health workers became jaded or uncaring from working day after day with the mentally ill, their perception would change witnessing this. I held back my own emotion, concentrating on what I was there to do. Adrenaline pushed me to perform. But when the mother of the deceased came to the front and described her daughter becoming sick with schizophrenia, and how relentlessly tormented she was by thoughts of being possessed by the devil, I nearly broke. I signed with tears sliding down my face.

After the service, Dallas told me she wanted to talk to the grieving parents. I interpreted as she told them their daughter was her friend and that she was sorry for their loss. At this, I could no longer control my emotions. Tears poured down my face, releasing an accumulation of exhaustion and stress from my body. There is a breaking point for everyone, and mine came at this unexpected time.

I tried to pull myself together before too many people noticed. They might have found it odd that the interpreter would melt down so unprofessionally into a weeping wreck. My nose was running, my glasses were wet and smeared, and I couldn't see a thing. Searching through my purse for tissues, I felt a tap on my arm. I looked up through the blur to see a patient offering me a piece of gum.

22

No Home To Return To

Leola bounded from her room into the hallway with her wet and tangled hair flipped forward over her face. She stopped short in front of me, where I was talking with one of the technicians. Pushing her hair away from her face, she stood staring at me as if her mission had been aborted by my presence. I tried to keep this sudden encounter friendly as the staff had warned me she could be violent.

"Hi, Leola." She managed a single-toothed smile at me and I stepped closer.

"Leola, go do your hygiene," the tech demanded.

Leola turned and headed back to her room. I took in a breath, relieved. On a psych ward you never know when a little thing can ignite into a big thing, so it's wise to be cautious. A short while later, when I was safely seated behind the staff desk, Leola reemerged with her arms wrapped around a bundle of wet towels, her hair still wet and uncombed. I watched her head for the dirty linen bin.

Leola never did get her hair combed that day. As noon approached, she sat at a table with a spiral notebook, her hair looking the same as it did hours earlier. With an intent stare at a blank page she held her pencil frozen in the air above the notebook. While she was stuck in this position, I noticed her move now and then, as if to write, but after 30 minutes she hadn't managed as much as a scribble.

The patients in the hospital were working on getting better. The goal was for them to get stabilized on medication, keep up their personal hygiene, and work with their social worker on a discharge plan to go home. If they had no home to return to, they would go to a group home until they could find a permanent place to live. Most of the patients accomplished this. However, some never got better, like Leola, Trenton, or Camille. It saddened me that there were no other more homey, less expensive, places for them to live, especially when our state (like most) had only a precious number of psychiatric beds available and so many others who needed them.

I thought about this on my drive home, and the next day, too, and on days when I drove past the hospital on my way to other jobs. I worried that every day Leola and the few other long-timers were still hospitalized, someone else with a serious mental disorder was on the street, or in a shelter, or getting picked up by the police and taken to jail because no psychiatric bed was available in the entire city.

* * *

With my heightened sensitivity to the problems permeating our mental health system, I often wondered if mental health professionals shared my opinion of our laws and my concern for the bed shortage. Though I longed for those conversations, there was little opportunity at the hospital to engage with the staff. One day, however, I seized an opportunity when a social worker and I both were eating lunch in the break room.

I asked her, "Why do some patients stay here so long?"

"It's different reasons for each one," she replied. "Some have burned all their bridges. They've been in different places and got kicked out or sent back here. No one wants them."

"That's so sad." I paused before posing my next question. I knew the answer, but I wanted to get her perspective on the housing issue, as she dealt with it daily. "Are there not enough group homes or other facilities for them to go to?"

"Yeah, it's that, too."

To my disappointment, she didn't elaborate. Perhaps she was resigned to the unfortunate reality, or maybe she just didn't want to get into the politics of the matter.

I ate my tuna sandwich, musing over how mind-numbingly dreadful it would be to live locked up in a hospital with little to do each day. I recalled the first time I worked on a locked ward. The loud electronics of the door startled me when it unlocked, allowing me entrance to the unit. Hesitant walking down a hall, I heard shouting behind a door to my left and glanced over my shoulder to see a patient through the small window in the door standing naked, waving his arms and yelling. I assumed he was naked because he had either disrobed, or the staff had taken away his clothing to prevent him from using it to harm himself. *How awful*, I thought, *to be stuck in that tiny room all day with nothing to do.*

When the social worker met me in the corridor, I gestured toward the room where the yelling was coming from and asked her, "Don't they get bored, locked in there all day?" Her reply quickly enlightened me about the severe cases of mental illness.

"They have so much going on inside their heads. They don't get bored."

That assignment was my first encounter with untreated psychosis—seeing how some patients arrive at the hospital, sick as rabid dogs. I realized then how terrifying it must be for them, struggling with jumbled, uncontrollable thoughts, so powerful as to cause them to become a danger to themselves and others. As sad as it was to see this patient tortured by demons inside his own mind, reduced to a state of naked confinement, at least he was safe in the hospital and society was safe from him.

After lunch I emerged from the break room and saw Dallas getting up from the table she was sharing with Leola and retreat to her room. So, while I had no interpreting to do, I studied Leola. Sitting alone, making colorful doodles in her notebook, Leola seemed so innocent. With her soft jumbled speech and intermittent catatonia she didn't seem dangerous or capable of being violent. However, I heeded the staff's warnings and kept a safe distance.

I watched her draw cartoonish figures and fill the rest of the page with colored rows of tiny circles, feeling twangs of sadness for her. What kind of life might she have had if not for the tragic turn she took developing mental illness? A once beautiful brain, intricately fragile, devastated by the terrible disease of schizophrenia. Now this was how she spent her days.

As Dallas still had not returned to the dayroom, I became more pensive about this mysterious disease—*was it only the brain that was damaged by schizo-*

phrenia, or was it the mind too? Or was there no difference between the brain and the mind?

I imagined Leola one day, with her hair neatly combed, wearing a flowing dress and a radiant smile, coming out of the darkness of her illness. She would shock us all when she said in a clear and lovely voice, "Hello everyone. Guess what? I'm not sick anymore."

We would see that her healthy mind, still intact, had been there all along, like the patients in the movie *Awakenings*, who suffered from catatonia resulting from an outbreak of encephalitis lethargica. After they received L-Dopa, the drug used to treat Parkinson's Disease, they suddenly came to life, able to move and speak again.

Envisioning such a cure for schizophrenia was a pleasant thought. But even if scientists do find a way to stop its progression, or at best prevent schizophrenia from developing in the first place, it would likely come too late for Leola and the others I saw coming and going from this hospital. Until then, our current medications will continue to help millions of people with mental illness. There is no more need for bloodletting and cold packs, insulin coma therapy, straitjackets, and lobotomies—the barbaric treatments of the past for psychiatric illness. For many, our modern medicines quell their hallucinations and psychotic delusions. For others, they help in avoiding hospitalization, and for millions more, they help us lead normal lives.

Twyla interrupted my thoughts by calling out to the patients, "Courtyard time," and Dallas suddenly appeared, getting in line as if she had heard Twyla's announcement. I followed behind her and Leola, going outside where we all were "just people" enjoying the fresh air.

23

Hallucinations

Mr. Rousseau got lost in his own bathroom this morning. It's not uncommon for a blind person to get lost occasionally in a familiar place. One or two miscalculated steps before turning right or left can set them off in the wrong direction. Mr. Rousseau thought he was headed toward the doorway to the hall, but when his cane met a wall instead, he got confused. He panicked when he couldn't find his way out. By the time I arrived he was all ruffled and didn't want to leave his room.

"Tell him he has to come with me *now*," Glory said, "He has an appointment."

I signed to Mr. Rousseau, but he still refused.

"I'm not going," he signed. "My hallucinations are bad."

"He has to," Glory insisted. "They're gonna check his eyes."

With much encouragement on my part, Mr. Rousseau relented. He took his fedora from the nightstand and with Glory leading, they headed out with one of the floor staff. I followed them outside, where Glory motioned for Mr. Rousseau to get into the waiting car. He folded his cane and climbed in, except he was facing the wrong way. He landed on the seat backward with his legs pushed up to his chest, looking confused and frustrated.

Glory had not directed his hand onto the top of the car door, so he would know which way the car was facing. Now, with both of them agitated, Glory pulled on Mr. Rousseau's arm to get him out of the car. Awkwardly unfolding himself, he climbed out, grabbed his hat and threw it to the ground, refusing to get back in.

"He's 'flustrated,'" Glory said, stating the obvious.

Through all of this the driver stood waiting until Mr. Rousseau calmed down and reentered the car. As they drove away I watched the car until it turned and disappeared, thinking how Mr. Rousseau was not to blame for his anger. Losing your independence, because of blindness, is a loss of privacy and dignity. I know I would feel that way as I'm fiercely independent.

Growing up as the youngest of four, until my mother got pregnant again when I was 13, came with many advantages. I learned things from my older siblings, like how to read when I was four. And I benefited by observing what they did. I followed in their footsteps if it was something good, or I avoided doing something if it had been a mistake for them.

Another benefit of being the youngest was that my mom was more lenient with me. Worn out from raising the first three, she was also dealing with my father, who was struggling with alcoholism. Consequently, we had a lot of freedom. In the summers we spent our time at the city swimming pool or going to a friend's house to play. I thought nothing of walking a mile or more to their homes.

I started babysitting when I was 11 and bought my clothes with the money I earned. Like my siblings, I was nearly self-sufficient by the time I was 17. My independence led me to seek and befriend others who were different and interesting to me. I learned about their religions and family backgrounds. Because of this independence, I was not shy about asking questions or speaking out.

Carrying this directness into my adult life gets me into trouble sometimes, when I speak of the elephant in the room when it is not politically correct. I get stern looks. Or, when I cross my professional boundaries because it's the kind, humanitarian thing to do, though I worry later whether I'm going to hear about it if someone complains.

Often, I receive praise for my outspokenness, but I've also received complaints, which is why my heart turned over one morning when the director of the care center asked to speak with me and Jani, one of the aides. Following the director into her office, my nerves were all a flutter, wondering what I'd done wrong.

"I'm glad you're both here today," she said. "I'd really like for the two of you to teach Mr. Rousseau how to find his way around here. We'd like him to be more independent."

I was pleasantly relieved that I wasn't in trouble, but even more pleased that the staff had recognized the necessity of this for Mr. Rousseau. I loved teaching, however, I knew my role. I was being paid to interpret, not teach. Jani, one of my favorite aides, was silent. I knew she had no experience working with deaf or blind people, but I needed to clarify what the director wanted.

"You mean you want Jani to teach him and me to interpret?" I asked, doubtful that Jani would know how to do this.

"Yes, the two of you work together," she said.

Jani and I agreed to do it, though I saw a look of panic on her face. When we told Mr. Rousseau about the plan, he was immediately receptive. With his cane in hand, he came with us into the corridor, but when the three of us just stood looking at one another, it was clear that Jani didn't have the first notion of how to proceed.

"We could start by showing him his room number and where to find the numbers on all the doors," I suggested.

Jani nodded, looking less panicked that at least one of us had an idea. In seconds it was apparent that Jani wasn't going to take the lead, and soon it was me who was teaching him.

"Here is your room number," I signed, showing him the plate on the wall with his name and room number.

He felt the plate, then leaned in closer to inspect the numbers and the letters of his name. As we proceeded down the corridor, taking time to read each room number and the names for the washroom and laundry room, I soon noticed Jani was no longer in sight. It was me who ended up orienting Mr. Rousseau around the entire floor of the care center.

In the days that followed, Mr. Rousseau practiced navigating around the unit with Glory until he was comfortable on his own. It was a step forward for Mr. Rousseau's independence and a step back for Glory's usefulness.

* * *

The next week, Glory decided Mr. Rousseau needed a schedule. "I'm going to make a schedule for the CNAs," she announced, pleased with her idea. "He needs a shower every day and exercise. Here's what I'm going to do…"

Mid-sentence, she left me and Mr. Rousseau alone in the activity room, while she went to the office. She returned with a blank sheet of paper and handed it to me.

"Here you write it," she said.

At first, I thought maybe she didn't know how to write. I knew she had trouble pronouncing a lot of words correctly. I could write for her, but just as I knew it wasn't my place to make decisions for the client, I doubted it was hers either. She was a sitter, whose job was to monitor an individual who is suicidal or an escape risk. Besides, the staff posted a daily activity schedule on the wall. I think Glory was overstepping her boundaries, though I wasn't there to tell her how to do her job.

"You can write it," I encouraged.

So Glory began, speaking aloud as she wrote: "Shower every day, then walk." She stopped writing after the one line and slid the paper and pen back to me. "What else?" she asked.

"Maybe you should ask him what he wants to do," I gestured with my head toward Mr. Rousseau who was busy unwrapping a piece of chewing gum, oblivious to what Glory was up to.

Glory took back the pen and paper.

"He could practice orienting himself in the hallway," I suggested.

"Yeah, that's good. How do you spell that?"

I spelled the word *orientation* for her, letter by letter, as Mr. Rousseau gazed out the window. When she finished writing, Glory looked up with a smile, "See, you shoulda wrote it."

Satisfied with her schedule, she took it to the nurse's station to post for the staff.

I let out a sigh. Glory made me tired. Mr. Rousseau made me tired. My back hurt and I felt exhausted. That morning, when I had first arrived, Mr. Rousseau had been lying on his back on the bed with his knees pulled up to his chest. Someone had told him that was the way to relieve low back pain.

When Glory showed up a few moments after me and saw him rocking back and forth, she immediately noticed his ankle.

"It's swollen," she said. "He's got to elevate that ankle."

She told me to ask him if he wanted some pillows or blankets to put under his leg.

Mr. Rousseau was still curled up, rocking. I knew that interrupting him to sign Glory's question, right then, wasn't a good idea. Mr. Rousseau hated being interrupted while he was busy with something, plus he rarely understood my signing in the dim light of his room. But Glory was insistent upon getting his leg elevated.

"Tell him I'm going to get him some blankets."

With her out of the room, I tried unsuccessfully to get Mr. Rousseau's attention. Mostly, I was grateful to have a moment of peace without Glory firing questions at him while he was focused on fixing his back pain.

Many people don't realize that deaf-blind people can focus on only one task at a time. Asking them several questions at once, or quickly changing the subject, is usually a recipe for mass confusion. Interpreters are aware that people who are deaf-blind are unable to pick up visual or audio cues from the environment as the rest of us do. Unless they are given this information they can easily misunderstand conversations. We need extra time to convey this, to set the stage, before we can ask a question or tell them something. And even though Glory and others have stood by watching me do this, they often didn't realize how difficult it could sometimes be to get a question or concept across to Mr. Rousseau. Not because he wasn't bright, but rather his diminishing vision affected his ability to see and understand sign language in the way he was accustomed to, and he had not yet made the transition to tactile communication. It seemed he was stuck somewhere in between.

But my job was to interpret what Glory said. So with her out of the room, I figured I'd have time to tell Mr. Rousseau about Glory's concern, and by the time she returned he would understand why she wanted him to elevate his leg. He'd be ready to comply. Except, he had brushed off my attempt to communicate with him, and Glory was back in a flash with a pile of blankets.

"Ask him if he wants these under his knee or his foot," she said.

"We haven't talked about the blankets yet," I said.

Mr. Rousseau had stopped rocking by then and had his legs stretched out, so Glory set the blankets on the bed and went ahead, lifting his leg onto them.

"Ask him if he's comfortable," she said.

I hadn't conveyed to him what the blankets were for. He just went along with having his leg propped up, probably assuming it would help his back pain. After a minute, he sat up and shoved the blankets onto the floor.

"Nooooo, tell him to keep the blankets," Glory ordered.

I signed and he replied, "No, my back is not hurting anymore."

To a fly on the wall, we probably looked like the three stooges. Each one thinking they were communicating, unaware that they weren't. Like the fly, I knew we weren't.

After lunch, Mr. Rousseau said he wanted to go to the exercise room. Glory showed him the equipment and he decided to try the stationary bicycle. To help him get started, she bent over to guide his feet into the toeholds of the pedals, which kept spinning and moving out of reach. All the while, she was talking. Eventually, she got his feet placed and Mr. Rousseau began pedaling. Glory stood up and noticed the electronic screen on the bike wasn't working. While she fussed with the screen, Mr. Rousseau contentedly pumped his legs, oblivious to the broken screen. But Glory was not content.

"Ask him if it's too hard or too easy," she said.

I was confident Mr. Rousseau would let us know if he wanted the resistance of the pedals increased or decreased. Nonetheless, I interpreted as she requested, though with Glory hovering over him, I had to move to the front of the bike first. I looked away for a second and heard Glory yelp. From the corner of my eye I saw Mr. Rousseau's hand sweep in front of her and heard Glory yelp again.

"He hit me," she yelled. "I'm not takin' it. Tell him he can't hit."

She backed away as Mr. Rousseau got off of the bicycle.

"Glory says you can't hit," I signed.

"I'm blind. I can't see," he signed, searching for his cane on the nearby table. He grabbed the cane and grasped onto my arm while pulling me away.

"That's no excuse," Glory scolded. "You can't hit me."

I interpreted her words, feeling uneasy. Glory's sudden change in demeanor scared me.

"He's agitated today, and I don't like it," she said. "He needs to sit and calm down."

Glory took Mr. Rousseau by the arm and led him to the table. She showed him a chair, but he wouldn't sit.

"Ask him why he hit me."

I signed her question, and Mr. Rousseau defended himself like a kid caught with his hand in the cookie jar.

"I did it lightly."

Glory continued her rant: "I'm not letting him get away with that, because then he'll think it's OK. I'm reporting him next time…"

Nearing exasperation, I glanced at my watch. I was glad to see that it was 4:30. My back was killing me and I wanted to go home. I told Mr. Rousseau it was time for me to go, and he nodded, but Glory was not finished.

"This is what he did," she said, giving me a hard shove on my upper chest. "He pushed me like that!"

"That was pretty hard," I said, more bothered by her behavior than the shove.

Glory knew my shift was over. She took Mr. Rousseau's arm.

"I'm takin' him to his room. He's agitated and he needs to relax," she said.

I watched them totter away, convinced that Glory was the one who was agitated and needed to relax. She was acting more like his mother than a professional sitter, and I was feeling more like a babysitter for the two of them, than an interpreter. Glory seemed to be more trouble than she was worth, but it wasn't my place to say anything.

The next morning Lashay told me Mr. Rousseau was lying down because he had a spell with low blood pressure. I found him sprawled out asleep on his bed. Glory was in a large comfy chair alongside him, with a box of tissues on her lap, wiping her eyes.

"I just feel so bad for him. He's gonna be blind pretty soon," she cried.

I patted her on the shoulder. "I know."

I told Glory a story about me first learning about Usher syndrome.

"I was in my 20s, working at a school with deaf students. One morning before the students arrived, the classroom teacher informed me that she'd just found out that our brightest student was going blind. She said the student had Usher syndrome and explained to me what it was. She said our student would eventually be deaf and blind. When I told my husband about it that evening, I fell sobbing onto our bed. I couldn't imagine anything more cruel and unfair. Now, after working with many deaf-blind people, I see how they adapt to a new way of living. It's not easy, for sure, but it's not all doom and gloom either. They can manage quite well. They can work and do most anything."

Glory didn't seem at all convinced by my attempted reassurance and kept sniffling until Mr. Rousseau woke up. He said he was feeling better and that he wanted to practice navigating around the care center. He was more focused and energetic than I'd ever seen him.

Mr. Rousseau proudly led us to the nurses' station, showing that he knew where he was going. He ran his fingers along the length of the counter. When he found a section with a closed glass window, he turned to me and, with an outstretched hand, gestured, "Come, come."

That is the deaf-blind way of saying, "Tell me, tell me more."

I explained that the window was where the nurse dispensed medication to the residents. Mr. Rousseau seemed delighted to learn this. He then led us to the exercise room and to the dining room. Glory's smile grew with amazement at his progress, and my heart swelled with joy, seeing him adapting so quickly.

* * *

Glory set a cup of water on the table for Mr. Rousseau and I slid it over to his hand, so he'd know it was there. Mr. Rousseau took a big gulp. Then he set the cup down and signed, "Do you think I would try to escape from here?"

I spoke his words for Glory.

"Do I think you would try to escape?" she asked.

I signed her question back to him.

"Yes," he replied, "because I can't. I can't run fast enough, because I can't see. They would come after me."

"No, I don't think you would try to do that. But that's not why I'm here," Glory said. "I'm just here for your safety."

This conversation came after the rough start we'd had 20 minutes earlier when Glory brought Mr. Rousseau here to the dining room. She tried to get him centered in front of the chair before he sat down, but he started to lower himself before the seat was under him. He was halfway to the floor when Glory caught him and shoved him onto the seat, which got him angry.

"Tell him he has to feel for the chair. I don't want him to fall," she said.

I relayed the message, but Mr. Rousseau was adamant.

"I felt the table," he insisted.

"No, you have to feel for the *chair*," Glory said.

"You're mean," he signed, "Not her, I'm talking to you." Mr. Rousseau darted his finger clearly at me.

"Oh noooooo," Glory said, shaking her head.

Mr. Rousseau stood and announced he was going to his room. He unfolded his cane and navigated his way out of the dining room on his own.

"Wait," Glory called, gathering her bag and phone. "I'm so sorry, Diane. This is not your fault," she said, heading after him.

Unfazed, I followed her as she trailed behind Mr. Rousseau. When we got to his room, Glory used a whiteboard and a black marker to explain to Mr. Rousseau that she was the one who had pushed him onto the chair. I stood watching from the hallway.

"I'll give him some space," I said. "Call, if you need me."

Before I made it to the common room, Glory beckoned me back.

"He's sorry," she said.

From the edge of his bed Mr. Rousseau looked at me. With a closed fist he rubbed circles on his chest, "Sorry."

At that Glory burst into tears, heartbroken, once again, over his disability.

"Things will get better," I told her.

Mr. Rousseau complained about his hallucinations. "The visions are bothering me. I can't do anything anymore. My eyes—there are too many distractions."

That's when Glory said we needed to go back to the dining room where we were headed initially to get some water.

Learning that Mr. Rousseau had thought of walking away from the care center surprised me. I doubted I would be happy living in a place like this either, but where would he go if he did leave? I would have been interested to hear more of his thoughts, but neither he nor Glory said anything more about it.

Mr. Rousseau finished drinking his water and said he wanted to go to the exercise room. He was the only person I ever saw using the fitness machines at the care center. Probably, because he was the only resident who had Glory. While he pedaled on the stationary bike, Glory went to refill his cup of water. She fetched him water all day long, as if he'd won a vacation at a health resort, complete with a personal attendant.

When Glory returned with the water, Mr. Rousseau got off the bike and began stretching his legs. Glory grabbed the back of a chair, spread her legs, and bent over.

"Tell him to spread his legs and bend this way."

I knew Mr. Rousseau was going to do his stretches his own way, but I did as instructed.

I didn't need to, however, because Mr. Rousseau could see Glory bent over.

"I can't do that," he signed. He took hold of the back of the chair and stretched his calves the way he wanted to. Then he got down to the floor and did some more hamstring stretches.

Meanwhile, Glory went to ask permission to take him outside to walk. She was gone before I could remind her that she was not supposed to leave Mr. Rousseau unattended, (interpreters don't count as staff). However, since it gave us a few moments break from her incessant talking, I didn't fuss.

By now I was used to Glory and we worked fine together, though she constantly worried about the day when she would no longer be needed there.

"I know other people won't take care of him the way I do," she said.

I was starting to believe that Glory needed Mr. Rousseau more than he needed her.

Glory returned from the nurses' station disappointed: "He can't go outside," she said. "He's still on the offspervation."

"You mean observation?"

"Yeah, obbspervation." She laughed trying to pronounce the word. "Well, I need to write my report now, anyway."

I thought we'd have some quiet while Glory wrote her report, but I was wrong.

"How do you spell allusions? she asked.

"Hallucinations?"

"Yeah."

"H-a-l-l-u-c-i..."

I woke up the next morning chuckling about the dream I had. I dreamt I was asking my junior high school teacher if she could open my locker. I told her I needed to get my spelling book to study for a test. Then Chandler Bing, the character on the TV show *Friends* suddenly appeared in a business suit, holding the spelling book I needed. I was trying to sweet-talk him into lending me the book when he blurted out, "I have leukemia." A second later he was sinking into a glass tank full of water. Submerged in his suit, I saw his panic-stricken face underwater and his arms and legs flailing. With no effort at all, I reached over the glass of the tank and pulled him out, saving him from drowning.

From the edge of my bed I now got the point of the dream. I'm a caretaker, just like Glory, and I was afraid of being a bad speller.

24

Be Free and Fly Away

I arrived at work to hear that Mr. Rousseau was having a bout of tantrums.

"Well, Glory is playing a part in it," Lashay explained. "She insists that she has to get Mr. Rousseau up and showered, and she expects the rest of us to get all the things she needs. We're trying to get Mr. Rousseau to be independent. Until he can do more for himself he cannot leave here. Glory is enabling him to be dependent."

I nodded as I took off my coat. While I agreed with her, it was not my place to say anything.

When I got to Mr. Rousseau's room, Glory was pacing back and forth while he was ensconced on the bed. She started in right away.

"He can't leave here. He can't do it. He can't live by himself."

Her eyes filled with tears and she broke down crying while Mr. Rousseau sat, oblivious to her emotional outburst.

"The staff told him he had to start doing everything himself. He's mad now, and he won't come out of his room."

"That's fine," I said. "I'll give him some space."

"All right, but tell him if he doesn't come out of his room they're going to send me away."

I knew this wasn't true. I felt an immediate clenching in my chest, having to interpret something I knew was wrong. Instead, I told Glory, "Since they want him to be more independent, I'm going—I'll be down the hall."

I told Mr. Rousseau that I'd be at the nurse's station if he needed me. He and Glory could write back and forth on his dry-erase board to communicate. He could still read large print if it was written with a thick black marker. Glory could tell him whatever she wanted now.

And so I wouldn't look like I was neglecting my job, just sitting around the nurse's station, I found Lashay and let her know what was going on.

"Yes," she said with a knowing nod, "it seems everyone is riled up today." Lashay thought it had something to do with the upcoming holidays. "Christmas time is hard for the residents. Many of them have no visitors on Christmas. It makes them depressed or angry, and they act up."

Mr. Rousseau finally came out of his room at lunchtime but he still seemed unhappy. In the dining room in between bites of his meatloaf he told me he planned to spend Christmas Day in his room because he was the only deaf person there and there was no one to talk to. He said he tried a few days ago to contact his daughter in Louisiana, but he didn't hear back from her. He blamed the nurse, who left the phone message, for not doing it correctly.

Jerry was still passing out lunch plates to the latecomers and some of them were complaining about the food. He did his best trying to lift everyone's spirits.

"Hey, everybody. It's two more days until Christmas. We'll have a party and lots of good food, and everyone will get a present."

I interpreted with enthusiasm, almost wishing I could be there for the party, but Mr. Rousseau seemed unmoved. I noticed he was no longer resisting my tactile signing like he used to. Lately, he welcomed it, usually, but right now like the other residents, he was spiritless.

The day dragged on. Still, it was hard at the end of my shift to say goodbye to Mr. Rousseau knowing he'd be mostly alone while I was enjoying time with family on Christmas. I wasn't sure what to say, though I tried to be positive.

"Enjoy your party and the good food, okay? I'll be back next week. Thursday."

"No," he signed, "tomorrow."

I knew he was teasing, but it was hard to feel jovial. "Thursday," I signed again. He grabbed onto my two outstretched fingers and held onto them. We both smiled as I gently pulled my fingers away.

* * *

Returning to work after Christmas I discovered that Mr. Rousseau no longer had a sitter. Glory was gone. He seemed sullen all day, though for me it was peaceful without all the drama that Glory manufactured. Near the end of my shift, however, Mr. Rousseau took a spill in his room. No one saw him fall, but he came out to tell Lashay what happened.

He was leaning forward toward his bed, which he thought was in front of him, but somehow he missed it and went straight to the floor. He fell onto his hands and shoulder. Mr. Rousseau seemed OK, but a doctor had to come and check him for injuries. Though no one could predict how long we'd have to wait, I stayed.

Fortunately, the doctor arrived in under 10 minutes, examined Mr. Rousseau, and determined that nothing was broken. As he was leaving, however, it dawned on me that the staff needed a way to communicate swiftly with Mr. Rousseau if there was an emergency at the care center and no interpreter was there. There's a universal signal that's used in the deaf-blind community that's quick and simple and doesn't require any knowledge of sign language. It can be used whenever the staff might have to move Mr. Rousseau without delay from an unsafe area. I told Mr. Rousseau I had an idea and needed to talk to the nurse.

"I'll be right back," I signed.

Tracking down Lashay, I told her about the emergency signal.

"All you need to do is draw a giant X on his back with your finger. It alerts the deaf-blind person that there is an urgent situation and they must come with you right away. They'll know you will explain what the emergency is as soon as you get to a safe place."

"That's an excellent idea," she said. "Can we teach it to him right now?"

I agreed and Lashay followed me back to Mr. Rousseau's room. He was sitting on his bed unwrapping a piece of gum. We waited for him to pop the gum into his mouth and stash the crumpled wrapper into his pocket before I explained the plan. I showed him the signal, pressing firmly with my finger drawing on his back so he'd feel it through his thick shirt.

"I get it," he signed.

"Can we practice?" Lashay asked.

Mr. Rousseau was game. He lay down and closed his eyes, pretending to be asleep, but then realized something and sat up. "What will they do if I'm on my back?" he asked.

"Yeah," Lashay asked. "What should I do?"

"What would you do?" I tested.

"I guess I'd roll him over," she said, answering her own question.

Mr. Rousseau also got it, without my needing to interpret for him. He lay down and closed his eyes again. Lashay leaned over and tapped him on the shoulder. He opened his eyes, and she took his hand, pulling and rolling him toward her just enough so she could draw the X on his back. Mr. Rousseau stood, grasped her arm, and the two marched out the door playing their roles perfectly!

That evening I drove home feeling like I'd actually accomplished something today. If the big X was my sole contribution to the care center and Mr. Rousseau's life, all my time spent there was worth it.

* * *

One morning I accompanied Mr. Rousseau to the dentist to repair his broken tooth. He was unhappy about going out on account of his hallucinations.

"They look like marbles," he told Jerry, who was driving us to the clinic. "They're different colors, shooting at me, getting bigger and bigger."

Sometimes, he ducked trying to avoid them.

Jerry was sympathetic. "I'm sorry to hear that," he said. "Sometimes it takes a while for the medicine to work to stop the visions. Try to ignore them."

Mr. Rousseau told the dentist about the marbles, too. "I wish they would go away," he signed.

"I wish they would, too," the dentist said. "But, I'd like to take a look at your tooth and see if we can take care of that."

The dentist got to work on the tooth, while Mr. Rousseau held onto my hand with his eyes closed to block out the flying marbles. There was little for me to interpret while the dentist did his work, but Mr. Rousseau wanted to make sure I didn't leave.

Thirty minutes later the dentist proclaimed the tooth "as good as new." When I shared the news with Mr. Rousseau, he simply nodded and asked for his hat and cane.

"Tell him he needs to brush more," the doctor added. "Twice a day."

But Mr. Rousseau ignored my signing. He got up from the chair, complaining about the marbles. His tooth problem was solved, but the hallucinations continued to plague him.

Back at the care center, a nurse asked Mr. Rousseau how it went at the dentist.

"Fine," he said.

I told Mr. Rousseau, then, what the dentist had said on our way out: "He said you need to brush more. Two times every day." I used my voice as I signed, so the nurse would know, too.

"All the residents need to brush more," she mumbled. "They all have bad teeth, and we don't have the time to monitor them to make sure they do it."

Mr. Rousseau had no comment about the brushing. He wasn't concerned about his teeth. He was bothered by his hallucinations. He asked the nurse, "Why won't they go away?" He asked me the same question over and over throughout the day.

Alongside having to deal with annoying visual images, Mr. Rousseau was worried about his eyes.

"What will happen if I become totally blind? What will I do?" When he asked me these questions, I could only suggest that he talk to the staff. I couldn't help him, which weighed heavily on me.

In the late afternoon, Mr. Rousseau and I sat on opposite ends of a couch near the nurses' station. It felt peaceful for a while, and then it became apparent that Mr. Rousseau was not the only person who was having a bad day. Kerri, a resident with fiery red hair, began screaming at a nurse.

"I want out of here! I've been here three years, and I don't have to listen to you. I'm not takin' that medicine!"

Kerri turned away from the nurse and directed her increasing ire at another resident. The two women got into a shouting match a few feet away from Mr. Rousseau and me. Expecting pushing and shoving to come next, a surge of adrenalin ran up my spine. As I considered fleeing to safety with Mr. Rousseau, staff came running. Half of them surrounded Kerri, and the other half circled the second woman.

Cognizant of my responsibility to interpret environmental information that's relevant to my client, in the midst of all that was happening, I had to consider what Mr. Rousseau would do if I told him two women were fighting in front of us. He might rise from the couch in a rush to get away and stumble into them. But it was not my job to filter out information that might upset him. Should I tell him what was going on, or wait for this to pass. Maybe this called for the Big X?

My calculations took place in a flash, and I reached for Mr. Rousseau's hands. He welcomed my tactile signing now, after so many weeks, as he realized my hands were the key to opening his closed world.

"A woman, Kerri, is upset and yelling," I signed, pointing in her direction, though Mr. Rousseau would have no idea how far away Kerri was by my mere pointing. Still, I continued. "Kerri and another woman are arguing and shouting."

Mr. Rousseau's eyes grew big. He sat up straight and clutched his folded cane to his chest. "Should we leave?" he asked.

"Wait," I signed, deciding it was best to sit tight, not add to the chaos. As the staff succeeded in separating the two women, I told Mr. Rousseau, "A male nurse is talking to Kerri, now."

No one had told us to stay or leave, but now that the nurse had Kerri's attention, I figured it was safe for us to move. We were walking toward the dining room when a resident in front of us began hollering at the staff. He wanted something but was told to wait. The staff was too busy dealing with Kerri to help him.

"No," the man shouted. "I won't wait. I always have to wait, and I'm sick of it. God damn it!" I halted with Mr. Rousseau, not sure it was safe to approach the agitated man, but then decided we should keep going and get past him. His swearing trailed behind us as we reached the dining room. Residents hovered in silence at the tables, listening to the yelling. Everyone could hear it except Mr. Rousseau.

"Is it 5:00?" he asked.

"Yes."

"Is dinner late?"

"Yes, it's late," I sign.

Every minute can feel dark and long for a person who cannot hear or see, and anything late is noticeable. On the secure unit of a residential care facility, a meal 15 minutes late was especially noticeable.

* * *

Mr. Rousseau looked exhausted. His hallucinations had not abated in weeks. I interpreted while Lashay explained what the clinicians thought was going on: "The medicines should have stopped your hallucinations, but they haven't, so we think your hallucinations are not coming from your brain. They are from your eye disease."

"Do other people here have hallucinations, too?" Mr. Rousseau asked.

"Yes, some do. They have hallucinations because something is not working properly inside their brain. But we don't think there's anything wrong with your brain. We think the visions you're seeing are from your deteriorating retinas. You have to remind yourself that they're not real and they won't hurt you. Simply distract yourself by keeping busy."

Mr. Rousseau was quiet for a while after their talk. A few hours passed before he shared what he was thinking.

"My eyes will get worse," he told me. "I see through a tunnel that is getting smaller and smaller, and someday it will close, and I will be blind. The light will become dark."

While I was well aware of what was happening to him, hearing him articulate it made me nearly cry.

At lunch, Mr. Rousseau scraped the sour cream off his burrito, as Alva, a resident with black, graying hair, asked to sit with us.

"Of course," I replied, without asking Mr. Rousseau's permission. I knew he didn't like to be bothered while he was eating. Plus, tactile communication during meal times isn't practical when hands are greasy and sticky. I was also aware when sitting with Alva, there was a risk of getting hit with one of her long, boisterous church sermons.

Alva pulled a chair out from the table. "Don't worry," she said, plopping herself onto it. For a second, I thought that she'd read my mind and was going to say, "I'm not going to preach today," but instead she surprised me. "I'm not going to steal your husband," she said.

"That's good to know," I said, with a laugh.

As Alva kept on talking, I stared at the little white whiskers on her chin.

"No more husbands for me. The only one I want is not of this Earth."

She opened a small bag of Lay's® potato chips and went quiet while she concentrated on eating them one by one. I was enjoying her silence when halfway through her bag of chips, a low Bob Dylan voice come from her throat, singing, *"Lay Lady Lay…"*

Her sense of humor made me smile.

Mr. Rousseau devoured his burrito, unaware of Alva. Wiping his chin with a napkin he signed, "That was good."

It was nice he'd found something he liked for a change. Since Glory left, there hadn't been much of anything that he liked.

Alva interrupted my thoughts. "You do such a nice job with him. He likes you," she said.

"Thank you, Alva."

"Yes, I can see it," she nodded.

A compliment coming from a resident was unexpected. So often the residents seemed focused on themselves and only took notice of others when someone crossed them in some perceived manner, then they got upset like children when something seemed unfair.

By now I was familiar with most of the residents—the ones who sat quiet, absorbed in their voices, and others who were overly loud talkers, like Alva and Jaelynn. Jaelynn changed her clothes frequently and acted as if she were intellectually superior to everyone, though it was hard to tell just how smart she was by some of the outlandish things she said.

At the end of my shift when I was gathering my belongings at the nurses' station, Jaelynn came asking for some of her cash from the locked box. She said she was going out shopping with her sister. I was ready for Lashay to let me out from the secure unit, but I had to wait while she counted out ones and twenties for Jaelynn. She got interrupted several times by other staff and by Jaelynn herself.

"I have more money than the others," Jaelynn said, "because I got two billion dollars from Crime Stoppers for telling them where to find Osama Bin-Laden."

Besides me, I don't think anyone else raised an eyebrow at Jaelynn claiming to have gotten two billion from Crime Stoppers. I'd heard her before telling other residents that she'd lived in Iraq where all of her family had been killed.

"My father is a terrorist," Jaelynn said.

Listening to her reminded me too much of Cindy and her delusions.

Lashay finished counting Jaelynn's money and handed her the bills. As she walked with me to unlock the door, she smiled and said, "Jaelynn's so crazy."

"Just think of happy things and keep smiling, Lashay. I'll see you tomorrow."

Lashay laughed. "Humor is what keeps us all going."

* * *

In the dining room with Mr. Rousseau one morning, I stared out the window. I didn't want to be there. I wanted to be out with the Canadian geese I saw lined up on the straw-colored field. One followed the other as they waddled along until one of them took flight, then upward they all went, free to come and go as they chose, unlike us who were locked inside. I could always leave at the end of the day, but the residents were locked in until someone else, a team of clinicians, decided they could leave or move somewhere else.

My daydream soon came to an abrupt halt. Kerri was having another bad day, hollering from the table next to ours.

"I'm gonna get a lawyer, and I'm gonna get out of here, God damn it." She got up, shoving her chair aside. "And I don't like her," she added, charging toward another resident who was now shouting back at Kerri.

I saw fire in Kerri's eyes, like this time she *really was* going to punch somebody. Without hesitation, I drew the big X on Mr. Rousseau's back. He stood up without question and came with me, leaving his lunch behind. We followed a flow of others to the far side of the dining room.

Away from the commotion, I explained to Mr. Rousseau that Kerri and another woman were yelling and fighting. I could tell his heart was pounding by the way he was breathing. I reassured him: "You're safe here."

The staff was quick to surround and calm Storm Kerri. One led her away, and we were told to go back to our tables.

I couldn't blame Kerri for feeling stuck there. The place was depressing. While I wasn't exactly stuck, I was feeling as though this temporary assignment was stretching into forever. My client wasn't becoming independent. He wasn't moving on. Another resident's eye was dripping guck. Alva was yelling for someone to unlock the bathroom. Mr. Rousseau was complaining of shooting marbles, and a new resident kept approaching me repeating his name, "I'm Heriberto, Herr-iii-berr-to, pronouncing it more slowly each time in case I didn't get it the first time. I felt like I would go crazy soon. In that moment I wanted to be free and fly away with the geese.

25

On Edge

Winter 2009

Our gloomy winter grew a bit dimmer when I saw the morning's headline on the Denver Post: "Psych units shutting doors," The article was about the University of Colorado Hospital being the latest in a string of hospitals in the metro area to close its psychiatric unit in the last 10 years. "With the beds at CU gone, the metro area will have about 380 general adult psychiatric beds—a drop of nearly two-thirds since 1990," the article said.

This was dreary news considering that "...40,000 mentally ill people show up in Colorado emergency rooms each year..." The shortage of psychiatric beds was creating an overflow in emergency rooms and jails where individuals with untreated mental illness were ending up. I wondered what it was going to take for our politicians to start paying attention to this humanitarian problem.

It was dreary outside, too. With snow falling like frozen raindrops, it was a good day to be inside even if it was on the locked unit of a care center. Though things looked a bit dreary there as well. Mr. Rousseau had grape juice spilled on his shirt and his hair looked more greasy than it had the previous week. It had to have been more than a week and a half since he'd bathed.

I assumed he was getting concerned about his hygiene as well, when he asked, "Can you smell me?"

I was less than two feet away though I hadn't yet caught a whiff.

"No," I signed.

"Because I found my deodorant," he said.

I guess he figured that's all he needed as far as taking care of his hygiene that day.

I often hear people in care facilities say that they want out. I understand and feel bad for them, including Mr. Rousseau, but when they do things like refuse to shower, it leads me to believe they aren't ready or capable of living independently. But then, Mr. Rousseau received three hot meals a day. He had a bed and a room to himself. There were nurses and people around, and an interpreter. Maybe it was too much for him to contemplate being sent back into the community to fear loneliness, darkness and silence, and no doubt other struggles. Maybe living on the secure unit of a residential care center wasn't so bad. And to get that, all you had to do was refuse to shower.

A new resident pulled my attention away from Mr. Rousseau, when he approached the nurses' station, shouting about a woman who stole the telephone poles from the hospital. I heard his name was JP. He had greasy hair, too, and no teeth. He needed dentures and some new jeans. His were ripped on both sides from his thighs to his ankles. They flapped loudly when he walked. When he sat, his bare legs were exposed.

The staff warned me to keep clear of him. "He's agitated, and he's going to the ER," someone said, as JP stormed through the halls. He yelled into the community telephone and hollered at the staff. Three hours later he was still roaming the halls. The only resident I saw going out was Alva. She was going with a social worker to look at another place to live. Maybe she would move soon and be freed from this locked fortress. She was going out in the cold, bare-legged, in a skirt and tennis shoes, with no coat. I worried she would be wet and frightfully cold by the time she got back.

In the meantime, Mr. Rousseau wanted to write a letter to his daughter and asked me to write it while he dictated it to me. *Dear Jackie*, he started, *I haven't seen you in a long time...*

I was glad Mr. Rousseau had someone he could reach out to. When we finished the letter we took it to the office and put it in the mail bin. Jaelynn was there asking if the mail had been delivered yet.

She said, "I'm waiting for some dog tags I ordered with my name engraved on them because my birth mother got me a green card when I was born..."

Jaelynn seemed more talkative than usual. I wondered if it was the predicted change in weather that was affecting people. Could changes in barometric pressure make people hyperactive? I was curious, too, how the staff felt at the end of a workday. Did they feel exhausted and defeated, or did they feel gratified that they'd helped the residents move a step closer to wellness and independence?

At 3:00 I asked myself if I'd accomplished anything productive. Yeah, I had, I realized. I'd written a letter.

* * *

I was feeling anxious. It seemed this was my last day, as I was not scheduled for any more work at the care center. It was past the time that I should have been contacted if they wanted additional interpreting services. I wondered if Mr. Rousseau was moving and why no one had informed me. I hadn't felt this anxious in a long time. For months I'd been immersed every day with people struggling with mental illness, I'd heard and seen the kinds of challenges they were dealing with. I'd watched some in aimless wander, listened to others complain, and rant. Some did crafts, but many did nothing at all. Perhaps this environment was starting to affect me, making me feel anxious, sad, and down.

Mr. Rousseau was still unshaven and not taking care of himself—he couldn't be leaving. And where would he go, anyway? So, why hadn't anyone contacted me for more work? Distracted and off my game, I stood staring at nothing. In my fog I heard a male voice behind me.

"How are you today?"

I turned to see Colin, one of the floor staff, busy writing on a clipboard. He couldn't have been addressing me. He must have been asking someone else how they were. He continued writing, looking at his clipboard.

I looked away, then heard him again.

"Are you OK?" he asked.

I realized then he *was* talking to me.

I must have looked like I was losing my mind, or maybe he was worried that I'd already lost it.

Apologetic, I managed a weak smile. "I'm sorry, I thought you were talking to someone else. Yes, yes, I'm fine. I was just thinking about something."

Colin, tall and with dark hair combed back, reminded me of musician Vince Gill. He always said good morning and would typically chat, where most of the other staff were too busy to talk to the interpreter. I wondered if Colin had heard anything, or knew if the administration had decided to discontinue Mr. Rousseau's interpreter, or if he was moving somewhere. Before I could muster the words to ask, Mr. Rousseau came asking for help with his laundry.

"I can help you," Colin said.

My hands came up, ready to interpret Colin's reply, but Lashay interrupted us, calling out from the office, "Mr. Rousseau has an X-ray scheduled, off-site. He needs to go now, and the interpreter has to go with him."

When I told Mr. Rousseau he raised his eyebrows in surprise.

"Now?" he asked.

I nodded my fist, "Yes."

It was freezing outside and with ice covering the ground, it slowed our careful steps to the van. I was quiet during the ride, worrying about my job ending. With Lashay riding in front I considered asking her if she knew anything, but soon we arrived at the clinic.

Two technicians took us to the x-ray room, and I directed Mr. Rousseau onto the table. One girl pushed and pulled the machine over his head, all the while talking as she tugged and shoved on him. The space between her and the machines was limited and too awkward for me to get close enough to interpret to him what she was saying. As it was, he got confused and irritated.

"I don't like this," he signed, abruptly sitting up and banging his head on the lowered machine.

Now *I* was irritated.

I found out the x-ray tech was a student. Had I known beforehand, I would have warned Mr. Rousseau so that he would know to be patient with her. We went back to the van after the x-ray and I resumed my worrying.

At lunch I ran into the facility director in the staff lounge. She broke the agonizing silence I'd felt over the possibility of Mr. Rousseau leaving.

"It's so hard finding another place for Mr. Rousseau to live," she said. "No one wants to take on the responsibility of a deaf-blind person."

"Yes, I understand."

"And when he goes, it's going to be hard for him to learn to navigate a new place."

I agreed, and since she brought it up, I felt okay asking her the question that had been nagging me for several days. "Is Mr. Rousseau leaving?"

"No, not yet.."

"I haven't been scheduled for any more assignments. Are you planning for Mr. Rousseau to continue having an interpreter?"

"That I don't know. I'll check on it."

Freelance work was like that. I often didn't know where or when my next job would be. It didn't typically bother me, but here, even though it wasn't the most uplifting environment and I was starting to feel ready to move on, the thought that I might be phased out like Glory, unnerved me—not just for myself, but for Mr. Rousseau. With his communication barriers it would be difficult for him to get along here with so many people, some with unpredictable behavior, and no interpreter.

After lunch I sat with Mr. Rousseau in the common room listening to JP talk with another male resident. "I'm trying to do good and not be crazy," JP said in a loud voice. "I used to do drugs."

The other man, who rarely spoke, asked JP, "What kind of drugs?"

"All kinds—methamphetamines…"

Seeing the results of JP's drug use on his teeth and his behavior, made me glad I never got involved with drugs. My brain was fragile enough already. I was interested in their conversation, but Mr. Rousseau wanted to go exercise, so we left.

While Mr. Rousseau tromped on the treadmill, I became Jaelynn's captive audience when she sauntered into the room.

"They caught Neanderlis and Bafflement," she said.

"Who are they?"

"They are the head of the secret society."

"The secret society?"

"Yeah, the dark side with all the demons, where I was before I came here."

"I see."

I honestly didn't see, but I knew my boundaries. I wasn't there to be engaging in conversations with the residents. But then Mr. Rousseau was occupied on the treadmill, and I was just sitting around and my curiosity piqued.

"What kind of demons?" I asked.

"Well, they were human but they were transformed by alkaloids."

I hadn't a clue what she was talking about. I figured it was her schizophrenia talking, or she was referring to some science fiction she'd read. Or perhaps it was a cult that she'd been involved in. I didn't read science fiction and knew next to nothing about the underworld, or secret societies, and the little I knew about religious and satanic cults, was that they were dreadful. Jaelynn didn't say anything more to help me understand, nor did I ask.

Driving home, I was still on edge, having heard nothing from the director on whether I'd have any more work at the care center. But even more pressing was who were Neanderlis and Bafflement?

26

Having Hope

Sometimes things simmer in the back of my mind, and I don't even know they're there until something spills out. At Christmas dinner, a few weeks ago, for example, my mother-in-law and I were the last two at the table finishing our dessert when I blurted out, "Some people have no insight."

"What's that?" she asked.

It surprised me that she asked that question. People with insight know what insight is. "It's when you just know something, without being told or shown," I said. "You can surmise something without having all the pieces to the puzzle."

"Oh," she said.

To be fair, my comment probably came from out of nowhere. I don't even remember what we'd been talking about. But, something I notice often when I'm with a deaf-blind person, hearing and sighted people will ask me things like: "Can he lip-read?" "Is he 'death,' too?" "Does he like to watch movies?" "What kind of music does he like to listen to?" Or, they let an x-ray technician, who is just learning how to do her job, practice on the patient who can neither hear nor see what's going on, and who is easily frightened.

Now, as I think about it, probably what had been on my mind when I blurted out to my mother-in-law about people's lack of insight was the time Mr. Rousseau asked an aide, "Who will help me with my laundry?" It was five minutes before lunch and I expected her to reply that she could help him after lunch, but she said, "I can do it right now."

My job is to interpret what she says, but instantly I saw the problem with what she had said. I saw the picture of Mr. Rousseau navigating back to his room with his cane, which would require several minutes, then five or 10 minutes more for him to locate and collect all of his soiled laundry and the basket, and more time to navigate back up the hall with his cane while carrying the loaded basket under the other arm, only to find just *me* standing there waiting for him.

He would then ask, "Where is the aide?"

And I would have to tell him she was not there because she would have gone to the dining room by now to help pass out lunch trays. Mr. Rousseau would be standing holding the basket, getting frustrated and confused because she had told him she would help him "right now."

Agitated, Mr. Rousseau would give up waiting, turn and carry his load of laundry back to his room. He would return several minutes later and ask me what time it was. When I'd tell him, he'd be upset because he would be 15 minutes late for lunch and then be upset about the aide and his unwashed laundry for the remainder of the day.

Because of the aide's lack of insight, I found myself stepping out of my interpreter role. Instead of signing her answer, I told Mr. Rousseau it was almost time for lunch and asked if he'd like to do his laundry after lunch.

"Yes," he replied.

So we went to the dining room on time with the other residents. There was no frustration, agitation, or confusion, except in my mind. I had not interpreted exactly what the aide said and allowed the cards to fall as they might. Instead, I had taken charge of the situation to avoid an unnecessary communication breakdown and a mess, which left me with conflicting guilt for the rest of the afternoon for not adhering to the tenets of our profession of which I have taken the following oath: *Do not advise, interject, or give personal opinions.* And definitely, *do not take charge of other people's lives.*

After lunch, Mr. Rousseau made his way up the hallway with his laundry squashed under one arm, while sweeping his cane across the floor with the other. As he approached I reached for the basket, but he insisted on carrying it himself, until it started slipping downward. Only then did he signal with a grimace and a nod toward the basket that I should take it. I held it for only a minute. He took it back and headed for the nurse's station, where he set the basket on the counter.

"Tell him he's not supposed to put his laundry up there," someone called out.

I signed to him, but he ignored me, standing steadfast and determined. Lashay finished what she was doing in the office and turned to see Mr. Rousseau standing next to the basket on the counter. "I can take a hint," she said good-naturedly. We both laughed. Lashay opened the laundry room for Mr. Rousseau and helped him get his soiled clothes into the washer. Unlike the aide, Lashay had insight.

I was no longer ruminating over people's lack of insight. I was in good spirits because I finally got scheduled for several more weeks at the care center. My paranoia about being phased out was all about nothing.

Colin was facilitating a wellness group this afternoon for the residents. I signed into Mr. Rousseau's hands as Colin spoke. "People can recover from mental illness," he said, naming the steps that are involved in recovery. When he got to the last one he said, "The tenth step is *hope*. It's the most important step because without *hope* you can't expect the other steps to help much in your recovery."

I was fully engaged in this topic. Colin asked each person in the group if they had hope. They all said yes, but when he got to us, Mr. Rousseau hesitated before he responded, "No."

I hadn't foreseen that answer. I thought hope was a natural survival instinct that everyone had. Admitting that you have none, raises red flags. I expected Colin to raise a few questions, at least, but Colin glossed over it and continued talking about recovery. Maybe he knew Mr. Rousseau's attention wouldn't last, and he was right, because soon Mr, Rousseau announced he'd had enough. His eyes were bothering him, so we left.

I felt disappointed that we had to leave as I was ready to interpret uplifting stories about people using hope to recover and move on with their lives. I wanted to hear that there is hope for everyone who struggles with mental illness. I wanted Mr. Rousseau to see and believe that he could get better and move on with his life, too.

* * *

It had been three weeks since Mr. Rousseau last bathed. In a non-subtle hint I asked him, "Would you like to ask the staff if you can shower today?"

"Yes," he signed, but when it came to doing so, he changed his mind. His hallucinations were bothering him again. So he sat, bored and locked up, unable to even step outside for a breath of fresh air when he wanted to. That can't be good for anyone's mental health. I knew it wasn't good for mine.

Alva came to sit with us. She hadn't moved out after all. I didn't really mind Alva. I knew she was a caring person even though a few minutes ago she was on the community telephone cussing and shouting, "American communists and socialists take your property and then give you a small part to live on so you are holed up in a tiny crowded spot where they give you pills and wait for you to die!"

She did have a polite side. She once asked me, "Do you want to work here?"

"I do work here, though I don't do the same work as they do," I said, nodding toward the aides who were passing out snacks.

"Yes, they're sweet," Alva said, "but not the people who steal behind your back when you're eating. They should not steal their clothes and steal their personalities and try to act like them. They should not covet their neighbors and worship false idols."

Alva held out her hand to receive a cup of tortilla chips with melted cheese from an aide. She bowed her head and prayed, "Dear heavenly Father, thank you for this food and these people who prepared it and serve it. Thank you for the Mormon Tabernacle choir and all that lays at his head. May some of it lay at my head. Amen."

Amen.

27

A Fragile Mind

It was 9:00, late for me to be eating breakfast. I stood at the kitchen sink in my bathrobe, staring at a banana in my hand. What was I doing with this piece of fruit? It was as if it had magically appeared there, as I suddenly had no recollection of picking it up, nor of what I had planned to do with it. My muddled thinking disturbed me. I shuffled to the table and sat peeling the banana, trying to force my thoughts to become clear.

I had an interpreting assignment that day, but I couldn't think for the life of me as to what it was. Downstairs my husband showered while I sat befuddled, eating a banana. Keetah, our tiger-striped cat, jumped into my lap, the way she always does when I'm in my robe. Drawing her paws up and down, she padded on the soft velour before settling down, purring as I rubbed the soft fur under her chin.

I knew I should be getting dressed for work, but where was I going, and at what time? My disconnected thoughts scared me, and I felt my heart beating fast. Keetah jumped from my lap, sensing my preoccupation, and I got up to search for my assignment information. I found the papers I'd been working on before I went to the kitchen, but I couldn't make sense of the words on the pages.

I headed downstairs to the shower. Perhaps I was just disoriented. We recently bought new furniture and moved our bedroom up from the basement, but we were still showering downstairs. Everything felt out of place. As the warm water beat against my body, I tried to tame my rapid heartbeat. My heart knew something was wrong.

While getting dressed, I told Jim, "Something weird is going on. I can't think straight, and I don't know why."

"Go lay down," he said. "Call in sick."

"I can't. This job is for a new agency. I can't not go."

I lay on the bed for a few minutes, then I got up. "I'm okay," I told him. "I think it's just our bedroom change that's got me rattled."

I figured I just needed to keep moving. That's all it was. Looking in the mirror, satisfied with my outfit and my hair, I told myself I was ready and would feel better once I got outside for some fresh air.

By now, I knew where I was going, but as I drove, I couldn't follow what the host on the radio was saying. I tried harder to concentrate, but couldn't make out the meaning of his words. I changed the station. Music was better, but still, I felt strange like I was dreaming.

Floating is what my brain seemed to be doing. My thoughts floated away before I could string them together. Tooling down the highway, I suddenly became frightened by my inability to understand my own thoughts. With a pounding heart, I broke into a cold sweat and felt a blackout coming on. Luckily, there was a shoulder on the side of the road and I was able to pull over quickly. I stopped the car just in time to lean over the console before my world went totally black. With my head down I felt the blood flowing back into my head and the tiny hole of light in front of my eyes widened again.

When I sat up a few moments later the panic was gone, though the haze lingered. I drove on with my mind in a swirl of blips of the past nights' dreams, unsure if I was truly awake.

I used to sleepwalk as a child. Once, when I was eight years old, I was sleeping on the couch, while my mother was in the kitchen cooking dinner. In the middle of a dream I got up and went to my mother and tried to ask her something about dominoes, but my question was not making any sense. Mom patiently tried to understand me, but my 13-year-old sister thought I was acting funny and laughed at me. She ticked me off, so I stomped back to the couch and went back to sleep. I finished my dream and woke up for real in time for dinner.

But this time I didn't think I was dreaming or sleep-driving, but I did think I should eat before I got to work. I stopped at a McDonald's, and while waiting in line, I noticed the woman in front of me had an unusual hair color of a pinkish rose. Normally, I wouldn't pay attention to a stranger's hair at McDonald's, but with my oddly heightened visual perception, her hair stood out. I blurted out, "Your hair is beautiful."

"Yeah, it used to be red, but I bleached it," she said.

I repeated aloud what she said to help myself understand, but I couldn't get my words out correctly. She said it again, more slowly. She and her friend must have thought I was crazy, but I was convinced I'd be all right after I ate.

Downtown had changed in the few years since I'd worked there with many new parking lots and structures. I found it confounding and didn't want this added stress of trying to figure out where to park. I hate parking garages and try to avoid them, but rather than have to have to think too much, I pulled into one feeling a familiar glint of pain behind my right eye. It was suddenly clear what had been going on. It was a migraine.

If I didn't take something right away, it would develop into a stabbing, throb in my head, followed by nausea. I couldn't be a last-minute no-show to this job. Fumbling for my purse, my fingers found my medicine easily in the dark garage. Swallowing the pill, I'd soon be OK.

I walked the six blocks to the Social Security office where the deaf client was waiting for me. He seemed happy to see me or at least relieved that an interpreter had arrived. I thought it was a miracle that I'd made it. He quickly struck up a conversation while we waited to be called. Mostly, he signed and I nodded.

Fortunately, our meeting with the representative was short and I only had to ask her to repeat something a couple of times when I lost my train of thought. Neither of them seemed to notice that their interpreter was not in top performance that day. When we left the building, I was eager to get back to my car, but the deaf man picked up the conversation he'd started with me earlier about politics. For several minutes we stood outside conversing in sign. More than once I lost my train of thought mid-sentence.

"I'm sorry," I apologized, "I had a migraine this morning, and I'm not thinking very clearly today."

"It's all right," he signed.

I figured we were good to end the conversation there, but he continued talking—about his family and his mother dying and how his relatives drank a lot and rejected him because he was deaf. I could see on his face the pain this had caused him. Though I'd known this man for many years through work, this was the first conversation I'd ever had with him. Sympathetic, I listened a moment longer before I said I needed to get going.

As it's common in the Deaf culture to hug people you know when saying hello or goodbye, I wasn't surprised when he stepped forward to hug me, but when I saw his face coming straight toward mine, I turned my head at the last second. His lips landed awkwardly on the corner of my mouth. That was odd, I thought, as I walked away, putting this very strange day behind me.

* * *

I inherited my fragile brain from my father. Depression, anxiety, and schizophrenia run in his side of the family and so do migraines. Out of us five siblings, I was the one to have inherited the classic migraine from him, which he'd inherited from his mother.

Since childhood, I've dealt with these incapacitating episodes, which I called "the throw-ups" when I was small. The headache pain and the dreadful vomiting that came with it would last all day. I would writhe in my mother's bed, so sick that I wanted to die. Even though my father had migraines, it seemed that neither he nor my mother knew what was going on with me when I was very young, perhaps because my father never experienced vomiting with his migraines. My caring and sympathetic mother appeared mystified by my spells and didn't know how to stop them.

It wasn't until junior high that I experienced the "aura" with the migraine, the symptoms that differentiate classic migraines from regular migraines. When this happened the first time, I didn't understand the strange symptoms, I only knew I was having a difficult time taking my 8th grade French vocabulary test.

While the teacher spoke the words in French, we were to write them in English. Partway through the quiz, I could no longer see the words I'd written on the page. I looked up at the teacher and could only see the right half of her body. I felt confused and frustrated, getting behind as she gave us more words. I raised my hand and tried to ask her to repeat them, but I couldn't get my own words out of my mouth. She looked at me with concern as I struggled to speak. When my right hand went to sleep and my fingers and mouth became numb, I left my desk and approached her.

"My mouth is mun," I said, unable to say the word *numb*.

"Do you want to go to the nurse?" she asked.

I indicated that I did and she had another student walk me to the nurse's office—a good thing because I doubt I would have been able to find the office by myself. I couldn't see or think straight. It would be interesting to know what the nurse thought was wrong with me because I couldn't tell her a thing. The nurse called my mom who came to pick me up. I don't remember the rest of that day, but I distinctly recall what had preceded the French test.

I had come to school that morning wearing my favorite outfit, a yellow quilted jumper I'd made myself and Capezio ballet flats. The Capezios were my sister's, but she let me wear them. They were expensive shoes, and I was saving up to buy my own. My first class that morning was English, and the teacher reminded us we were going to the library. Right away I knew I was in trouble. I'd forgotten it was library day, and I'd left my book at home. It didn't matter that I was wearing my favorite outfit. Even the beloved Capezios that made me feel confident and good about myself couldn't change the fact that I was going to have to face Miss Berry, the librarian.

Miss Berry was a little old biddy, whom all the kids were afraid of. She didn't care what kind of shoes you wore. She only cared about her books and she guarded them like the gold at Fort Knox. Never mind her skinny arms and her 4'11" stature. Miss Berry had tight, curly hair and beady eyes that sent out laser beams when she lectured kids who forgot to bring their books back. She hollered and punished kids for all kinds of minor infractions, like whispering or giggling in her library.

As the English teacher led our class to the library that morning, I shook with terror. I was going to have to tell Miss Berry that I'd forgotten my library book. There was no way out. We filed into the library and sat silently, four to a table, waiting for our name to be called, so we could march up to her desk with our book. I prayed she might overlook me and not call my name, but, of course, she did. With wobbly legs, I walked up empty-handed.

"Where's your book?" she demanded.

My voice came out in a scratchy whisper. "I forgot it."

She bellowed out for all to hear, "You forgot your book?"

I was sure every head in the library had turned to see me shake and nearly fall into tears, but the tears were stuck behind my face, which felt like a red hot balloon. The pulsing and pounding in my head drowned out the rest of her admonition. She sent me to sit at the "bad kids" table.

My "throw-up days" often occurred around times like this when something was worrying me, like a test or an oral book report, or having to bring in the diorama I made that I thought looked stupid and caused me embarrassment. Things other kids get stomach aches over, caused me to get migraines. The doctor told my mother I was having tension headaches and prescribed some little white pills in a dark brown bottle. I was supposed to ask for one when I felt I was having tension, or when I thought I might get sick. I don't know if they helped. I didn't take them often. By the end of junior high, my parents were convinced I was experiencing migraines.

From the 1960s through the 1990s I suffered through each attack, for there were no effective medications back then. I became very familiar with the aura that precedes the headache. Though scientists still don't understand why it happens, they know the aura begins when an area in the lower back of the brain releases a surge of chemicals that overexcite certain nerves in the brainstem. This can cause distorted vision, narrowing of the blood vessels, and symptoms similar to a stroke: numbing of one hand and fingers, confused thinking, and garbled speech. The aura can last up to 60 minutes or more before it fades and the headache begins.

I never understood this brain physiology until I met Dr. Judy Lane, a neurologist who specializes in migraine. I was 46 years old, and I'd looked her up after watching the Denver Broncos play against the Green Bay Packers in Super Bowl XXXII. During the second quarter, Denver's running back, Terrell Davis, was struck blind with a migraine and had to step out of the game. After taking some medication at halftime, he recovered enough to go back on the field. He ended up scoring the winning touchdown for the Broncos and was named "Most Valuable Player" of the year.

I thought it was a miracle and wanted to know the name of the medication Terrell Davis had taken. It was two years later when my sister came across a newspaper article, which mentioned the name of the doctor who was treating Davis and showed it to me. It was Dr. Lane. I made an appointment and when I saw her not only did she tell me the name of the medication, she also explained the migraine process to me, showing me pictures of how certain chemicals slowly spread across the brain during the aura, causing the stroke-like symptoms, and how that led to the headache. Understanding the neurophysiology of migraines made them less mysterious to me and finally getting medicine to treat them made me less fearful of them.

A migraineur is what I'm called. We have overly sensitive nervous systems. Emotional stress, hormonal changes, too much sleep, not enough sleep, or skipped meals can trigger a migraine. It's been said that migraineurs have common personality traits, too. We've been described as intensely driven, conscientious, achievement-oriented, perfectionistic, and rigid. We're also known to be creative and sensitive to the feelings of others. Albert Einstein, Thomas Jefferson, and Elvis Presley were migraineurs, and some modern-day celebrities like Ben Affleck, Whoopi Goldberg, and Kareem Abdul Jabaar suffer from them, too. Perhaps I have some personality traits in common with them. However, where we differ is I'm not famous.

Whether science can actually link personality traits with migraines, I don't know, though they have established a link between migraines and anxiety and depression. Changes in the level of serotonin in the brain, which happens during migraines, can eventually lead to anxiety and depression. Having dealt with migraines for almost 50 years, and anxiety and depression for the last decade and a half, I can attest to this.

Considering this link it occurs to me, after my recent episode of confusion and inability to understand the words coming from the radio while driving to my interpreting assignment, might there also be a link between migraine and schizophrenia? Could frequent migraines contribute to developing this brain disease?

Stunned by this idea, I plunged into articles, trying to find out but failed to turn up anything that alluded to migraines leading to schizophrenia. I was reassured by an explanation that said the confusion and language difficulty that can happen during a migraine aura was transient and reversible aphasia. Fortunately, that altered mental state fades, as mine did after several hours that day, and since then I haven't experienced an episode like it.

So fragile is the mind that when the brain's chemicals are not in perfect balance, it plays tricks on you. It wreaks havoc on your mental health. We have no cure for migraines. No crutches, wheelchairs, bandages, or casts can support us while we wait for the mind to heal. A migraineur finds her own ways to cope with this disability. Mine is a tendency to be independent, not to follow the crowd. Others may see me as "rigid," as we have been described, but for me it's a self-protective mechanism. An attempt to control my environment to avoid tipping the scale toward a dreaded migraine. Despite having to live life as a migraineur, I'm grateful for the medications we have today to treat migraines and other mental disorders.

28

Crashing

Two deer nuzzled, heads together, noses down in the snow. I watched them from my kitchen at dawn while coffee steamed from my cup. The larger one locked his rack onto the smaller one's single antler, tussling, and pulling him side to side. The small one pulled away and Big Rack followed, niggling for more. They made circles in the snow, playing their game as the sun rose.

The deer were soon a memory replaced by the activity on Unit 6. I hadn't been there for several months. Dallas had been discharged to home with her husband until this latest admission. She was wailing because they'd taken away her crutches. She couldn't walk without them due to a recent "surgery" on her leg that she performed on herself at home, gashing her calf with a knife.

"Dallas, you need to quiet down, or you're going to the isolation room," Patty warned.

I interpreted to Dallas, and with flailing arms and hands she signed, "I want my crutches. Why did you take them?"

"Because you were threatening people with them," Patty said. "You can't have them until you calm down. When you're quiet, you can come to the table and eat."

Patty took the crutches to the nurse's station, leaving Dallas stranded on the couch and wailing even louder. Like everyone else, I tried to ignore Dallas' noise while feeling sad for whatever reason was making her behave in such self-destructive ways. I watched Patty pass out lunch trays to the patients at the tables and to Leola who was sitting alone.

A second later, Leola was standing in front of the open food cart.

"Go sit down Leola," Patty called over her shoulder as she set a tray on a table.

It seemed people said this to poor Leola all day long. Whenever she approached anyone, someone would invariably call out, "Leola, go sit down."

Usually, she complied, but this time Leola didn't move from the food cart. She reached in, boldly helping herself to a plate of vegetables. Patty rushed to the cart, and Leola held the plate out to her, as though she were being helpful.

"For the love of God, Leola," Patty exclaimed.

I'd never seen Patty lose her cool like this.

"She's contaminated somebody else's plate," Patty complained, as Twyla stepped in to help.

"Come on, Leola. Let's go this way," Twyla said.

Leola gladly followed. The staff was quick to back each other up whenever someone had a problem with a patient, taking the heat off in the moment. Dallas eventually calmed down, and a male worker helped her hop on one foot to a table, as I slipped away to the break room.

A bedraggled-looking nurse followed me in. "Those borderlines," she sighed, "they can get under your skin."

"You mean Dallas?"

"Yes. Every time she leaves, she goes home and injures herself and ends up right back here."

"Yeah, it's sad and hard to understand."

"What can we do?" she said, shrugging her shoulders. "All it does is give us job security."

"Yeah and depression," I added.

* * *

I sat with Mr. Rousseau at lunchtime, making sure he knew what items were on his tray and where his drink was. I wouldn't want him to accidentally knock his glass of cherry red punch onto another unwary resident. His hair was unwashed and the smell was off-putting. Nevertheless, I let him hold my arm when we went out after lunch with the group. I knew he enjoyed getting outside and having someone walk with him. Maneuvering around the patches of snow he caught with his cane, he finger-spelled, "i-c-e," at the crook of my arm.

Jaelynn walked alongside us to the enclosed yard next to the building.

"I have a lot of email accounts in my name," she said. "They were betrothed to me when my mother passed away. Her name was Betty White. Now, I own her company—the Betty Ford Company."

I thought *betrothed* meant engaged to be married, but whatever. "What kind of company is it?" I asked.

"Look it up," Jaelynn said, traipsing away. "It's complicated," she added under her breath as though she was too tired to explain it, or she thought I was too dumb to understand. Jaelynn still made me think of Cyndi, so confident in her delusions that she left me second-guessing my own good sense, trying to make sense out of her nonsense.

As for Cyndi, I hadn't heard from her in a long time. She stopped calling me, and I her. I had to say, I certainly didn't miss the way she sapped the energy out of me. I could see why families sometimes abandoned their mentally ill loved ones. The emotional drain from trying to help them function in society, only to see them relapse into illness again and again, would be exhausting. You can only go so long before you break and have to distance yourself from them.

When we returned to the building, Mr. Rousseau and I sat in the common room doing nothing. I studied him with his greasy hair and dull expression. *Is this all you want for your life? To live here with no one to talk to, and nothing to do?* I wondered.

I wished I could say, "It's hard to see from this perspective, but there is a life out there for deaf-blind people. With Braille, tactile sign language, new technology, and SSPs (support service providers), deaf-blind people are living productive lives."

The question was, would Mr. Rousseau ever get there? Right now it seemed the only thing holding him back was greasy hair. *Refusing to bathe makes people think you are mentally ill. The world outside is waiting for you, don't you want it?* I wondered.

***

My hair was wet, and it was still half dark when I left the house. Four inches of snow had fallen on the driveway, and it was still coming down. We needed the moisture, I conceded as my stomach reminded me that I hadn't eaten breakfast. As usual, I was in my morning rush to get on the road.

Arriving at the care center the rush was over. For people who are deaf-blind, the pace is always slow. When you can't hear and you can't see, you can't rush. In some ways, I liked the slow pace and enjoyed working with Mr. Rousseau, though I feared my skills were getting rusty. I noticed it recently while interpreting for a professional board meeting. After months of working at the care center, it was jarring to be tossed into high gear. My signing was jerky and awkward at first. The words flowing from my ears to my brain were not flowing back out through my hands and fingers as smoothly as they should. Like an old car, I had to kick-start myself to get up to speed.

It made me realize I missed working in the community with people who have attended to their hygiene, where no one passes gas, where no one has scars on their arms from cutting or burning themselves, and where people talk about current events and world problems. It occurred to me that it might be time to move on from the care center. But then who would be with Mr. Rousseau?

There aren't many interpreters experienced in working with deaf-blind clients. You have to adapt the visual mode of communication used by the deaf to one who can no longer see it, and it requires more of our time, energy, and patience. I would feel guilty abandoning Mr. Rousseau, yet this environment was pulling me down. Or perhaps it was just the gray days of winter that were making me feel doleful. I decided it was time to use the gift certificate I received at Christmas for a massage at the Tall Grass Spa.

I drove along Upper Bear Creek past million-dollar homes and properties on the way to the spa. Despite the afternoon sunshine, patches of snow lingered on the ground and more snow was predicted for the next day. For now the sky was a perfect blue, presenting a panorama of snow-capped mountains in the distance. The sign for the spa was up ahead. I slowed down just in time for a band of elk crossing the road in front of me.

I counted more than 50 of them while I waited for them to cross. They were in no hurry. With my care idling, I grew impatient, thinking they were going to make me late for my appointment. Why was I always in a rush? I should be more like them.

The spa is located inside a cottage, tucked away in this wilderness. I always feel nervous entering places like these. Fancy spas where rich ladies pamper themselves are not places I'm used to frequenting.

A young girl at the front desk greeted me.

"Hello. Are you here for a massage?"

"Yes."

"Here are some spa slippers for you. Would you like a tour?"

"Um, yeah, sure."

She showed me an impressive hair salon where ladies were getting highlights and cuts, and make-up stalls with face products to buy. There were nicely decorated bathrooms and dressing rooms and rooms with individual steam showers. There was even a clothing boutique. She handed me a white robe to put on and told me I could choose whichever dressing room I wanted.

The luxurious bathrobe must have weighed several pounds. I didn't understand why a bathrobe needed to weigh so much, but I put it on and when I came out of the dressing room, she took me to the great room where a fire was burning in the fireplace and calming waterfall music played in the background.

"You can sit here and start relaxing," she said, handing me a cup of cold water with a slice of lemon.

A young man in a black bathrobe was already relaxing in front of the fire. I felt awkward sitting across from him, a stranger, both of us in bathrobes. I flipped through the pages of a ladies' magazine until the therapist came for me.

"Hi, I'm Cami," she said with an accent, extending her hand. "I'm going to do your massage."

"Hi, I'm—"

Cami squeezed and shook my hand with a firmness I didn't expect. After hearing it crack I yelped, "Ouch." Embarrassed, I explained, "Sorry. I have a problem with my thumb."

"It was out of place," she said. "It's back in place now."

"Yes," I said, rubbing the back of my hand. "It's been hurting for some time."

In the dim light of the therapy room Cami asked, "When was your last massage?"

I was hesitant to admit that I'd only had a professional massage once, years ago, so I found myself saying, "I've never had a massage. Well, my husband gives me one from time to time."

Cami nodded. "Any surgeries I should be aware of?"

"I've had 11. Do you want to know about all of them?"

Cami's eyes widened, like she was shocked, but she kept her response professional. "Just the most recent one."

I point to my throat. "It's here. Just be careful of my neck, that's all."

I was glad she didn't ask about the others.

"Do you have an aroma preference—lavender, sage, mint?"

"You pick one."

She picked lavender and stepped out to allow me time to get on the table. Cami's strong, confident hands began finding the painful knots in my back and shoulders. She knew where they were without me saying a word. She worked in silence, rubbing out all the stuff I'd been holding onto for years. I was glad I didn't have to talk, be friendly, or interesting. I just wanted to melt into the table.

Never have I found pain so heavenly. My muscles immediately adored her, and I knew I would return to this spa. She worked on the back of my neck, stretching and lengthening the taut muscles.

Finally, she spoke: "Your body feels like it's been to war."

I was aware that I hadn't been taking care of myself. I was almost afraid to ask, but I did: "What are you finding?"

"A lot of hurt from what you've been through."

She sounded so sad. *Was I that sickly?* She worked past the 35 minutes I'd requested, saying, "I went over because there is so much more you need. Take a bath with Epsom salts tonight, and at least once per week to get the lactic acid out of your muscles. You have blockages from holding so much in."

Tears began rolling down my temples, into my hair. A stranger knew me better than I knew myself—a stranger whose fingers listened to my body, whose hands learned my story. I tried not to cry. She'd broken through the shell I'd built: pushing myself, ignoring my body, being there for others, always showing up. Never slowing, never stopping. Yet, she knew.

Though honestly, what could Cami possibly know about me? Did she think all the hurt and pain in my body was from all the surgeries? The hurt was from holding worry for my friend, Harriette, who lost her battle against breast cancer, and for her daughter Cyndi, whose life I promised I would stay involved in,

My pain and hurt were also for my husband, for his health, and my son the entrepreneur, worrying whether he would succeed. And for my daughter, her trials and tribulations getting established in her career. And for the deaf, homeless man ridden with cancer for whom I interpreted and bought lunch just before Christmas, and the beautiful young deaf woman I had to tell that she had a brain tumor. My pain was for Mr. Rousseau and for all the deaf-blind people who are shut-ins. It was for Dallas, who thinks cutting herself is the only way to survive in this world.

My session with Cami was over. I was embarrassed and sad. As Cami left the room, she told me I could take as much time as I wanted before I came out. I wanted to lie there and sob for an hour. I wanted to scream and wail for all the suffering in the world. I wanted to cleanse it from my soul.

I was crashing and I knew it.

29

Somewhere Out There

Fresh snow lay on the ground. The thermometer outside held at 15° while the last few snowflakes floated to the ground. The refrigerator smelled of mold and the house looked a mess. I hadn't talked to my siblings in months. I was behind on paperwork and answering e-mails. I hurt all over. Jim was going with our daughter and her husband to look at houses. I told him I was going to soak in the tub while he was out.

My old feelings of depression seeped through me, the kind where I couldn't move. I wanted to sit, do nothing, and cry for no reason. Pouring Epsom Salts into the whirlpool bath, I told myself I was just burned out from working in psychiatric facilities. I soaked in the warm water, remembering how I felt after Harriette died. For a while I'd thought I was just burned out from working so much. "Interpreter burnout" is a common theme in our profession, something I'd never experienced before. But when the sad feelings didn't go away and six months of insomnia took over, I realized something else was going on. I finally saw a doctor, who diagnosed me with anxiety and depression. With medication, I had been doing well for several years.

Immersed in the water, I let my body go limp. Maybe a lack of vitamin D was causing this sadness, I reasoned, rather than believing my medicine might not be working anymore. I had no other reason to be feeling so glum, the way Ivy, the patient at the hospital, described in a poem she wrote and gave to me: "All I want is the love of Jesus Christ. I run to you, cry for you, cry and cry." The rest of her poem was a nonsensical verse of rain, pain, hurt, and cloudy, titled "Wonderful Unhandy." "That's me now," I announced in the tub. "Wonderful unhandy."

By Monday, I'd recovered from my weekend low. When I showed up for work at the hospital the staff told me Dallas was still in bed. I had nothing to do then except watch a student nurse taking patients' blood pressures and listen to Philomena talk to JP about being in prison.

"I've never been in prison," JP said.

I noticed he was more calm today than I'd ever seen him. I gathered his medications were working for him now, as he was no longer running around hollering at staff, nor wearing the loud-flapping jeans anymore.

"I was in for six years for burglary," Philomena said.

"Really?" JP inquired.

"Yeah, and altogether for nine years." Philomena continued, jumping from one subject to another, including something about her sister, and was not making much sense. Maybe that's why she was there. It makes sense that you can get stuck in a psychiatric facility when you don't make sense. Yet, in clean clothes with her hair neatly combed there was nothing about her looks that suggested mental illness.

The student nurse who'd been doing blood pressure checks approached me with his rolling pole monitor. "Excuse me, ma'am, may I take your blood pressure?"

"Yes, you can, but I'm not a patient. Do you still want to take it?"

"Oh, no, I'm so sorry," he said, "I thought you were a patient."

Did I look like a patient? I was clean and neatly dressed, but maybe I *was* starting to look depressed. The nurse sure thought so.

Dallas got out of bed in time for recreational therapy. Danica, a recent graduate from college, led the group.

"Today we're going to talk about things you can do for free after you leave the hospital," she said. "There are a lot of things you can do in your leisure time that don't cost any money." She asked Danny, a newly admitted patient, "Can you think of one?"

He was slow to answer, but came up with one: "Count money?"

I glanced up and caught Danica's eye as I was interpreting. A smile broke from my face. I wanted to let the laughter burst from my belly, feel its uproarious joy, delight in its release. But no one else was laughing, so I held it in.

With a sunny grin Danica said, "Yes, Danny, you can count money, but you don't have any, so what else could you do?"

His next idea sounded more sensible. "Listen to music?"

"Yes, that's a good one," Danica said.

A female patient suggested bowling.

"Well, bowling costs money, too," Danica reminded. "Can you think of something else you and I do every morning?"

The woman paused for a moment before she came up with it. "We take a walk."

Dallas was more realistic when it was her turn. "Do crafts or play video games," she signed.

Despite the difficulty some patients had thinking of things to do that don't cost money, I saw it as progress. At the very least, I felt lifted from my doldrums. My smile lasted the rest of the day.

Later that week, Danica brought out art supplies for patients to make cards for Valentine's Day. It was rare to see Camille involved in anything, but she joined us, bringing an awful cough with her. In between forceful expulsions from her lungs, Camille watched Dallas cut heart shapes out of red construction paper with scissors that make scalloped edges. Dallas held up a frame with a heart-shaped cut from the center.

"Leola," she signed, "Would you like this?"

I spoke for Dallas, looking to Leola beside me, hiding behind her hair. When Dallas placed the frame on a pink sheet of paper in front of Leola, it triggered her out of her frozen state. Mumbling, Leola began gluing the pieces together. She wrote "Happy Valentine's Day" on her card, pushed her chair back, and stood. She was finished making Valentines, though Dallas continued cutting, pasting, and tying bows out of pink ribbon. As she glued the bows onto several cards we heard someone singing, "Somewhere Out There."

I turned and saw Leola singing as clear as Linda Ronstadt herself. Danica and I looked at one another, my eyes growing wide.

"Wow," I mouthed, as though an angel had just revealed herself. Danica gave me a nod that said, "Yes, she sings."

The special moment vanished when Tony suddenly lurched from his seat at the staff's desk, dashing down the hall where someone was yelling. As we all scattered from the art table, I could see inside the room where a patient, banging her hands against some cabinets, towered over Ivy, crouched below her.

"Stop it, stop it!" the woman yelled.

The staff rushed in surrounding the woman while Ivy crawled out from under her, escaping into the hall. For everyone's safety, Danica shepherded Ivy and the rest of us into a conference room, amidst complaints from patients.

"When someone is having an issue, we need to be respectful and give them privacy," Danica said.

I interpreted this for Dallas, though I believed the real reason we had been herded into this room was to avoid a brawl breaking out and people getting hurt. With all of us crammed together, Danica tried to distract the patients from complaining.

"What's your favorite season?" she asked.

A few patients obliged her, but not Dallas.

"How long do we have to stay in here?" she asked.

"I'll go check," Danica said. As she departed I was acutely aware that she had left a room full of psychiatric patients with just me, a non-staff person. I could have left with her, yet I stayed interpreting for Dallas as the patients began interacting.

"I don't even know what happened," one said.

"Yeah, what happened?" another one asked.

"I was picking up my clothes and she pushed me down and started yelling," Ivy explained.

The patients spoke clearly, talking with each other. There was no mumbling or slurring of words the way they usually did in group meetings, where I struggled to hear and understand them while interpreting.

Like lethargic students who liven up when the teacher steps out of the room, the others asked more questions, speaking freely in front of me. When Danica stepped back into the room, however, everyone became quiet. Soon we heard the "all clear," and filed out, with me humming, "Somewhere Out There."

30

Scared

Mr. Rousseau languidly stirred a cup of coffee one morning, unaware of Alva grumbling right next to us. She was cranky and irritated by every little thing it seemed.

"I'm tired of this place," she complained. "These people are weird and this place gets weirder and weirder every day."

I was not amused by her anymore. I was tired of the place, too, and Alva was right. The place did get weirder every day.

When Mr. Rousseau finished his coffee, Alva got immediately upset about his empty cup, the napkin, and the spoon left in front of him.

"Tell him to clean it up," she said, with her eyes pointed at me.

Did Mr. Rousseau have to take orders from Alva? Did I? Did his cup have to be picked up right this second? I had not interpreted any of Alva's ranting to Mr. Rousseau. He was oblivious to her foul mood that was grating on my nerves. It was a relief when he announced that he was going to his room. As he turned to leave I scooped up the trash from the table, not because it was my responsibility, but to avoid Alva's wrath if I didn't. Then I retired to the nurses' station, where I wouldn't have to listen to her for a while. Soon, though, we could all hear Alva coming down the hall, roaring like a lion.

"I was raped 100 times! Do you want my baby?" Her voice reverberated off the walls to the windows and back down the halls. "Jesus Christ is your savior. Do you love the Lord Jesus Christ?"

Alva ambled toward a visitor standing near me.

"I prostrate myself before him," she proclaimed, lowering herself, hands and knees to the floor touching her forehead to the cold vinyl.

Someone came from behind to help her up. Her skirt askew, her tangled hair hanging in her face, she grabbed it in fistfuls, pulling as hard as she could. With her body shaking and her face turning red, she screamed, "You can't take my baby. They kill babies. They steal your money and your babies!"

Staff surrounded Alva, talking to her in soft voices, trying to calm her. But she ignored them.

"Who are you?" Alva called to the visitor. "Did you come to visit me?"

The man with sunken cheeks tried to smile.

"Bless your soul. Hallelujah!"

With the staff leading her away, Alva shouted over her shoulder to the visitor, "Did you steal my mind?"

Her rumbling faded as he nervously jingled the keys in his pocket and headed to the front door.

* * *

In the morning Lashay greeted me with her usual shining smile. "Mr. Rousseau's in a meeting with his daughter," she said.

"His daughter? Jackie? I thought she was in Louisiana."

"Yes, she's here."

Lashay took me to the meeting room and opened the door. I peeked inside and saw Mr. Rousseau sitting across the table from a young woman and a man. They'd brought coffee and donuts.

"Hello, I'm the interpreter. Would you like an interpreter for your visit?"

"I don't know if we need one," Jackie said.

"How about I ask him?" I suggested, pointing to Mr. Rousseau.

Mr. Rousseau said he did, so I settled into a chair in front of him as he took the last bite of a chocolate-covered donut and downed the rest of his coffee. I was curious if Jackie had come to help her father find another place to live, or maybe advocate for training in independent living for him, or perhaps some lessons in Braille. But there was no mention of these things. Soon Jackie and her male companion prepared to leave and she thanked me for interpreting.

"It's so hard to communicate with him now. We live in Louisiana and haven't seen him for a while. It seems like his vision has gotten a lot worse. I guess he needs that hands-on signing now."

"Yes, he does. I'm sure he appreciates that you came to visit, though."

Jackie nodded and then said goodbye to her father, tearing up a little on her way out.

Mr. Rousseau said nothing about his daughter or their visit after they left. His only inquiry pertained to Bingo.

"Are they playing now?"

I nodded my fist under his hand: "Yes."

They play Bingo every Saturday at the residential care center, and it was one thing Mr. Rousseau enjoyed. With him sweeping his cane back and forth across the floor, we headed to the common room where he bumped his hip into an empty chair. He pulled it back from the table and took a seat. He didn't see well enough to identify who else was at the table, but I couldn't help noticing, among all the residents at the care center, we always managed somehow to be sitting next to Alva.

"You have to help him," she said, as I slid a couple of Bingo cards toward him. I didn't need Alva telling me how to do my job, though I took it kindly, knowing she and the other residents were sensitive to his disabilities. Jaelynn, with her hair pulled into a haphazard array of pigtails with different colored scrunchies, was the other person at our table. She looked up at us briefly from her two cards, as the game was already underway.

"B-12," said the caller.

I signed to Mr. Rousseau. Watching him struggle to read his card, I realized we were going to get behind and rushed to grab a sheet of paper and a pen to keep track of the numbers being called. Mr. Rousseau was still looking for B-12 when the next one was called. However, we weren't the only ones getting behind.

"Did you call B-10?" Jaelynn hollered.

"What about I-29?" another person asked.

"Bingo!" someone yelled.

Mr. Rousseau gave up searching for numbers in the second game and asked me to play the card for him. Alva started complaining that she couldn't focus and Jaelynn questioned the caller once again, "Did you call G-4?"

"You have to focus, Jaelynn," he replied.

But she couldn't focus. She quit the game and padded over to the TV in her stockinged feet. Looking at her reflection on the black TV screen, she pulled the scrunchies from all her pigtails and redid them into new configurations. I would have preferred to be doing something other than Bingo, too, but I made myself focus instead of watching Jaelynn or wishing I were at the beach. Still, every so often I'd glance over and see Jaelynn playing with her hair, which she did until Bingo was over.

The weather had finally warmed enough to go outside, so after Bingo we all filed out. Mr. Rousseau panted softly as we walked in determined circles around the perimeter of the courtyard until he said he was tired. Then we sat, breathing in the sunshine.

Alva shuffled over in her slippers, carrying something in her hands. "May I sit with you?" she asked.

"Of course," I said.

"What's your name, beautiful lady?"

She asked a fair question. Though I'm here often, I'd never introduced myself to the other residents.

"My name is Diane."

"Diane, would Mr. Rousseau like some of this candy?"

Alva took a chocolate-covered piece of candy out of the package.

I signed to Mr. Rousseau, "Alva is asking if you would like some candy."

He nodded "yes" with his fist.

Alva struggled to break the round flat piece of candy, pressing with her thumbs until it finally broke, and I saw the white inside.

"Mint," I said aloud, fingerspelling to Mr. Rousseau, "chocolate mint."

As Alva reached out with the candy as far as her arm could go, I guided Mr. Rousseau's hand outward. Stretching as far as he could, a gap still separated them.

"Take it. Take the big half," Alva said.

Finally, she stepped forward and placed the candy in his palm. The chocolate mint made its way to Mr. Rousseau's palette, and we savored the goodness of Alva's gesture for several minutes.

Mr. Rousseau, enjoying the confectionery asked, "Do you have more candy?"

"Honey, if I did have some stashed and hidden away, I wouldn't know it," Alva replied. "My mind is shattered from all them electric shock treatments. I can't remember where I put things."

I interpreted, signing into Mr. Rousseau's hands. Since he had no response for Alva, I was wondering if he was thinking about the candy or what she said about the electroconvulsive therapy. I hoped he didn't start worrying about it, thinking they might give it to him, too. Though it sounds frightening, ECT is often an effective treatment for those whose mental disorders have been resistant to other treatments. I half-expected Mr. Rousseau to ask me about it, but he didn't.

At lunch, Alva sat with us in the dining room eating cottage cheese with pineapples. She swallowed several spoonfuls and paused. Holding her spoon upward, she looked directly at me and said, "You need to control your jealousy."

"What?" I asked, as if I didn't hear her right.

"You need to control your jealousy. It will destroy you."

Alva had been silently minding her own business for 15 minutes and suddenly blurted this out. She comes up with some perceptive observations now and then, but this one startled me. What could I be jealous of *here* that she picked up on?

"Do not let your jealousy lead to anger and hatred. Love the Lord Jesus Christ. Do not think about your greed. Do not covet thy neighbor…"

Seeing how Alva's words now seemed to be directed more toward "the congregation," than at me personally, I turned my attention away from her.

Mr. Rousseau, impervious as usual to her preaching, finished eating and put down his fork.

"My eyes are getting worse," he signed. "The tunnel is getting smaller and smaller. I don't want to be blind."

Ignoring Alva's ongoing sermon, I reached for Mr. Rousseau's hand. "I don't want that for you either," I signed.

There was no sugarcoating the inevitable, though the worry must have been torturous for Mr. Rousseau. While it wasn't my role to counsel him, I could refer him to someone who could.

"Do you want to talk to Jerry?"

"Yes," he nodded, so we went to look for him. I knew Jerry understood this issue because of his father's vision problems. Jerry would know what to say.

Jerry said he'd come to talk with us as soon as he got a chance and asked us to wait in the common room, but Mr. Rousseau couldn't contain his worries and fears. They come pouring out to me.

"What if tomorrow I wake up blind? What am I going to do?…"

I wanted to tell him that many deaf-blind people get training to learn how to navigate independently with a cane. They learn how to cook, how to read Braille, and how to ride the bus. They hold jobs and even travel on vacations with support service providers who sign. With new technology, deaf-blind people can communicate with others and are not nearly so isolated as they were in the past. With all of these advantages, Mr. Rousseau didn't have to be so scared. Yet in my role, I couldn't say any of these things. I could only mention them to the social worker and hope that she would follow up on them.

Eventually, Jerry found us and Mr. Rousseau repeated what he'd said to me.

"We know you're scared," Jerry said. "It's normal that you would feel afraid. But we're here and we can help you."

Mr. Rousseau broke into tears talking about his hallucinations, the red and black shapes that start small and grow and multiply into rows and columns, then turn into monsters with ugly faces who throw things at him.

"You just need to remind yourself that those things are not real, and they can't hurt you," Jerry said. "It's from your deteriorating retinas. Your brain is trying to make sense of your vision loss. There's a name for it. It's called Charles Bonnet syndrome."

Mr. Rousseau was quiet, thinking perhaps about what Jerry had said. Jerry then patted him on the back.

"Maybe we can play cards later, okay, Sport?"

Jerry gave him a firm handshake and Mr. Rousseau held on, not wanting to let go. Witnessing this brawny outdoorsman comfort Mr. Rousseau, my regard for Jerry went even higher. I felt better knowing that Mr. Rousseau had an ally in the battle against the demons he was fighting.

I glanced at my watch and noticed my shift was over. I let the two of them know it was time for me to go.

Don't leave," Mr. Rousseau signed. "Stay here."

"I'll be back on Thursday," I signed, looking at Jerry with my eyes plaintive.

"He's comfortable with you," Jerry said.

I smiled, wishing I could do more.

31

Out of Balance

Forty-five minutes into my shift at the hospital I had done nothing but sit in the dayroom watching patients. One of the new admits from last night shouted into the patients' shared phone,

"I ain't signin' no fucking papers. I want to talk to my attorney about my fucking mistreatment. The only papers I want are my 'walking papers!"

With a finger to her lips, Patty approached the woman, urging her to speak more softly. The woman slammed the phone down and stomped away yelling, "I ain't no crazy person. I don't belong here."

Patients who arrived in a manic state were often angry about being locked up. While their yelling, arm flailing, and feet stomping always felt unnerving to me, the staff confronted their behavior with calm. It wasn't an easy job, working on a psych ward.

As Patty gathered the patients for the community meeting, Dallas came out of her room so finally, I had something to do.

"Let's talk about our goals," Patty began. "What one thing would each of you like to get accomplished today?"

A few patients shared their plans: take a shower, talk to the doctor, meet with a social worker.

When she asked Tyrone, another new admit, he paused for a second before responding, emphatically, "To not bash in some motherfucker's head!"

I interpreted using strong facial expressions and signs to match Tyrone's harsh language. On the outside, I stayed cool, doing my job, but inside my guard was up.

Tyrone's voice betrayed a boiling anger inside him. Along with his ponderous size his anger scared me and I was the one sitting closest to him, less than two feet away. A glance at the other patients told me they weren't particularly concerned about Tyrone, but the expression on Patty's face was similar to how I was feeling.

Normally, Patty would respond with redirecting words like, "Let's keep focused on something appropriate," but she seemed thrown off her game. Straightening herself in her chair she moved on to the next patient, as if she didn't hear Tyrone, perhaps choosing not to stir a steaming pot.

While the meeting ended with no further threatening comments from Tyrone, I felt on edge all morning with him around. As patients milled about the dayroom, Tyrone, with his heavy body overflowing the seat, stayed in one spot eyeing everyone. He leaned back in his chair complaining loudly about the staff and the hospital while boasting of how much smarter he was than everybody else except his lawyer.

"I'm filing a lawsuit against these motherfuckers. They have no idea what they're doing," he said.

Neither the staff nor other patients indicated any unease with him, but Tyrone made me nervous. I split my energy between interpreting for Dallas and keeping an eye out for Tyrone. My disquiet lengthened into the afternoon. The minutes ticked by in an eerie calm. An hour passed and then another. The air thickening around Tyrone seemed to be expanding, stretching like a balloon that could burst any second. I felt like he was going to lurch from his chair, break through the membrane, and bash into a table, a wall, or someone's head.

Anxious to leave before something happened, I noted the time. 3:15. Fifteen more minutes until my shift was over. Tyrone hadn't budged from the spot he'd been in all day, boasting about his superior intelligence. He made it known to all that he had just informed his lawyer that he was "not staying at this nuthouse. I instructed him to call this hospital and tell them they have to let me out," he said.

At 3:30 I was gathering my purse and coat from the office when the uniformed officers showed up. Typically, they travel in pairs, but there were six. No one had warned me, though I knew why they came. The office suddenly felt crowded as the entire staff poured in, catching me in a huddle of whispers. It was as though a rocket was on the countdown to launch. We stood waiting for its engine to fire with our eyes on the officers making their way to the only one left in the dayroom.

We all knew what was coming, yet the element of suspense had us holding our breath, watching to see who would make the first move. Then it happened. Tyrone lurched from his seat. In seconds four of the men had Tyrone pinned against the wall. Two others secured his arms behind his back, cuffing his wrists. Someone else pulled a wheelchair up behind Tyrone and the men maneuvered the hefty man onto its seat. They pulled him facing backward down the hall, his feet dragging in untied shoes along the floor. The social worker standing next to me leaned into my ear.

"They've been through this hundreds of times," she said.

No one mentioned where they were taking Tyrone. All I knew is that it was obvious he was too dangerous to stay there.

* * *

Talking with Patty in the patients' hallway one morning, it occurred to me that I was spending more time with persons with mental illness than not. My life was out of balance. I'd slid into the unhealthy zone. Patty's voice faded as my mind drifted to contemplating alternative options for myself, but I didn't get very far. We were interrupted when Leola suddenly bounded from her room the way she does with her hair flung over her face. With an abrupt halt, she brushed her hair aside, then stepped toward us as if she had something important to tell us.

"Hey, you guys," she said with a delighted grin and a glowing face. It was the clearest thing I'd heard her say since the day she sang like Linda Ronstadt. Her joy lasted only seconds, as Patty shooed her away.

Leola's glow, however, lingered in the sunlight behind her affecting me in a serendipitous way. I felt appreciated, like I mattered to someone. Suddenly, my life didn't feel so out of balance.

Patty and I followed Leola to where the other patients were gathered for the morning meeting. We got seated and Patty said, "Good Morning, everyone. I'd like to read you a quote, and I'd like to hear what you think about it.

Here's the quote: 'Instead of giving myself reasons why I can't, I give myself reasons why I can.'"

One of the female patients responded first. "That quote encourages me to change my thinking, to stop dwelling on negative thoughts."

"Good," Patty said, moving to the next person.

"Leola, what do you think about the quote?"

Frozen on the couch, Leola was silent. Her hand covered her eyes. I signed to Dallas wiggling my fingers, "We're waiting."

But Dallas didn't wait for Leola. Skipping her, she signed, "I think it's a good quote because you can do a lot of things to help yourself. I think it's awesome."

Next to her, Trenton had been sitting with his eyes closed, yet he wasn't asleep. He'd heard everything.

"Awesome," he repeated. "Awesome makes me think of my dad, who always said it was a horse with a good temperament. And there are drugs, and if I take them maybe I can return to normal, like cooking and eating good things. Like Denise and Dawn and Debbie, they all have the same letter..."

Patty didn't allow Trenton to meander too long. She thanked him and moved on to the next patient.

"Camille, what do you think of the quote?" she asked.

I hadn't noticed that Camille had joined us. It's such a rarity that I turned to look and saw her wrapped, as usual, in a blanket. She was also wearing mittens.

"What's that?" she asked Patty.

"The quote," Patty repeated. "We're discussing what we think this quote means. Do you have something to say about it?"

Camille mumbled something and a male patient interrupted, "My grandfather committed suicide. It runs in the family."

Another patient, laughing at his voices, strode past, distracting us all. Patty was either losing control over the discussion, or she'd grown weary of it. Whatever the case, she wrapped up the meeting early.

Some days, group meetings go better than others.

32

A Quiet Rage

Mr. Rousseau was not always oblivious to the activity going on around him. His vision fluctuated throughout the day, depending on the light, but when the light was just right, he took in his environment. I realized this when he said one day, "That lady changes her clothes, over and over."

"Yes, it's Jaelynn," I said. "She does that."

On days when he was interested, I would tell him things about the other residents or the staff that everyone else in the common room was privy to. Jaelynn was no longer at the care center and even though I'd informed him of this, today he asked me, "Is that Jaelynn over there? I recognize her shirt."

"No, that's not her," I said.

He kept looking for Jaelynn, anyway. He didn't like her much when she was there and would ask me sometimes if she was a boy or a girl. But now that Jaelynn was gone he called her his friend because she knew a few signs. I wished Mr. Rousseau had more friends. Then I wouldn't feel so responsible for him. I wouldn't waste so much energy thinking about ways I could help him or feeling frustrated because I couldn't. I would find work elsewhere, knowing he would be fine without me.

On my break that morning I stepped into the staff lounge where Colin was pouring himself a cup of coffee. I noticed something different about him. He was not his cheerful self. He was quiet and his eyes didn't have their usual brightness. I wondered what was up.

"How's it goin' Colin?"

"I'm tired. Tired of working here," he said, sprinkling a packet of sugar into his coffee. "I'm a certified mental health counselor, but I'm not getting to do that here." He leaned against the counter and sipped his coffee. "I'm just killing time until I can find something else."

This surprised me, as I hadn't imagined that he was unhappy working here. I thought of him as a longtimer on the staff.

The only words I had for him seemed paltry, but I said them anyway. "I understand. Still, I'd hate to see you go, Colin."

At the same time, it was almost a relief to learn I wasn't the only person who found this place emotionally draining. Yet, despite my despair over Mr. Rousseau's lack of progress, and my life feeling out of balance, I was more than taken aback when the care center director shared something with me later that day.

Holding out a piece of paper over her desk, she said, "I thought I should let you know about this."

I took the paper. It was a letter from the company's chief financial officer informing her that, *"Due to budget constraints, we will no longer be able to provide ongoing interpreting services for Mr. Rousseau."*

I felt my heart sink and the blood drain from my face. Without reading the rest of the letter, I asked, "Is this true? Is it definite?"

"I'm afraid so, but it's not happening right away, not till next month."

With a pounding heart and my breath coming up short, I protested: "They can't do this. Can they really take away his interpreter?"

"It's what the letter says."

"But—how's he going to communicate? How will the staff—"

"I know. I'll talk to them, but I wanted you to know what's going on."

A quiet rage burned inside me at the insensitivity, the disservice to this deaf-blind person. And what about my job? I *loved* this job. I knew the environment had been getting me down, but how could my job just disappear? My thoughts spun as I tried to catch my breath.

When I spoke, my voice crackled: "Mr. Rousseau's afraid. He can't *hear*, and he's going *blind*. I can't tell you how many times he startles and reaches out for me with a look of panic on his face, and when I offer my hand or he suddenly sees me he says, 'I thought you were gone!'"

Seeing the tears escaping my eyes, she offered me a box of tissues. "I understand that he's scared. We all understand it. I can't imagine what it must be like for him."

"What about the ADA?" I sputtered, pulling out a tissue, while fully cognizant that real professionals do not cry at work.

"The what?"

"The Americans with Disabilities Act—his right to equal access to communication."

"Yes, I will remind them."

"And you said next month. That's only a few days. It's almost April."

"I'll see what I can do," she promised.

In a somber mood for the rest of the day, I sat with Mr. Rousseau wondering how the staff was going to tell him they were taking away his interpreter. I spoke to no one about the letter, though the clerk, who typically stayed in the back office, must have noticed something different about me. She approached me in the common room. "How are you?" she asked. "You seemed troubled."

My voice sounded pale and scratchy with my body shaking again. "Yes, because they're taking away his interpreter."

"You're kidding!"

Mr. Rousseau interrupted us. His hallucinations were bothering him. He asked me to get the nurse. I went to Lashay because she understood what was going on with his eyes. She told him, "Your hallucinations are different from what a psychotic person experiences. Yours are visual disturbances, common to people who are losing their vision."

Lashay patiently explained this to Mr. Rousseau, as she had done a few times before.

"It's like the phantom limb syndrome in people who have had their foot amputated. The foot is gone, but still, it itches. The brain is not yet used to the foot being gone. For you, it's your eyes. Your brain is confused by your deteriorating retinas."

Aside, Lashay told me, "The best we can do is give him medicine to help with his anxiety." She shared that she was aware of the letter from the center's headquarters. Like me, she was upset.

"Mr. Rousseau backslides every time you're away," she lamented. "This is going to be awful."

Sensing my distress, she asked, "What can I do for *you*?"

I shook my head. "Don't worry about me. Go to bat for Mr. Rousseau."

All day people came up to me: "You were the topic of discussion at the staff meeting this morning," Colin said. "We all see how Mr. Rousseau responds to you. To others he's lost. He doesn't understand us, and we can't communicate with him."

It was heartening to know the staff, at least, understood his plight.

"Maybe this is a crusade you need to take on, "Colin suggested. "You need to speak out, instigate change for deaf-blind people's sake. "

"I don't know," I said. "I hope you all can do something. I'm not going to be here much longer."

The saddest day was when they told Mr. Rousseau what will happen. They told him he had to be more independent. I knew he was struggling with his blindness, his fears, and his loneliness, yet he accepted what they told him. In the dining room an aide handed him a cup of milk with his silverware from the service window. I knew the new rules. I could not carry things for him or guide him anymore. I also knew, with his hands full, without his cane, he probably couldn't make it back to his table on his own in the dim light. I stood back, hiding my fistful of used tissues. My role now was to be a robot, to sign what I heard and voice what I saw. Robots do not feel, do not react, do not help. But this robot knew this was stupid and cruel.

Mr. Rousseau turned from the service window to return to his table, where his food waited and lost his direction. He stood looking confused. I could have easily taken his arm and guided him to the table, but now I wasn't allowed to.

He walked in the wrong direction, signing with one hand, "Where's my table?" Where's my food?"

I barked out his questions, hoping some busy staff person would hear me and notice Mr. Rousseau floundering. I felt how wrong this was and hated myself for standing still, watching and doing nothing.

Jerry, helping other residents, realized what was going on.

"Oh, God," he said, coming to retrieve Mr. Rousseau. "Your table's over here, Sport."

The whole thing was stupid and awkward.

When I saw Jerry in the staff lounge, I apologized for barking out earlier.

"I'm sorry I sounded rude. I didn't mean to. It's just that I got orders not to guide Mr. Rousseau anymore."

"I know," he said, "We all know."

That night I tossed and turned, unable to sleep. Throwing off the covers, I went to the computer and poured my feelings onto the keys about how cruel it is to ignore a deaf-blind person in a common area full of people. How inhumane to leave him in silence and darkness, isolated in a crowd. Isolation from other humans is torture and detrimental to one's soul.

My job is to connect a deaf-blind person to people and activities. To neglect to do so shows either a complete lack of understanding of deaf-blindness or a total disregard for that person's humanity. I filled three pages with my frustration and anger. I didn't know who I was writing to or who I was mad at. At midnight I turned off the computer, went back to bed, and fell asleep.

On my last day at the care center the social worker told me she had spent hours on the phone trying to expedite Mr. Rousseau's moving out.

"Where will he go?" I asked.

"Someplace where he can get services for his blindness," she said. "Probably out of the state."

I didn't know whether to be sad or happy hearing this: "I wish our state had better services for deaf-blind people, so they wouldn't have to move away," I confided. "I've seen it happen to others."

The next day I stayed home, and for five days after that I scheduled no work for myself as depression settled into my bones. Was it depression brewing inside me that caused my emotional breakdown over the care center's decision? Did I overreact, or would any reasonable person respond the same way? I asked myself, wondering if there was something else I should have said or done before I left. Feeling guilty that I abandoned Mr. Rousseau, I pondered over what else I could still do. I'd been so distraught that last day, I didn't even say goodbye.

* * *

April came with a citation delivered in the mail. The photo radar speeding ticket was addressed to my husband, but the photo was of me behind the wheel. The date was the same as my last day at the care center—the photo taken 12 minutes after I'd left. Just what I needed, a speeding ticket to remind me of that ugly day. It was the second ticket I'd received in three months in the same neighborhood. Like schizophrenic voices, negative putdowns reeled through my mind, "You're so careless. A stupid idiot. Nobody needs you."

The negative words swam through my head for days and into the evenings. At night sleep was fitful, but the words were there on my pillow when I awoke, along with fresh warm tears. I fought them, reminding myself, "I'm neither deaf-blind nor homeless, so why am I so sad, so depressed? Why do I feel like the whole world is sinking?"

I was still hurting and angry about what happened at the care center, about the way I had to leave. It was not how I'd expected my time to end there. I thought I would leave when Mr. Rousseau left, when he was moving on to a better place and everyone was happy. Instead, it left me with another war wound for the massage therapist to find.

At home I kept the TV off to avoid any negative news. It only made me feel worse. My husband understood my sadness about abandoning "the deaf-blind man," whose name I never uttered at home. He felt sad about it too.

I went back to the Tall Grass Spa. I had a different therapist this time. She rubbed away my blues, pushed my thoughts and cares away until nothing bothered me anymore. When she encountered a sore place on the outer edge of my foot, the pressure of her finger took me right out of my blissful state.

"Eeaaoooww."

"That hurts here?"

"Eeee-yeah."

"That's your shoulder," she said. "Your left shoulder."

"I could have sworn it was my foot."

She went back to rubbing the spot more gently, explaining how reflexology works. I decided to let her think it was my shoulder. She could think whatever she wanted as long as she kept rubbing. After she did my feet, she worked her magic on my arms and hands. She was nothing short of amazing.

In the morning, I woke up feeling different. My stomach was no longer in knots. Food tasted better again. And as the week progressed, I realized I'd stopped losing weight. The ugly words floating in my mind were gone and I was no longer speeding. Best of all, my heart was quiet.

I went on a medical assignment where my client, a deaf man on crutches, told me he traveled four hours to come to this appointment.

"I'm so happy I have an interpreter," he signed. "Last week, I drove four hours to get here and had to reschedule because there was no interpreter." Now he was smiling.

It always makes me happy when I have made someone else happy. I realize I had compromised my health by becoming too emotionally involved with Mr. Rousseau, wanting so much more for him. I stayed out of loyalty to deaf-blind people. But what good is loyalty if you are not helping someone? Mr. Rousseau was stuck in his misery, and I was sinking in the surrounding quicksand. Sometimes it's only after you've left a place that you truly know where you've been.

Spring 2009

The care center contacted me three weeks after I left, asking me to return to work. I can't say it was unexpected. I agreed to come back but on a limited basis. By choosing more diverse assignments, my depression had disappeared. I was no longer sad and frustrated by what I could not do within my professional boundaries. Driving to the care center, I felt carefree.

I was glad to see that Jerry was working that weekend. He had a way with the residents, especially Mr. Rousseau, and I loved how knowledgeable he was about a lot of things including mental illness. While the morning was slow, I brought up something I'd been thinking about.

"Jerry, I'm reading Dr. Kay Redfield Jamison's book, *An Unquiet Mind*. Have you read it?"

"Yeah, I've read that."

"Dr. Jamison says that bipolar disorder, or manic depressive illness as she prefers to call it, is often fatal. I'm not sure what she means. Can the disease itself kill you?"

Jerry thought for a moment. With residents coming by the desk asking for things like tape and Tylenol, I expected his response to be short, but it was more reflective.

"The reality is, without medication there's a high rate of suicide for people with bipolar, or any mental illness," he said. "And when they're not medicated, they're more likely to self-medicate with street drugs and alcohol. An overdose of either of those can be lethal, or it's an accident from being mentally impaired that kills them."

"So it's suicide rather than a disease process itself that makes it fatal?"

"Yes. You also need to remember that the medicines we have today haven't been around all that long, and medicines like lithium used to treat bipolar illness can be toxic at higher levels. People on lithium need monitoring with blood tests."

"I know medications can be harsh on the body."

"True, and we're still learning about psychiatric medicines," he said, leaning back in his chair. "Our system is so broken. When families can no longer cope with a mentally ill family member, they take them to the ER, or the police take them, but the hospitals don't want to keep them. So, they discharge them with medication, but the follow-through just isn't there."

"You mean the support in the community that's supposed to help them stay on the meds?"

"Exactly." Jerry sat forward again, tapping his pen on the desk. "Not only that, there's the idea that a mentally ill adult has the right to make his own decisions and live freely in the community. That's idealistic, and it doesn't work. They've closed too many of the psych facilities and now the waiting lists for beds are too long and families throw up their hands."

"Yes, deinstitutionalization—"

Jerry interrupted, "It's why we see so many mentally ill people incarcerated. They're stuck in jail without treatment. They become chronically mentally ill, and they end up here or in some other long-term care facility."

Jerry was as passionate about this problem as I was. For months, I'd wanted to discuss this with someone in mental health—pick their brain, get their opinion. I was overflowing with questions to ask, things I wanted to say.

"It seems people are silent about this issue, like they don't even notice that we have this problem in our society. I think we should band together and go speak to our legislators about the lack of attention to this."

Jerry shook his head, looking disheartened, "They don't do anything because nobody wants their taxes raised to pay for the mentally ill."

He focused his glance down the hall, where we saw Mr. Rousseau fast approaching, his cane sweeping back and forth across the floor. Jerry stood and pushed his chair back to the desk. I felt our conversation hanging in the air as I switched my attention to Mr. Rousseau. There was so much more to say.

Summer 2009

It took longer than anyone expected for the arrangements, but things finally came together. Mr. Rousseau was leaving Colorado. Packed and ready to go, he sat near the nurses' station wearing his old leather bomber jacket and felt fedora, while Jackie wrapped things up in the office. "I won't be seeing you anymore," he signed to me, "I will live in Louisiana now."

"Yes, I know. You'll be near your daughter and can see her more."

He shrugged his shoulders, showing little emotion. I hadn't seen Mr. Rousseau much in the last few months, but I knew he was ready for this.

Mr. Rousseau's daughter, Jackie, approached us from the office. She looked exhausted. Taking a breath, she said in a raspy smoker's voice, "We're finished. We can go now."

I signed into Mr. Rousseau's hands, "Your daughter is ready. It's time to go."

"Now?" He asked, as if he couldn't really believe the time had come.

I nod my fist in his hand.

He stood and unfolded his cane as Jackie extended her arm for him, her hand shaking. An aide waited by the door with a cart loaded with a few boxes of Mr. Rousseau's belongings. I thought Mr. Rousseau might say something to me like "thank you" or "it was nice having you as my interpreter," but he was quiet. I couldn't let him leave just like that. So, I reached for his hand. "Enjoy your life in Louisiana. I will miss you," I signed.

Mr. Rousseau tapped my hand, then took his daughter's arm. Jerry unlocked the door and we accompanied them to the front of the building and stepped outside.

"Well, good luck to you, Sport," Jerry said, offering Mr. Rousseau a handshake. A shiver spread up my arms and across my back. I interpreted for Mr. Rousseau while looking at Jerry. We both had watery eyes. There was nothing else to say as we watched them go hand-in-hand to her car.

33

A Fragile Mind Has Limits

September 2010

Our plane from Boston touched down at Denver International Airport at 12:54 p.m. I led Mara, my deaf-blind friend, through the concourse around the people flowing in the opposite direction. A sign pointed to baggage claim, but suddenly I got confused.

"Which way to United's baggage claim?" I asked a woman walking next to me. She shot me an irritated look and pointed to the sign. "Baggage claim," she answered.

She was not helpful. A streak of panic shot through my mind. I could no longer think for myself. I needed someone to take me by the hand and show me where to go.

"But, where's United's?"

The woman ignored me and kept walking. A man in a uniform, who stood directing people, overheard my question. He pointed to the escalator on his left, "It's this way, ma'am."

I thanked God for his kindness. My momentary freak-out dissolved as we followed the flow of people onto the downward escalator. At the bottom there was no new decision I had to make. There was only one way, straight ahead to the doors to wait for the train that would take us to the terminal. It was only the timing thing I needed to concentrate on now. When the train pulled in, there were just a few seconds in which to get myself and Mara onto the train with both our suitcases before the door closed. I would guide her hand onto one of the poles to steady herself before the high-speed train took off.

Just as I had guided her the last six days through airports, onto planes and shuttles, through hotels, up elevators, down hallways, along sidewalks, across streets, through restaurants, onto trolleys, and even a boat, we boarded the train safely.

At the terminal, the train slowed as a female digital voice announced the stop. "This is the baggage claim."

The doors opened and I led Mara off the train to the ascending escalator. Attached at the crook of my arm, by now we were well practiced on getting onto escalators with suitcases.

The tension in my body relaxed for the first time in a week. I no longer needed maps or needed to ask passing strangers stupid questions. Back on familiar ground, I knew where we were going. Mara trudged alongside me, wordlessly trusting as she had all week while we toured Boston. After several trips, we'd become good traveling buddies, despite my intermittent moments of panic. Often, when I returned home from these trips, my family and friends would ask me, "Why do you do that?" Why does a deaf-blind person like to travel when she can't see?"

"She can see a little," I tell them. "She wants to visit as many places as possible before she goes totally blind. And anyway, deaf-blind people get a lot out of traveling."

I explained how there are different feels to different places and changes in ambience and environments. There are lots of things to touch and smell and interesting facts for deaf-blind people to learn when traveling with a support service provider (SSP) who can interpret information. Still, it was difficult for my family to understand this, even when I added, "It's rewarding for both of us."

Unpacking my bags at home, I saw the two of us in my mind, hopping on the trolley, getting off at Faneuil Hall and exploring the Marketplace. I saw us touring the Old State House and Paul Revere's House, then eating burgers and buying souvenirs at the famous Cheers bar. I saw myself driving the rental car to Gloucester, where we visited another deaf-blind friend. We even took a harbor cruise. We did more during this trip than I had in either of my two previous visits to that city with my family. The reveries filled me with warmth until I saw myself at the end of the trip, on what should have been a simple errand. Instead, my stomach turned sour.

Six days and nights of being the eyes and ears for two, I'd been on duty for practically 144 hours when I left Mara at the hotel while I went to return the rental car. I'd told her I'd be back in 15 minutes, but soon after I left I remembered I needed to fill the car's gas tank. By the time I found a gas station, I was a mile and a half from the hotel. The outdated gas station didn't accept credit cards at the tank, so after I filled the car I went inside to pay.

That's when I discovered I didn't have my wallet. "I can't believe this," I said to the attendant. "I must have left my wallet at the hotel! It's just a mile away. I can go get it and come right back."

The muscular man stood shaking his head, surely not buying my story. "What can you leave with me while you go get it?" he asked. "Do you have a GPS?"

I looked at his face, into his eyes. I had a Garmin with me, but suddenly I didn't trust him any more than he trusted me, the out-of-state tourist.

"No, I have nothing," I said, feeling anger rise from my gut, mad at myself for my mistake. I knew I had only one choice. I went back to the rental car, moved it away from the tank, and left it parked next to a fence. As I stomped off the property, I heard the attendant calling after me, but I was too proud and too mad to turn around.

Pounding the pavement, I headed east through a residential neighborhood, figuring it couldn't be hard to find my way back. If I walked straight for one mile, I should come to the hotel. That would have been true, however, at three-quarters of the way I came to a huge fenced-in high school campus. Not seeing any shortcut through, I would have to take a detour around it.

No doubt Mara was wondering what was taking me so long, worrying perhaps that I'd been kidnapped or murdered, leaving her to fend for herself. I tried sending her an email, but it wouldn't go through. When it finally did, she didn't reply. Had something happened to her?

By the time I reached the hotel, I was steaming mad and sweaty. I found Mara happily watching captioned TV and my wallet sitting on my bed. Stripping off my sandals, I began putting on my tennis shoes. She looked up from her program as I finished tying them. "I'm sorry. I'm so mad," I signed.

"Why?" she asked,

"Didn't you get my email?"

She shook her head. On TV, Lucy and Ethel were jumping around barefoot inside a huge vat of grapes. Mara looked back to the TV and started laughing at Lucy. I wished I could stay and watch Lucy and Ethel with her. It was my favorite episode of *I Love Lucy*. But I had to get going before it got dark. Signing large and fast, I explained to Mara what happened at the gas station and why I had been gone so long. She hadn't even noticed. She'd been too engrossed in the show.

"Now, I have to walk back there to pay him!"

"Okay," she signed. "Fine."

With nothing more to worry about and the sun shining in the evening sky, I didn't mind the walk back to the gas station. I even felt a moment of victory when I handed the $17 in cash to the gas station attendant. Still, the whole incident, including my momentary mental lapse at the Denver airport the next morning, reminded me that my fragile mind has limits. I'm forced to ask myself, am I too fragile to take on responsibility for a deaf-blind person traveling across the country? Tossing the last of the dirty clothes from my suitcase into the washing machine, I saved the question for another day.

* * *

"I think I want purple calla lilies for my bouquet," my daughter, Heather, said.

We were having lunch out on our deck in Conifer, talking over her wedding plans. Having recently inquired as to the cost of flowers, I learned that calla lilies are the most expensive flower. Even so, I wasn't going to tell her she couldn't have them. I was pleased that she had made a decision. Each one for this wedding had come painstakingly for my 30-year-old daughter, who was trying to stay within our budget.

"Great, just let the florist know what your budget is, and they can make up the bouquet accordingly. Then, what about the centerpieces?"

I'd already researched ideas for these too. "They can be expensive, but we could—"

"I don't even *care* anymore," she renounced, with a downfallen face into her palms. Her shining auburn hair fell lightly over her hands. She had hit her overload point. "I can't think about centerpieces. You can do whatever you want."

"I saw some with submerged flowers. I could—"

She pulled her head back from her hands. "Fine, those will be fine."

Thank goodness. We had both worn thin. After months of looking at wedding venues, Heather chose a house on the top of a mountain with a stunning view of the Breckenridge ski slopes, available to rent. We had reserved the place and rented the tables, linens, dishes, and chairs. We'd also ordered food and the cake. As for the dress, our search for the perfect one ended a few weeks ago, with an ivory Pronovias gown with a modest lace train.

In the 70s when Jim and I said our vows in front of a justice of the peace, I wore a long forest green velvet skirt with a matching peplum that laced up the front. I made it myself. No one witnessed our promises to each other, except the court's clerk, and no one celebrated with us afterward. That was long ago, when things were more simple.

* * *

The golden aspens glimmered in the afternoon sun. Heather stood with eyes sparkling like the beading on her gown. With her dark hair pulled back and cowboy boots peeking from the hem of her ivory lace, she was an elegant western bride. Guests, waiting under the turquoise sky, turned to witness her father walk her down the path to the patio.

I was still savoring the memory of the wedding a week later when the phone rang. It was my friend, Emily.

"Hi, Emily. It's been so long. How are you?"

"Good. I've gotten married since I last talked to you," she said.

It was wonderful catching up with Emily, exchanging details of her wedding along with my daughter's ceremony. We talked about many things, though I was the first to bring up Cyndi.

"Have you seen her recently?"

"No, not in a long time," Emily said. "She quit talking to me, too, after she did you. In fact, that's what I was calling you about. I happened to be reading an old *Denver Post*, from July 25th, and I came across the Obituaries. It says, 'Cyndi Grober, Denver. Daughter of the late Harriette and Stanley Grober. Sister of Jeff (Jill) Grober. Services were held.'"

It was hard to believe what I was hearing. "She died?"

"Yes, on Monday, July 19th."

"My gosh. And we weren't informed? So…that's it?"

"Yes, the services have already been held."

With her poor health and her sad circumstances I'd always known that Cyndi wouldn't have a long life, still, learning she had passed was a shock. I felt rueful that I hadn't known she was dying. I might have visited her, or maybe she hadn't wanted to see people, at least not Emily or me.

I tried to picture who may have been at the service, aside from a few family members. I didn't think she had many friends left. The ultimate mystery of Cyndi left me to imagine how many other people with mental illness die friendless, so their obituaries simply read: *Services were held*.

Part 3

34

Unbalanced People

January 8, 2011

Heading into the new year with a fresh direction in my community interpreting, I felt invigorated. I was no longer working with Mr. Rousseau and hadn't worked on a psychiatric unit in four months. My concerns about our broken mental health system had been put aside. I was not worrying about the dearth of psychiatric beds in hospitals anymore, or the lack of group homes for persons with mental illness, or our faulty laws and the resulting problems of allowing seriously mentally ill people to go without treatment. Cyndi was completely out of my life, and I had moved on.

My focus on the morning of January 8th was on my monthly meeting with the ladies of the Denver Branch of the National League of American Pen Women (NLAPW). As the president of the group, I enjoyed spending time with these women of the arts. With our common goals we supported each other's projects, and it was where I went to get recharged and find inspiration. I was always eager to get home afterward to work on my own creative endeavors. That afternoon, however, my inspiration was swept away in a blink of an eye when I arrived back home and walked in the door. Learning what had happened that morning in Tucson, Arizona, all my concerns came rolling back in one gigantic bundle. Little did I know this would set me on a crusade to influence change in our mental health laws.

It was midafternoon when I pulled up in front of the house. Inside, I found Jim standing in the kitchen watching breaking news on TV. I turned to look and heard them say, "Giffords was shot in the head. She's been taken to the hospital and other people have been hurt as well." The anchorman was talking about Congresswoman Gabby Giffords of Arizona. This morning she was hosting a "Congress on Your Corner" event in front of a supermarket near Tucson. She'd been talking with a couple of her constituents around 10:00 a.m. when a gunman started firing.

"Oh, my God. This is awful!" I cried, feeling a flush creeping up the back of my neck, burning the rims of my ears. "If she's still alive, I can't imagine—"

Not one to show his emotions, my husband was silent, though his expression told me his sentiments were like mine.

"We're not going to speculate on what the motive may have been, or who the target may have been," the reporter said.

I had not heard of Gabby Giffords before this, but the afternoon anchorwoman related that Gabby is, "—an exemplary congresswoman, a hard worker, a selfless woman who put herself last—" We were also told that the person who shot her was a 22-year-old from the local area and that he was in custody.

When I heard the shooter's age, I knew in my gut what it was before anyone had spoken it.

"It's schizophrenia."

"What?" Jim said.

He was passing through the kitchen trying to get back to his Saturday chores.

"Schizophrenia, I bet you the shooter has schizophrenia."

Jim stopped for a moment. Looking at the TV, he shook his head then turned away. He'd heard enough from the broadcasters. I remained stuck in front of the TV, full of anger and disbelief that a shooting like this had happened again.

By the end of the day we'd learned that Congresswoman Giffords was alive, but in critical condition after surgery. Six people had died, and 14 others were injured. Police had identified the gunman as Jared Loughner.

Though it was unconfirmed, I had no doubt this horrendous act was a result of untreated severe mental illness. No 22-year-old of sound mind would do this. I knew schizophrenia can develop at any age, though, in males the late teens to early 20s was a common age for it to manifest.

The media and the internet were abuzz with reports that supported my suspicion. Students who knew Loughner at Pima Community College alluded to him as being mentally unstable. One student even said she was *terrified* of him.

The day after the shooting, anger grew more rampant. Some in the media were blaming Loughner's violent act on politics, accusing the right wing, and Sarah Palin, for "targeting" Giffords, saying something about "crosshairs" on an electoral map over Giffords' district.

Pima County's Sheriff, Clarence W. Dupnik vocalized his anger in a news conference: "When you look at unbalanced people, how they respond to the vitriol that comes out of certain mouths about tearing down the government—the anger, the hatred, the bigotry that goes on in this country is getting to be outrageous…"

I understood the sheriff's anger. I was angry, too, yet I couldn't agree that this shooting was a result of someone reacting to political statements. It was something deeper than politics.

In the days following the shooting, Gabrielle Giffords was fighting for her life. A week before I'd never heard of this woman, but now I looked for daily reports on her condition as debates fired up over gun control and political attacks against the Tea Party movement and conservatives increased. Meanwhile, I watched the videos Jared Loughner had posted on YouTube.

In the video he called, "Genocide School," Loughner was walking the college campus in the dark, saying incoherent things like, "… *This is my genocide school, where I'm gonna be homeless… … If the student is unable to locate the external universe, and the student is unable to locate the internal universe, where is all my subjects?… all the teachers that you have are being paid illegally… This is genocide in America…*"

I found his other videos equally incoherent and disturbing. The next day while walking into the post office, I saw his mug shot on the front page of the newspaper inside a kiosk. His haunting eyes, wide open and buggy, were accentuated by his cleanly shaven head. His lips formed an inappropriate smile, as if he had something over us. Looking at the photo made me uncomfortable. I wanted to hate him.

Every day the news was of the violence and carnage of the Tucson shooting. I felt disdain toward the media for showing this over and over, making me sick. I could have changed the channel, yet I kept watching, hoping to hear some mention of the real cause of this tragedy.

As the days went on, it bothered me more and more that no one was talking about untreated severe mental illness being at the root of these senseless acts. While I questioned the reasons for the silence, I couldn't allow my anger and frustration to fester inside me. Instead, I would do something constructive with it.

35

On A Crusade

On my crusade I armed myself by reading all the books I could find on mental illness. The one that resonated with me the most was Nathaniel Lachenmeyer's memoir, *The Outsider*. Lachenmeyer writes about his father, Charles Lachenmeyer, a sociology professor, who became afflicted with schizophrenia. After Nathaniel learned of his father's death in Burlington, Vermont, he went there to try to find out what happened. What he learned was astonishing and profoundly sad.

As Professor Charles Lachenmeyer became ill, he developed delusional and paranoid thinking. He believed that people were conspiring against him, trying to steal his research on "thought control." The professor didn't trust anyone, because he thought people were trying to hospitalize him for a mental illness he did not believe he had. He avoided everyone, including an appointed legal guardian, from whom he would have been able to collect disability checks. This led to him becoming destitute and homeless.

Through the harsh winter of 1993, as he slept outside in subzero temperatures, the merchants of Church Street and the Burlington police felt sorry for him, but there was nothing they could do since he ran away from everyone. The police were unable to take action until Charles committed a crime, and they feared he would freeze to death before they could arrest him for something. Eventually, Charles was arrested for a small crime and the police took him to the state hospital, where he stayed for several months. It was less than two months after his discharge from the state hospital that Charles Lachenmeyer was found dead from an apparent heart attack.

It struck me how Charles Lachenmeyer had survived homelessness and near starvation through a freezing winter, only to succumb shortly after regaining his health. It made me wonder if the stress of paranoid schizophrenia, homelessness, and malnutrition due to the failure of our laws and our mental health system was the real cause of death for Professor Lachenmeyer.

I had been to Burlington and walked along brick-paved Church Street with my husband. In my mind I could see the straggly-haired Professor Lachenmeyer, in his filthy overcoat, rambling along that street, and I thought of the psychotic woman I had interpreted for at the hospital, who was refusing to take medication. My mind went to the doctor who said, if she refused treatment, after 72 hours, they had to let her go. I still wonder what happened to that woman as I never saw her again. Hers and the story of Charles Lachenmeyer have stayed with me. They speak the shameful truth about the forgotten ones in our society.

Along with books, I read articles online and one day fell upon the website of the Treatment Advocacy Center (TAC). It said Dr. E. Fuller Torrey, a research psychiatrist who specialized in schizophrenia and bipolar disorder founded the TAC in 1998. The site looked familiar. When I read that the focus of this organization was on "eliminating barriers to the timely and effective treatment of severe mental illness," I recalled visiting this site before. It had been two years since then. This time, I was drawn in like a magnet. At the bottom of the page it said, "You can make a difference." Below it was a box with the words, "Become an Advocate."

I clicked on the box.

May 16, 2011

Since they transferred Gabby Giffords to a rehabilitation center in Texas four months ago, I'd seen little publicity on her, but, today, she made news again. An article said Gabby had progressed in her ability to walk, read, and speak in short phrases, so her doctors allowed her to travel to the Kennedy Space Center in Florida to watch the launch of the Space Shuttle Endeavour, being that her astronaut husband was the commander of the crew. After the rocket's successful takeoff, she remarked, "Good stuff."

Gabby Giffords inspired me and because of her, I was even more determined to effect change in our mental health laws to prevent others from having to go through what she had.

I was no less interested in the legal case against her perpetrator, Jared Loughner, but I had neither the time nor mental energy to follow all the proceedings. Since Loughner had pleaded "not guilty" to all charges against him (January 24th, 2011), I predicted a long court battle ahead, though, ultimately, I knew he was going to end up in prison or a mental institution.

Periodically, however, I'd catch the headlines and read updates on him. On May 25th, 2011, a judge found Loughner incompetent to stand trial after two experts diagnosed him with paranoid schizophrenia. The judge sent him to the Medical Center for Federal Prisoners in Springfield, Missouri. Subsequently, he was court ordered to take antipsychotic medication for aggressive behavior.

On July 7, 2011, Loughner's defense lawyers were arguing in court against his forced medication, claiming there were no limits set on the type or quantity of psychotropic medication given to him. They said it violated his constitutional rights and intensified brain-altering changes he did not desire. The prosecuting attorneys maintained he had been ordered to take medication because he was a danger to himself and others.

A three-judge panel ruled on the argument on July 12th, saying that Loughner had the right to refuse antipsychotic medication and allowed him to stop.

Two weeks later, the prosecutors argued that Loughner was having screaming and crying fits and had harmed himself. They said he believed the radio was inserting thoughts into his head. Now he was back to being involuntarily medicated.

It saddened me how "the law," intended to allow for fairness, actually allowed for a lot of nonconstructive, tactical delays that didn't serve anyone's best interest.

* * *

I rarely looked at new books on display at the library, because they can only be checked out for a week, but one day a title jumped out at me as I walked by: *Gabby: A Story of Courage and Hope*. It was written by her husband, Mark Kelly. That evening I started reading what he wrote about her: "Gabby was a talker... she was so animated, using her hands as punctuation marks, and she'd speak with passion, clarity, and good humor..." He described her brain injury as "a kind of hurricane, blowing away some words and phrases, and leaving others almost within reach, but buried deep, under debris or in a different place." While she still struggles for words, he said, "... she's still contagiously animated and usually upbeat, using her one good hand for emphasis."

Five pages into the book I was already moved to tears. When I finished it, I felt as though I knew the congresswoman personally. It was as if Gabby belonged to all of us, not just to Arizona. She was "America's congresswoman." Before her injury Gabrielle Gifford's priorities were border security, economic security, national security, energy security, and ironically, fixing our broken mental health system: the same issues that were important to me.

* * *

A year and a half had passed since that awful day in Tucson. Like many others, my mind was on other things. We were delighting in the birth of our first grandchild, Emerson Grace. I was taking care of her two days a week and doing my community interpreting on the other days. Life was good.

But then it happened again. On Friday morning, July 20, 2012, we woke up to the horrible news. Another mass shooting and it was in Colorado. I heard the details as I was driving to work.

During the previous night's midnight screening of the film *The Dark Knight Rises*, a man wearing a ballistic helmet, gas mask, and body shields entered the emergency exit of a movie theater in Aurora, where he set off tear gas grenades and shot at people in the audience. Now 12 people were dead and more than 50 were wounded. My throat tightened into a lump as my heart sunk in my chest. This was the worst of the worse. How were we going to stop these awful and senseless bloodbaths from occurring?

Again, the shooter was a young man. His name was James Holmes. The devastation he'd caused to his victims, their families, his own family, and the community was reprehensible and irreparable.

I wanted to hate this shooter, too, but he was most likely another young person suffering from untreated mental illness. He was another victim of our broken laws. This never should have happened. We had learned nothing from the murderous rampage in Arizona and made no progress in addressing the dangers of untreated serious mental illness.

Once again, the debates rose up, even louder than before, between those who were against guns and those who stood up for our right to bear arms. Buyers were flocking to gun stores as they had after the shootings in Arizona and at Virginia Tech University, saying, "… if someone in that theater that night had had a gun, James Holmes could have been stopped…we have a right to defend ourselves…"

Whichever side of the debate we were on, everyone knew the healing of the Aurora community was going to take a long time. Meanwhile, there would be lawsuits filed, and a huge murder trial was gearing up. It was enough to distract us all from the underlying issue behind all of these tragedies: What to do about untreated serious mental illness?

* * *

Eighteen days after the Holmes massacre in the theater, we were still reading about Jared Loughner in the news. The psychologist who evaluated him, Dr. Christina Pietz, confirmed what I had believed all along. She told the judge that Loughner was "one of the worst" mentally ill patients she'd ever seen. Since receiving involuntary medication for schizophrenia, Loughner was no longer hearing voices. He had been declared competent to stand trial and had pleaded guilty to 19 charges in exchange for no death penalty. At his sentencing, he understood he was to spend the rest of his life in prison.

36

Blatantly Absent

Overlapping the political debates over guns was the election. After spending two billion dollars on their presidential campaigns, the election of 2012 was finally over. I wished we could have used the two billion instead to reopen all the state psychiatric hospitals and provide more group homes for homeless, mentally ill people. The problems in our country troubled me. We had too much corruption, too much debt, too many unemployed, and too many people who were homeless. While people everywhere were celebrating the results of the election, worry seeped deep into my bones. Tears streamed down my face as I pushed my empty shopping cart through the aisles at Costco. I never shopped at Costco and started wondering what I was doing there. I couldn't even see through the watery blur in my eyes and couldn't remember what I'd come in for. Pushing the cart back to the front of the store, I returned it to the rows and exited the store.

For weeks, a heavy cloud hung over me like a fog I couldn't see through. Despite my antidepressant medication I felt myself sinking into bleakness. In the mornings I woke crying into my pillow and could hardly eat, with my stomach in knots. I felt weak and achy and was losing weight. I knew I couldn't keep going like this. Somehow, I had to clear this dreadful gloom from my head and rid myself of the negative thoughts that were making me ill.

Forcing myself out of bed, I went to the closet and stood looking at the purple, black, and gray tops I wore for interpreting. The clothes were depressing. I couldn't wear those drab colors. I needed something bright. Something uplifting, and I needed it, NOW.

I went to the mall searching for something pink, but there was nothing pink in the entire mall. Pink was not a fall color, but I was sick and I *had* to have it. Before collapsing into an embarrassing heap of tears, I finally spotted something in neon pink on a clearance rack and bought it.

At home, I slipped on the pink polyester top. It was too big, but it didn't matter, the color was good. Still, it wasn't enough to pull me out of the dark. Maybe some pearls would help, the *real* pearls that belonged to my grandmother. I could see no reason they should sit in the jewelry box. This was the perfect day to wear them. I lifted the strand of ivory beads and hooked them around my neck, pleased by their reflection in the mirror, though the heaviness hanging over me was not fooled. The negative thoughts still nagged. To force them out of my head and shake them from my body, I needed to move.

I put on a Phil Vasser CD and opened the door to the deck. The sun and warm air invited me outside. With the music playing and holding Keetah with her paws on my shoulder and soft fur to my face, she was my dancing partner. Labored at first, our movement came easier with each swing and sway. My shy notes grew bolder as I sang and danced with my cat. If my husband were home to see me, he would think I was crazy, but I was doing this so I *didn't* go crazy. Keetah and I twirled under the blue sky, singing for the audience of lodgepole pines. My timid voice grew confident singing, "Lucky As Me."

Dancing with Keetah was lovely, though pulling out of a depression this low required more than pearls and dancing with the cat. It required reprogramming my brain to stop the negative thoughts that had been playing over and over in my head since the election. It took work and focus to take them down, one by one, as they rolled into my mind. I replaced each one with a positive thought. I reminded myself to be thankful for our 70-degree weather in the middle of winter, my husband, my beautiful family, and our country.

Soon I was singing in the shower again, like I used to when I was not depressed. I told my husband I appreciated him. I hugged and kissed four-and-a-half-month-old Emerson and told her I loved her. After a couple of weeks, I noticed my depression was gone. I was productive again. Whether it was my strategy of positive self-talk that brought my brain chemicals back in balance, or my depressive state simply wore itself out, I couldn't say, though I believed I had a powerful new tool to conquer depression whenever medicine was not enough.

December 18, 2012

I caught the news bite on my way to work: "Governor John Hickenlooper has proposed an $18.5 million plan to redesign and strengthen our state's mental health services and supports." I turned up the volume on the radio to hear more, but there was nothing, and listening again on my drive home, still nothing. I expected news like this to merit more than a three-second soundbite, or at least be mentioned later on local talk radio, but no one was discussing how this money was going to improve mental health services. Nevertheless, it was clear I had not been alone in my concern for the woeful inattention to mental health in our state.

In the six months since the Aurora Theater shooting, the media had continued with their focus on "gun violence," offering scant analysis of the underlying reasons for the violence. I knew that much of the time mental illness, drug or alcohol abuse, or poverty, was involved with gun violence, but these things were seldom mentioned in the news. Drug addiction, poverty, and especially, mental illness, carried a stigma. So, instead of drawing attention to these unpleasant truths, the media labeled the problem as "gun violence."

I understood the reluctance to talk about mental illness. I seldom talked about my depression and anxiety. The reality was, mental illness was affecting millions of Americans and families at an exorbitant emotional and financial cost, and the only way to shed light on these issues was to be public about them.

Governor Hickenlooper's announcement was welcome news, and I was curious how he planned to spend the $18.5 million. Was he recommending changing the psychiatric commitment laws in Colorado and adding more beds to our psychiatric hospitals? His proposal seemed like a topic that would have generated a good deal of attention, but weeks went by, and I heard not a single conversation about it. Still, I didn't forget it.

Another month passed and after no news, I finally looked up the specifics of the plan for myself, discovering that it was the Aurora Theater shooting that had instigated the action from the governor. He met with his advisors shortly after the shooting in July to discuss mental health in our state, and five months later presented the new design for services. A reporter who covered the governor's speech that day wrote, "… the governor acknowledged that the dollar amount we spend on mental health in our state has been declining for many years and, as a result, public safety has been at stake." Finally, we had the government's ear and even an admission of the state's negligence.

The governor's remedy, among other things, was to set up drop-in crisis stabilization centers and provide two new 15-bed facilities for psychiatric patients transitioning out of inpatient care. These were good measures, though what I saw as most important was his calling for Colorado's legislators to align our three statutes on mental health commitment into one law, which could lower the threshold for who may be considered dangerous. This could be a game changer in reducing violent crimes by persons with untreated serious mental illness.

Out of all the proposed measures in the governor's plan, one thing was blatantly absent. There was no mention of modifying the language in our privacy laws to allow families and caregivers access to the health information of a seriously mentally ill loved one. Without this, we could not assist them with treatment, and the consequences could be dire. This was the crucial missing piece in the entire plan. If our lawmakers addressed this one issue, all the other measures might not even be necessary!

December 20, 2012

Governor Hickenlooper's plan to improve Colorado's mental health services should have been the plan for our entire country, for we were once again in mourning, this time grieving for children killed at a school in Newtown, Connecticut. Six days earlier 20-year-old Adam Lanza had shot his way into Sandy Hook elementary and killed 20 children with a semi-automatic assault rifle before he shot and killed himself. Funerals for some of the children were today.

While gut-wrenching sadness filled our hearts, the media was wildly abuzz. The conversations I heard on TV and radio were all the same—about guns. Adam Lanza had used guns registered to his mother, whom he killed earlier that same morning. Now, distraught residents of Newtown were pressuring legislators to ban assault weapons. Political debates over gun control, the definition of "assault weapons," and the second amendment rights were spreading once again, like wildfires throughout the country.

While I wished for a magical end to these atrocities and the endless conversations about them while we did nothing to stop them, I read people's theories online as to why Adam Lanza did this. Some were saying Adam Lanza was obsessed with violent video games. Others said Adam did this because Mrs. Lanza was petitioning for conservatorship, which would have given her legal authority over her "gravely disabled," or mentally ill adult son. He was afraid his mother was trying to get him committed to a mental institution, so he took his anger out on her and the children at the school where she worked.

If this second theory was accurate, I wondered how long Mrs. Lanza had been dealing with her son's mental problems and going through this legal process? The wheels of government turned so slowly, and, in the meantime, a person with an untreated, serious, mental disorder could do a lot of harm.

Through all the public discussions, I heard no one addressing the families who were struggling to get a seriously mentally ill loved one the care they needed. The silence puzzled me. Perhaps people were unaware of the obstacles families face, though I found this hard to believe, given the prevalence of mental illness.

The tragedy at Sandy Hook Elementary was the result of our faulty mental health system and tedious legal system. Adam Lanza, his mother, the children he killed, their families, and their community, were all victims of his illness and our legislators' refusal to act in the best interest of everyone's safety.

From the news and commentary on the internet, I knew these issues were weighing heavily on the minds of thousands, if not millions of us. One courageous mother, named Liza Long spoke out, posting on her blog the day after the shooting at Sandy Hook. "I Am Adam Lanza's Mother," she wrote, telling how her son had pulled a knife and threatened to kill her and himself one day after she asked him to return his overdue library books. While his young siblings ran to the car, safely locking themselves inside, she managed to get the knife away from him while he screamed insults and threats. It ended when he was taken away in an ambulance to the ER. They discharged him with a prescription for an antipsychotic medication.

Liza Long ended her post saying, "It's time for a nationwide conversation about mental health…"

I agreed with Liza Long. But, two days after her posting, another blogger criticized her for speaking publicly about her son. Hanna Rosin, from NPR, snapped back at Long saying, "Don't compare your son to Adam Lanza." Rosin berated Long for identifying her son as "belligerent and mentally ill," and for saying, "he terrifies me." Rosin claims this kind of humiliation is likely to prevent the kid from getting a job in the future, adding that perhaps it's time to tack onto the children's rights movement, "a subcategory protecting them from libel, by their own parents."

Liza Long was sympathizing with Adam Lanza's mother, but it seemed Ms. Rosin didn't get that impression. Ms. Rosin summed up Ms. Long's attitude to having "some kind of mommy blogger Munchhausen syndrome…"

I couldn't understand someone dismissing mental illness so snidely. Perhaps Ms. Rosin was not aware of the number of youth who are so troubled by mental disorders they never make it to adulthood but die by suicide. I sighed and rolled my eyes. Truthfully, I felt like pulling my hair out. The problems with our laws and the breakdown of our mental health system merited more than mothers bad-mouthing other mothers.

37

Not A Weakness of Character

January 2013

With a jar of pureed prunes and six-month-old Emerson in my lap, I found the baby spoon missing its mark as she wiggled, turning her face this way and that. Purple purée smeared her face and hands. I took care of Emerson a couple of days each week. Babysitting a grandchild might be a chore to some, but to me, it was a celebration that I'd made it to grandmotherhood. Babysitting countered my tendency to overwork or fall into depression over social and political issues. I had forgotten, though, how quick little prune hands and fingers can be at six months. They were faster than Grandma's hands. I now had purple smudges all over my pants.

How could there be so much purple in just two baby spoonfuls? Maybe it was the canker sore on her tongue that didn't like the prunes. Or perhaps it had nothing to do with not liking prunes. Emerson's first tooth was just poking through the gum. Maybe it was the spoon in her mouth she was protesting. Her mom, Heather, wanted her to eat prunes because she was worried the baby was constipated from the oatmeal she fed her.

I gave up on the prunes and rinsed Emerson's tiny hands at the sink and wiped the purple spots from my pants. Why did people always think babies were constipated anyway?

* * *

Yesterday's prunes were a fading memory, as I chatted with one of the technicians at work. She sat with her legs crossed, twirling her foot. Twenty years younger than I, she out-ranked me with her master's degree in psychology and, I assumed, her knowledge of the field. As I was always interested in the professionals' perspectives on the issues I cared about, like the lack of housing and supervision for homeless psychiatric patients who are being released from prison or hospitals, I asked her how many group homes we had in Denver. "I know of four in Denver, there's probably 10," she replied.

I nodded, thinking she was probably right, as I knew of six. "How many do you think are in the whole state?"

"Not enough," she replied glibly.

"I'm just curious, like, how many people need housing compared to how many places are available?" I said, feeling the need to explain my question. "I'm trying to get a picture of the structure of our system and the extent of the problems. It seems so many people want to blame our society's problems on guns instead of looking at mental illness and our mental health system or the lack of services."

"I think it's our culture—too many video games with too much killing," she said.

"I know video games could play a part, but what about families who are powerless to get treatment for a mentally ill member?"

"That mother taught her son how to use guns and she had them in the house," she snapped.

Assuming she was speaking of Adam Lanza's mother, I was a bit shocked that she would be blaming the mother for what he did.

"I understand that, but what about Gabby Giffords? You know—the guy who shot her? Don't you think somebody knew that kid needed help?"

"That psychiatrist at CU, she's gonna get it. She knew—he told her he was gonna kill people. She's in trouble."

I noted she was now referring to a different shooting, the one that happened in our state. As part of my brain searched for the Aurora Theater shooter's name—Holmes, James Holmes—whom we knew by now had been a neuroscience doctoral student at the University of Colorado and had been seeing a university psychiatrist for treatment, another part tries to recall if that psychiatrist had warned anyone of her concerns about him before the shooting… or if our HIPAA laws had prevented her from doing so. I told myself to research this while thinking maybe this technician doesn't know who Gabby Giffords is. Or maybe her mind just jumps around a lot.

I kept trying to make my point.

"Yes, I'm aware of that dilemma with the psychiatrist, but I'm thinking about the families of these shooters. The Columbine shooters and others like them. Do you think their families were aware that their sons had problems? I think the law is against the *families*."

"It's no different with the police. They can't help…"

I tried to follow this women's train of thought, which didn't seem aligned with mine. She went on, blaming the NRA, the guys who she said were afraid of their guns being taken away. "They're afraid for their 'right to bear arms,'" she proclaimed, with a sarcastic stab in her voice.

I let the conversation go at that. Obviously, these were emotionally charged issues. Many people saw the problem as only about guns. Even if it were possible to sweep away all the guns in the world, or at least keep them from mentally unstable individuals, those people would still be mentally unstable. And those who are violent can still set fires to their parents' homes or stab and chop people up with knives and saws, or throw themselves in front of buses and trains. I was neither a lover nor a hater of guns. I loved our freedoms and the rights we are afforded and allowed to exercise through responsible behavior. And I was in favor of empowering families, so they could assist their mentally sick loved ones access treatment.

Why was I so passionate about this issue, when it didn't directly affect me or my family? Because it did affect me. For more than two years, I had tried to deal rationally with Cyndi, but found it impossible, because she was not rational. I didn't realize for a long time that her irrationality was because she had a mental disorder. In the meantime, her nonsensical phone calls and illogical requests twirled me into a frenzy. I began suffering from mental stress, which affected my family. I could have turned my back on Cyndi and walked away from her craziness. But I knew she needed help, and I had promised her mother before she died that I would stay in her family's life. There was no one else speaking up on Cyndi's behalf. She would not give permission for her brother to be involved with her care, and he was at a loss as to what to do.

Even if family members are estranged or blocked from being involved with a mentally ill loved one, they don't just walk away and forget them. The loved one is always in the back of their minds. Looking the other way on the forgotten ones in society does not make them go away.

* * *

For a long time I'd heard that mental illness was caused by a chemical imbalance in the brain. It sounded like some vague term people used to try to sound intelligent. But today the term is no longer vague. Using advanced imaging technology scientists can see the structure of the brain and watch the chemical and electrical activity. Researchers have seen evidence of neurotransmitter abnormalities in patients with bipolar disorder and major depression.

As a person afflicted with anxiety and depression, I find this research exciting. It's reassuring to learn that my condition is not due to a weakness of character, as some people believe. They say things like, "Get over it," or "Just snap out of it." Persons suffering from depression or anxiety would love to be able to snap out of it. Clinical depression can be incapacitating, yet it's sneaky how it develops.

A poor night's sleep is dismissed at first as a random event. The same with a bit of anxiety over a social or work event. And who doesn't have a stab of panic once in a while over a scary thought or some mishap? Vague stirrings of fear with some intermittent heart pounding are hardly noticed as they come and go, but then, they become surges of fear and panic that keep popping up at inconvenient times in the day, at work, in a meeting, or when talking with a friend. Your heart pounds and your voice gets scratchy and you're out of breath, wondering what you are so scared of all of a sudden, doing something that you've done hundreds of times before.

The nights of poor sleep start coming more often. Your pounding heart keeps you awake until four or five in the morning when you finally doze off. You have to rise an hour later to get ready for work. When night comes again, you go to bed exhausted from only two hours of sleep the night before, and the night before that. You close your eyes, but the pounding in your ears is so loud you cannot fall asleep. You cannot find the peace to quiet your body and mind. You lay waiting and waiting for sleep, which might come any second if you could just turn off your mind. But it won't turn off. You think about people, every person you have ever known. People you haven't thought about since you were in elementary school. Memories of all sorts, events long forgotten, roll through your mind as you toss and turn.

The more you watch the minutes on the clock ticking away into the wee hours of the morning, the more anxious you become, worried that if you don't sleep, you won't be able to perform at work, you will make mistakes, you will be found out, you will be criticized for your incompetence, you will be embarrassed, maybe even fired. Why can't you just relax? You turn on the light and try to read, but you are too tired to concentrate, too tired to hold the book.

You get up, walk the halls, search the cupboards for something that will help you sleep. You're disappointed, finding nothing that will help. You are not a drinker, but you see your hand reaching for a bottle of beer in the refrigerator. Back in bed at 4:00 a.m., you finally fall into the comfortable sleep your body craves, only to be awakened at 5:00 a.m. by the sounds of your husband stirring in the kitchen. You'd left his bed hours ago thinking a different bed might help. At 6:00 a.m. you get up, get ready for work, feeling like crap.

Your daily focus becomes consumed by actions intended to assure a good night's sleep. Sometimes it works. Still, you are struggling to accomplish everyday things that are supposed to be simple, wondering why every task seems so overwhelmingly difficult. And you are left wondering why is your heart always pounding? What is it that you are so frightened by?

You see a doctor, and he gives you a prescription for Valium to help you sleep, but two weeks later when you ask for a refill, he says no, it wasn't meant to be a long-term solution. Next, he gives you Ambien. Ah, finally, you get some sleep. But when the prescription runs out and you ask for a refill, the doctor says no. It wasn't meant to be a long-term solution. So, you are back to where you started, lying awake all night with your heart pounding, afraid to go to work in the morning.

Now, you are afraid of going out at all. You are afraid of talking to anyone because you are such a mess. You've lost so much weight, your wedding ring hangs upside down on your finger. You have difficulty making decisions and the tiniest task, trying to print labels with your computer, has you overwhelmed and sobbing. It's too hard. Life is too hard. You question whether you can go on. You think, if you had a gun, you might use it to put an end to it all. Still, you push onward, despite the horrible drag and havoc insomnia is wrecking on your life because blood tests show there is nothing wrong with you.

How long can a person go on like this before they crack? Before they begin to hallucinate from lack of sleep, experiencing their first psychotic break? When voices start telling them to strip off their clothes and run from the monsters who are chasing them, to when the police are eventually called and they are brought to the emergency psychiatric department or taken to jail? These are the questions I asked myself because this person was me. I was one of the lucky ones. I got help before I cracked up.

It was the physician's assistant whom I credit with saving my life. It had been two weeks since I'd been to the physician's office complaining, again, about my sleeping problem. When the doctor suggested I try a depression medication I broke down, believing he was not listening to me. "I'm not depressed," I cried. "I have anxiety!" I did not want the medicine he offered to prescribe for me. I left empty-handed in tears.

But I continued spiraling down to where I could no longer deny that I was sick. I called his office again. The doctor must have been expecting my return. Without hesitation the receptionist said, "Can you be here at 2:00?" Never have I gotten in to see a doctor so quickly. The entire staff must have been on alert for me.

I met with the physician's assistant. Unlike the two doctors I'd seen previously, this woman with a fresh-looking face and strawberry blond curls, rolled her stool close and looked into my eyes.

"What's going on?" she asked.

"I can't sleep. It's been going on for six months. I can't function, and I'm afraid to go to work."

She looked at me, attentive, as I told her I'd been to the library searching for answers for why I couldn't sleep, trying to find out if it was related to menopause as my husband had suggested. I'd found a book on anxiety and depression and sat on the floor in the stacks of the library reading what described me perfectly. I finally understood what was wrong with me. It wasn't menopausal symptoms I was suffering from. It was depression. I even brought the book with me to show her.

"I'm at the end of my rope," I said, letting go of any pride I had left. "I can't keep going like this."

"What do you mean you're at the 'end of your rope'? Are you thinking of hurting yourself?"

I flashed back to the few times I'd thought if I'd had a gun, I might have used it on myself. At the same time, I'd never imagined myself sitting in front of a doctor who would be asking me about intentions of killing myself. I was not that kind of person. But here I was. With her, I felt safe, relieved.

"No," I replied. "I would never do that."

"I can help you," she said. She left the room and when she came back, she had some samples of an antidepressant medication, a different one than the doctor had offered me the first time.

I recognized the name of the medication, the same one a fellow breast cancer survivor had mentioned once that she was taking. She was a doctor herself, so if this medication was all right for her, I trusted it to be all right for me.

"I hadn't wanted to take an antidepressant earlier. I thought my problem was just anxiety, not depression," I commented. "I always thought depression meant that you stayed in your pajamas all day. I always get dressed. I work. I published a book."

"Depression and anxiety usually go hand in hand," the physician's assistant said.

I believed her, and she turned out to be right about me. I responded well to the medication. In a matter of weeks, I had my life back and have been forever grateful to her.

Three of my cousins, however, were not as fortunate as I have been in dealing with their mental health issues. Their illnesses occurred more than 30 years ago before the newer antidepressant medicines came out. One cousin suffered a psychotic break while away at college and was subsequently diagnosed with schizophrenia. Two others killed themselves. All were in their early twenties. I never learned the reasons for my cousins' suicides, however, 90% of people who die by suicide have clinical depression or another underlying mental disorder. Substance abuse is often a factor.

These events in my family happened in the '70s when people didn't speak openly about mental illness or emotional problems, and the links to suicide weren't mentioned either. Today, even with our increased understanding of mental illness, there is still a lack of awareness of its symptoms, and suicide rates continue to increase every year. Suicide is not a topic that can be addressed or prevented without addressing mental illness. I never seriously contemplated taking my own life, yet having experienced the incapacitating effects of clinical depression, it's not hard for me to understand how some people get to that point.

38

A Voice in the Fight

Soon after my disjointed conversation with the mental health technician at work, my curiosity had me plowing through internet articles on James Holmes and the psychiatrist who had been treating him. Referring to the psychiatrist, the technician had said, "She knew... she's in trouble." But was she? Had the psychiatrist done something wrong? Was she the one responsible for what Holmes had done? I didn't think so, and I wanted to find out.

In my search I stumbled across a paper titled, "Reforming Colorado Mental Health Law," by professor Clayton Cramer, author of *My Brother Ron: A Personal and Social History of the Deinstitutionalization of the Mentally Ill.* There was no date on the paper, though I gathered from the dates of the resources cited that Cramer had written it sometime in August 2012, one month after the shooting. Discussing how the commitment law in Colorado failed our citizens that night in Aurora, Mr. Cramer wrote:

"... the killer had given clear signs of serious mental illness problems to acquaintances—serious enough for Mr. Holmes' psychiatrist at the medical school to alert police. While the details of exactly who said what to whom and when are likely to be locked up in understandable efforts to protect individuals and institutions from civil suits, what is clear is that Dr. Lynne Fenton's efforts would indicate that she perceived Holmes to be at least at level 4 of the Behavioral Evaluation and Threat Assessment (BETA) matrix: "High Risk."

So, Dr. Fenton *had* contacted the police about Holmes. But they didn't take him in for a 72-hour hold. The reason, Mr. Cramer surmised, was because Holmes did not fit the description of "gravely disabled," nor was there evidence (at the time) that Holmes was of "imminent" danger to self or others.

This was where the breakdown occurred. Because of the limitations of the law, neither Dr. Fenton nor the police could do anything about James Holmes. They could not stop him from going on to murder, maim, and terrorize the moviegoers in the theater that night. Unlike the technician at work, I did not believe Dr. Fenton was at fault.

To me, these murders were all the evidence anyone needed to know that it was time to change the language of "imminent danger" in our law. Cramer went even further, beyond the reason of just protecting the public's safety. Outlining all the financial costs to taxpayers, including those associated with a capital murder trial, he figured, "… a mentally ill prisoner will cost about $1.77 million over a thirty-year term of imprisonment."

His numbers did not surprise me. The losses created by severe untreated mental illness are great. In addition to the financial cost, the individuals who are suffering lose their chance to live normal lives. Their families are robbed of happiness, and society loses valuable contributing members.

January 16, 2013

While people everywhere were still talking about what happened in Newton, Connecticut, and the issues surrounding it, President Obama was considering 19 executive orders on gun control, including tighter background checks on gun buyers. The NRA was calling for increased school security. Activists were emailing circulars listing the school shootings since 1988 to 2011—from Australia to Finland, Japan to France, Canada to England and Belgium, and every state in the United States—showing the names of antidepressant medications the gunmen were taking (or were in withdrawal from) before committing their mass shootings. Gun owners, Pharma, and video games were getting the blame for causing young males to go berserk and run on shooting rampages.

Other people claimed fatherlessness was the reason for the gun violence. As I listened to Mike Gallagher on my drive home, he read from Lee Habeeb's column in the *National Review*. "Fatherlessness causes boys to join gangs and get guns and kill each other. Violence is a huge problem in Chicago," Gallagher read. "In Chicago, it's Newtown every month."

Everyone knew gang violence in certain neighborhoods of Chicago was out of control with young people shooting each other in fights over turf, or in retaliation over perceived transgressions, defending their egos and reputations. But Chicago was a separate issue from mass shootings. Or was it? I asked myself.

As I drove through Turkey Creek Canyon, I imagined what the stress must feel like living in such an environment filled with violence, where you were in constant fear just trying to survive on the streets in your own neighborhood. It had to affect a person mentally. Given that Chicago's Cook County jail is the largest in the United States, I wondered how many of its inmates had mental disorders.

I looked it up when I got home. I found the statistics in a *New York Times* article (February 18, 2012), with Chicago's Cook County Sheriff, Tom Dart, claiming that nearly 2,000 out of their 11,000 inmates suffered from mental illness. The number was almost three times the number of psychiatric patients at the state's Elgin Mental Health Center, which had 582 beds. The sheriff believed the number was going to increase because the city was planning to close six of its 12 mental health centers to save a couple million dollars. The fear was that patients might not be able to get to the remaining clinics, which were farther away, and without access to treatment many would likely end up in dealings with the police.

It struck me how lawmakers could think that downsizing the number of mental health centers to save money was a good thing when the consequences would most likely end up costing the city way more.

While the cause of violence and mass shootings was debatable, it was undebatable that untreated mental illness contributed to homelessness, crime, and violence; leading to overcrowded jails and prisons and overflowing hospital emergency rooms.

Even in my wholehearted belief that reforming our involuntary commitment statute would reduce most of these problems, I knew it would not be a simple fix. Since deinstitutionalization, we no longer had enough psychiatric beds to meet the need throughout the country. Getting legislators to rebuild our facilities would not be easy, but improving access to mental health care for all those in need was worth the fight.

    I vowed to be a voice in that fight.

39

Numerous Red Flags

How do you influence change of a system with a longheld belief? A system that believes it is civil and humane to allow someone severely mentally ill to refuse treatment because they don't believe they are ill. A society that incarcerates people whose real crime was they'd lost their minds. These questions and more swirled through my mind.

I didn't wish to do away with the laws protecting our civil rights and individual freedoms. I was a firm believer in personal freedom, yet there had to be an exception regarding persons with serious mental illnesses who are at high risk of harming themselves or others. For families and friends who were desperate to help an adult loved one, who had lost clarity of mind and become unsafe because of a mental illness, HIPAA was standing in their way. HIPAA prevented them from accessing medical information or making healthcare decisions for that person without their permission. But didn't evidence show that someone in the throes of psychosis was unlikely to give that permission?

There was no doubt that privacy laws were putting the public's safety at risk. When health professionals, school officials, and law enforcement felt prohibited from communicating amongst each other regarding a person who was posing a threat to the community, there were tragic consequences. We saw evidence of this with the Columbine High School shootings in 1999, and again at Virginia Tech in 2007. And it happened in Arizona at a "Congress on Your Corner" event, and a year and a half later in Colorado, in a movie theater.

I concluded that all of these shootings could have been prevented, as I turned the last page of Dr. Lucinda Roy's book, *No Right to Remain Silent*. Once I started reading her account of what led up to that horrific day when

Seung-Hui Cho opened fire inside classrooms at Virginia Tech, I couldn't put the book down.

Dr. Roy was an English professor at the university when Cho murdered 32 people on the campus and wounded more before he shot and killed himself. Prior to that day, however, there had been numerous red flags that he was dangerous. Many people at the university had noticed him as angry, withdrawn, and hostile. Faculty members had started reporting him to various offices. One professor was so disturbed by the violence in his writings in her class she got him removed from her class. Dr. Roy also became concerned about his strange behavior and alerted several departments about him, including the Virginia Tech police. And several female students reported that Cho had harassed them.

After he left a message for a roommate, containing a suicide threat, Cho was picked up by the police, who deemed him "an imminent danger to self or others." A magistrate ordered a psychological evaluation for him. He spent only one night in the psychiatric facility and was released with a court order for outpatient counseling. Records from the counseling center show only that he went through triage.

While many people noticed and reported Cho's inappropriate behavior, no single agency had all the pieces of information on him to see the real threat that he was. And soon after all of America saw what happened as a result.

I closed Dr. Roy's book and sat at my desk, unable to move. It was a beautiful day outside, perfect for a hike, and I didn't have any work scheduled. I could go walking in the woods outside my door and clear my head of this sadly disturbing story. Or I could call up one of my siblings whom I haven't talked to in a while. Instead, I felt compelled to stay inside and look up the report that Dr. Roy referred to in her book, written by a review panel appointed by the Governor of Virginia in the aftermath of the massacre at Virginia Tech.

I found photographs of each person who lost their life that day on the first page of the report. I didn't know any of these people, yet it seemed disrespectful to pass over their photos, each one showing an optimistic smile. It was so cruel what Cho had done to them—stealing their futures. A guilty knot turned in my stomach. Why hadn't we done something before this happened? Why had I not spoken to my lawmakers about fixing our broken laws and mental health system? Perhaps, if more of us had, those students and two professors would still be alive pursuing their dreams, while Cho would be getting the help he needed. The fact that each student had been awarded a posthumous degree, did nothing to quiet the guilty pang in my ears.

The stillness ached around me as I sifted through the rest of the report, putting together the story of Seung-Hui Cho. Wading through torrid details, and recounts of family members, teachers, administrators, students, roommates, and law enforcement who had encounters with Cho, I saw that hundreds of people were interviewed, yet few were friends of his.

Cho was a loner.

I felt as though I were watching a horror movie, shivering on the edge of my seat. Many opportunities had been missed when this mentally disturbed young man could have been apprehended had his mental health problem been taken more seriously. Seung-Hui Cho fell through the cracks. The result was 32 people lost their lives on a spring day in April 2007.

The how and the why of this tragedy, and others like it, boiled down to breakdowns in communication due to fear of violating our privacy laws. Given the complexity of them and the inconsistencies between the state laws and the federal laws, of when it's permitted or not permitted to disclose information, it was no wonder why so many of us were confused about them. Rather than worrying about to whom you can say what to, or of whom you may inquire about, and under what circumstances, it was apparent that most people, including professionals and persons of authority, decided it was easier and safer to just keep quiet.

I understood the fear. I was afraid when I went to the hospital where Cyndi was to speak to the social worker about her. I was nervous going behind Cyndi's back and afraid that I might be wrong. Maybe Cyndi was not delusional or mentally ill. What could happen to *me* then, for saying such things? Could I be in legal trouble? Even the social worker appeared afraid to talk to me. But what were the risks of not speaking up?

Back when I worried over Cyndi and the foolish decisions she was making, I racked my brain over who I could talk to about her. It was clear I could not talk to Cyndi herself. I understood that the law prohibited me from obtaining her health information without her permission, though without it, I didn't know if she had a mental health diagnosis, or if she was being treated for one. I didn't know if anyone was monitoring her, or if I was taking on worry for nothing. When I'd tried, in roundabout ways, to get the name of her case manager, Cyndi eluded my questions. Since I had gotten nowhere when I'd tried to confront her on her delusions, I didn't feel confident of having any success in trying to talk her into getting a mental health evaluation either. I had a strong hunch that broaching that subject would backfire. Hence, the only recourse was to persuade her brother to file a petition for a court-ordered mental health evaluation on her, or petition for it myself.

I was reluctant to petition the court on her behalf and never did get to the point of persuading Cyndi's brother to do it. I felt similar to how the police must feel. Our hands were tied. The law states there is nothing we can do about someone simply because they are mentally ill. We must wait until they commit a crime or get hurt.

I had an alternative solution. I waited for Cyndi to get sick. She frequently went into the hospital with one infection or another, and at the hospital, I knew there would be someone accessible for me to talk to.

I was correct in that. When Cyndi did get sick and went into the hospital, I tracked down a social worker to listen to my concern and she acted upon it. I know that much. But I don't know what happened afterward. That was another problem with our privacy law. When you reported a person of concern, you were not contacted later about what steps had been taken and what the result was. How were you to know if anyone investigated what you reported? Too often no one did.

The drama with Cyndi had passed and no longer affected my life. Still, nothing had changed with our laws regarding easier access to for the mentally ill. And for the privacy laws with all their bullet points, we had taken away common sense and replaced it with convoluted laws that scared us into silence, and it wasn't good.

* * *

No one could say whether mental health treatment would have prevented Cho, or Jared Loughner, Adam Lanza, or James Holmes, from committing murders, but I had seen the difference treatment made. I saw how people come into the hospital after a suicide attempt, in a manic or psychotic state, or wrapped in depression so deep they couldn't move. I was not privy to their personal stories, yet, after months of observing them, and seeing the difference between how they were upon admission, compared to how they were after attending groups and becoming stabilized on medication, was striking. Upon discharge, they were clean and dressed with combed hair. They were also conversant and calm, behaving the way we expect adults to behave.

From what I observed working on hospital psychiatric wards, and from my own personal experience, I could attest that treatment benefits most individuals with mental illness. It gives them another chance at life, where before they were only going downhill. No one chooses to be sick, and when they are, if treatment is available, they usually accept it. When someone who is seriously mentally ill refuses treatment, he is choosing to be sick. Proponents of our law believed that a person has a right to exercise his civil liberties. This may be civil, but, to me, allowing someone who is not rational to deteriorate from a brain disease when treatment options are available is inhumane. And so is waiting until someone becomes dangerous before he can receive treatment.

Along the way on my crusade, I read the story of a man named Edward Holder (not his real name). A retired army officer and psychologist, Holder had two mentally ill sons. One of them was working on his Ph.D. in physics when he became afflicted with schizophrenia. The other son had been a student in law school when his schizophrenia developed. At times during their illnesses, each son had been homeless, living on the streets of Washington, D.C. Over the years, Holder and his wife had tried 15 times to get their sons committed for treatment. The courts would not commit them, because they were not deemed imminently dangerous. Holder had rented apartments for one of his sons, but it never worked out, because his son would always wander back to the streets. In 1988, when researchers interviewed Edward Holder about the situation, he said, "The authorities say it is their choice and their right to live like stray animals. Why is rapid suicide illegal and gradual suicide a right?"

If Holder was bitter about our law then, I could imagine how he might feel today, 44 years later, knowing that nothing had changed. Today, the law still did not address whether an individual *needs* treatment. It is only if they are imminently dangerous that they will gain attention from the law. By then, even if the person has not yet harmed himself or others, it's likely their illness has progressed so far that it has become irreversible by treatment. If laws are supposed to be fair, where was the fairness in this one?

Even remorse from one crafter of the law, (Lanterman-Petris-Short Act), has not brought reform. Late in his life, Frank Lanterman admitted the law had been a failure when he said, "I wanted the LPS Act to help the mentally ill. I never meant for it to prevent those who need care from receiving it…"

Lanterman, Petris, and Short may have had noble intentions when they drafted the law, but they were shortsighted. They did not foresee the homelessness it created, nor did they imagine that our jails, prisons, and hospitals would be overflowing with mentally ill persons who have nowhere else to go.

40

Time to Act

March 6, 2013

Emerson played at my feet while I sent off an email. Eight months old and mobile, it was only a matter of seconds until this 13-pound cherub would have me out of my seat, redirecting her away from the bookshelves. She liked to pull the books down, and some were heavy. I didn't want them falling on her. She went after everything in sight of her bright blue eyes. The time it took to send one email was about all the time she allowed me. When I stood up, I realized she had untied my shoes.

I'd forgotten how these little ones keep you busy every waking moment with feeding, diaper changes, and walks in the stroller. She wanted constant stimulation. Already, her favorite diversion was watching nursery song videos on the computer. Our cats were a big draw too. Acting silly together brought giggles from her small belly. It was a joy I hadn't felt in years. Too much time inside psychiatric facilities had dimmed my perspective to where I'd almost forgotten how to laugh, but my giggling with her was real—not the forced kind you muster at the hospital or the residential care center, where you laugh because otherwise, you might cry.

Meanwhile, the news thickened with stories of the shootings in Tucson and in Aurora. Through Freedom of Information requests, the media had brought the Pima County Sheriff's department to release 2,700 pages on the investigation of the shooting in Tucson. In *The New York Times*, I read parts of the transcripts of law enforcement's interviews with Jared Loughner's parents. Their statements indicated they were having trouble communicating with their son and struggling with his odd behavior in the months leading up to the shooting.

Sadly, what they had to say sounded too familiar. His mother, Amy Loughner, described her son as a "loner" who talked to himself. She said, "Sometimes you'd hear him in his room, like, having conversations… and sometimes he would look like he was having a conversation with someone right there…" She says she told him he "needed to go see someone about it," but he never did. His father said he had become so concerned that he'd been disabling Jared's vehicle at night to prevent him from going out.

It was evident that Loughner's parents were very aware their son had serious problems, but they either felt powerless over him or simply didn't know how to go about getting help for his "odd behavior." Nor were they given much help or direction from Pima Community College when they suspended their son for disruptive behavior and "run-ins" with the campus police. I'm not inferring that the college should shoulder the blame for what Jared Loughner did, but this appears to be where the breakdown occurred. This was the final point where mental health intervention for Jared Loughner may have prevented the tragedy at the "Congress on Your Corner" event. However, because of our laws, his parents had no legal authority to force their adult son to get evaluated, nor did the college.

My guess is that most families dealing with the onset of mental illness feel powerless and don't know what to do either.

* * *

June 4, 2013

On the morning's drive to work I heard the announcement: "James Holmes' attorneys entered a plea of not guilty by reason of insanity today for their client." It left me wondering if the trial would be to decide if he was guilty of murder and wounding and terrorizing people in the Aurora theater, or to decide if he was insane. And if he were to be found sane, meaning "not insane" at the time of the murders, must there be another trial to prove he was guilty or does his earlier plea mean he has already admitted guilt and therefore he will go straight to prison instead of a mental hospital?

The legalities were confusing. Especially because, in my mind, it was so clear that Holmes was mentally disturbed. No one of sound mind does what he did. Fortunately, the dialog flooding the internet over this case included legal experts, who clarified what would happen next. If the jury decided Holmes was not guilty by reason of insanity, he would be committed to a mental institution. On the other hand, if they decided he was guilty, they would have to decide whether he would get the death penalty or spend the rest of his life in prison.

In the meantime, all the proceedings were delayed. Judge Carlos Samour Jr. and the defense attorneys were going back and forth over Holmes' constitutional rights regarding the Colorado insanity plea and whether he or his attorneys were required to sign a statement saying they understood the five-page list of consequences of the plea. The judge eventually determined they were not required to sign it.

I speculated whether that might leave the door open for a mistrial if the defense later claimed they hadn't understood all the consequences of the insanity plea. What then? Would James Holmes go free? I hadn't the mind, nor the patience, for all the legal intricacies involved. I just hoped justice would be served for the families who had suffered by what James Holmes had done.

September 16, 2013

Padding into the kitchen for my morning coffee, I was met with flashing lights and sirens. It was Breaking News on Fox. "It's pretty frightening here, chaotic, ambulances—an all-black armored vehicle escorted by police cars. You don't like to see this on a Monday morning. A man in full fatigues with a helmet running down the street. He's got a long gun… fire trucks, sirens, officers driving as fast as they can…"

Please, not again, I prayed, hoping it was not happening live while knowing that it was. Peter Ducey was reporting live at 9:08 ET from Washington D.C.

I switched the channel to CNN where Wolf Blitzer was reporting the same news: An active shooter in a building had witnesses shaking. "… he was on the fourth floor shooting down into the cafeteria, people are running everywhere, falling down… don't know if people are hurt or dead…" Blitzer said. Schools were on lockdown. Flights and baseball games were being delayed.

Soon they confirmed that thirteen people were dead at the Washington Navy Yard. The gunman was dead, too. His name: Aaron Alexis, a 34-year-old who had a history of mental illness. I couldn't handle listening to any more of this. I turned off the TV.

The next day, stories came out about the Navy Yard shooter, saying he had been suffering from serious mental issues. One claimed a Rhode Island police sergeant had reported Alexis just last month to the naval station police because Alexis had "told cops he was 'hearing voices' through his hotel room wall. He said that three people were following him and sending vibrations into his body…using 'some sort of microwave machine' to keep him awake."

Flashing back to the mental health technician at work who believed that violent video games and guns were responsible for these senseless shootings, whether she was right or I was for believing that untreated mental illness was to blame, the media was playing a big part in their proliferation. Those with fragile minds, vulnerable to interpreting this kind of media coverage as sensational or thrilling, are prone to want to act out their own mass shootings. I didn't need to see or hear of another shooting to know that it was time to act to prevent more of them.

* * *

When I heard that the Colorado legislature had approved the expansion of mental health services, I immediately went searching for the bill online, hoping to see a change to our involuntary commitment law or a modification of the language in our privacy laws. When I located it, I saw that the legislature approved had funds for most of the proposed measures as I expected. However, they had taken the part concerning the civil commitment statutes and made it into a separate bill. It was nine pages long. I read the entire bill looking for changes in the law. There were none. Rather, it called for a task force to examine our current statutes on involuntary commitment for mental health and alcohol and substance use disorders and to make recommendations on consolidating them into one law. They were also to "clarify and codify" the definitions of "danger to self or others" and "gravely disabled."

This was what my heart had been screaming for, since the day I heard it was against the law to keep a mentally ill person locked up for more than 72 hours against her will. It was unfathomable to me why a person who was actively psychotic would be allowed to walk freely out of a hospital. That was years ago, and I still believed that someone seriously mentally ill was worthy of treatment and deserving of supervision for their's and the public's safety.

For all the time I'd felt myself as part of a silent minority of Coloradans bothered by the lack of attention to mental health and its association with these mass shootings, I now knew we were not a minority. Finally, we had the governor's attention. I read that the task force was to submit a report of their recommendations by November 1, 2013. That was one week ago.

* * *

I soon learned that not everyone was celebrating the governor's expansion of mental health services. Professionals in the field didn't believe the $18.5 million was going to help much. The needs were too great. Referring to the number of mentally ill patients that were crowding his emergency department at Denver Health, the director, Chris Colwell, stated, "I don't think people understand the crisis that we're in. Most are homeless and have nowhere to go after they are released from the hospital except back to the streets." The president of the Colorado Coalition for the Homeless, John Parvensky, said his organization stopped carrying a waiting list for mental health services when it reached 2,000 people.

While my heart ached, wondering how all those people could survive living on the streets, my mother-in-law told me stories of the people who came into the homeless shelter where she volunteered. "Some are just down on their luck," she said. "They've lost their jobs or just got divorced and need some help, but many are mentally ill and can't work. They come to the facility to receive mail, take showers, or make phone calls." Over the years she'd seen the numbers increase, to where she was often handing out mail to more than 900 people in a day.

The burgeoning number of homeless people was disconcerting. I'd see them huddled in alleys, or sitting on sidewalks against buildings when I worked downtown. On warm days they congregated on the grass across the street from Urban Peak, the homeless shelter on Broadway, or they idled in Civic Center Park across the street from the capitol building.

On cold days, I'd see them inside McDonald's on the west side of town where I stopped in for lunch sometimes, detecting the smell of body odor and grease before I noticed the lone soul in a corner of the restaurant, dressed in layers of soiled clothing and a torn jacket, hunched over, sleeping, or talking to someone only he could see. One frigid morning I stood in line wearing my red faux-sheep-lined coat from L.L.Bean when a young woman approached me.

"How much was your coat?" she asked.

"I don't know," I replied. "It was a gift."

"Oh," she said and walked off.

In an upscale mall on the east side of town, such a question from a stranger would be rather unusual, but at McDonald's on the poor side of town, I was not at all shocked or off-put by her question. My husband bought me the coat, and I honestly didn't know how much it cost. If I had known, I'm not sure what I would have said. The other notable difference about this part of town, I'd never seen a manager run off a fragile-minded soul finding warmth and respite inside McDonald's. Maybe this was how the homeless survived.

Of course, the $18.5 million allocation for mental health services was not going to solve Denver's homeless problem, but it was a start.

May 2014

Sipping a second cup of coffee, I finished replying to my morning email and realized that it'd been months since I'd read or heard anything about reforming our mental health laws. A year had passed since the governor's task force began reviewing the civil commitment statutes. Their report would have been out months ago. Between work and taking care of the grandkids, I'd fallen behind and didn't even know what they'd recommended.

With some minutes to spare before leaving for work, I did a quick search for the report. It looked like the task force had done its job. They considered each aspect and perspective on involuntary commitment from the adverse effects it has on a person deprived of their liberty, to the safety and concern for the public. From their extensive analysis, they had come up with a new bill. I was eager to read it, but I had to get to work.

It was after dinner when I looked at the bill again. I was excited to see in HB 14-1386 they had removed the word *imminent* from the previous term "imminent danger." This meant an individual no longer had to be strictly "of immediate danger" to be placed on a 72-hour mental-health hold. Instead, a person could be held if they posed a substantial risk of physical harm to themselves or others by evidence of recent threats or suicide attempts, or recent homicidal or violent behavior toward another, or had placed others in reasonable fear because of their behavior. Added on was the language that the act was "necessary for the preservation of the public peace, health, and safety."

HB 14-1386 made so much sense. I was hopeful that it would pass.

As I dug in further, however, my hope quickly faded. I discovered that the bill had already passed through the House of Representatives nearly a month before. The Senate had received it the following day, but three days later, the Senate voted 5-0 to postpone it indefinitely. Not only was I disappointed by the Senate's action, I felt puzzled. What would be the reason for their inaction on such an important piece of legislation? I scrambled to find something more to tell me why they had shelved this bill but came up with nothing.

* * *

Sometime later I learned it was a gun-rights group that had raised opposition to HB-14-1386. I would not have been surprised had it been civil rights activists who halted the momentum, but I was surprised that it was gun owners. This bill was about mental health, not guns! Yet it seemed much of society could not separate the two issues. The Rocky Mountain Gun Owners were in a rage over the bill and the fact that it passed through the House. They posted a Legislative Alert on their Facebook page:

"… This bill dramatically expands the definition of 'gravely disabled,' even going as far as to include those who 'lack judgment' in the conduct of their 'social relations' to be potentially committed."

The gun owners were afraid that the proposed law was so vague that anyone could be called "dangerous to society" for the "slightest potential threat" and have their guns and their second amendment rights taken away. They were scared, not for those who were at risk of being innocent victims of an out-of-control, violent, mentally deranged person, but for themselves.

Wow. It seemed that emotions got in the way of common sense when it came to politics, but perhaps I was naïve, believing that law-abiding, mentally sound gun owners needn't fear this law.

41

Fighting for Families

June 1, 2014

Wrapped in my robe, I sat typing invoices for last week's assignments. I heard the email land in my morning inbox. The subject line asked for "Immediate Action," I didn't often allow incoming emails to interrupt me while I was busy, even one asking for immediate action, but this was from the Treatment Advocacy Center. So I stopped what I was doing and opened it. It was a press release introducing "The Helping Families in Mental Health Crisis Act." I read, "For the first time in 50 years, real solutions have been proposed to fix America's broken mental health system… this bill, HR 3717… is designed to reduce the barriers to treatment for those who need it most."

Below, in bold letters, it said, "H.R. 3717 will: EMPOWER parents and caregivers, ADDRESS the shortage of psychiatric beds, and STABILIZE patients beyond the emergency room…" I felt my heart beat faster when I read these next words: "H.R. 3717 clarifies HIPAA to permit a "caregiver" to receive protected health information when a mental health care provider reasonably believes disclosure to the caregiver is necessary…"

"Oh, my gosh, this is it!" I shouted into my quiet house. "These are the exact issues I've been concerned about for so long."

The press release urged me to contact my representative to tell him how important this legislation was. Whether it was excitement over this new development or a sense of urgency that compelled me, I wasn't sure, but the next thing I knew, I had put the invoices aside and was searching online for something that would tell me more. It led me to Congressman Tim Murphy's webpage, where I found the bill summary. After reading it, I believed it made perfect sense.

But, I didn't stop there.

I continued searching and saw that this bill had been introduced six months ago after a yearlong investigation into our nation's broken mental health system. Clicking on one link and then another, I landed upon a 10-page memorandum that outlined the results of Murphy's Subcommittee's investigation into our federal programs addressing severe mental illness. I had things planned for the day and needed to get dressed; yet, this information seemed important, so I printed a copy to read later. Before getting ready, I stole another minute to read an OP-ED that caught my eye. Representative Murphy had written it a month after they had introduced this bill.

He said, "I was profoundly shocked to learn just how archaic and ineffective federal mental-health policy is in our country…Easily two million patients with serious and persistent mental illness, many of whom lack insight into their schizophrenia or bipolar disorder, go without medical treatment. Why? Because the federal government has never approached serious mental illness as a healthcare issue. This laissez-faire approach to brain illness has directly resulted in growing rates of homelessness and incarceration for the mentally ill over the last 20 years. Sadly, it has also led to numerous tragedies, including 38,000 annual suicides."

Like many of us, this congressman had heard and seen enough. While I believed this Act was long overdue as a solution to many problems, my mind wandered to the next step, considering what would happen if this law passed. If treatment suddenly became obtainable to those previously unable to access it, where would all these patients go to receive it? Many states had closed their psychiatric institutions long ago. They'd torn them down or turned them into something else. Where would the money come from to rebuild psychiatric hospitals? Despite my questions, I felt convinced that passing this bill was the right thing to do. I committed to support Murphy's bill even before I read the memorandum sitting on my desk.

It was after dinner when I went back to the press release I'd read that morning. It included a form letter, making it easy to contact Congress. I sent the letter to Senators Michael Bennet and Mark Udall, urging them to support "The Helping Families in Mental Health Crisis Act," and I signed up to receive Representative Murphy's weekly e-News. I didn't know if I was in the majority, or the minority, in my support of Murphy's Act, though I felt elated to be joining the force that was fighting for families dealing with the challenges of mental illness.

* * *

It was several weeks before I had a chance to look at the memorandum by Murphy's Oversight and Investigations Subcommittee. When I picked it up, I tromped through notes and citations to get to all the details they'd gathered through forums and hearings into how federal dollars for mental health programs were being spent. I dove in, realizing that most people would find reading material such as this highly boring, while I was engrossed reading facts that validated things I'd believed to be true, and in stories that deepened my perspective into all that was wrong with our mental health system.

In a forum they hosted on March 5, 2013, on how effective care continues to elude many Americans suffering from serious mental illness, it was revealed that even for people who have insurance or the means to pay for care, it is 110 weeks, on average, from when the individual first experiences symptoms to when they enter into treatment. While this statistic didn't surprise me, I found it disturbing, considering that the earlier a person receives treatment following their first psychotic break, the higher their chance is for recovery.

Then it was the title of one of the hearings that drew me in further as I believed HIPPA was at the crux of our problems: "Does HIPAA Help or Hinder Patient Care and Public Safety?" When I saw there was a video available, I abandoned the written summary, opting to watch the entire hearing instead. After my husband went to bed, I clicked on the YouTube video and sat in the dark listening to a blond, mustached man named Edward F. Kelley, testify about his son:

> "My son has thought he has been a U.S. Marshal looking for his gun.

> He has thought the aliens were invading him. He thought he was a secret agent. He thinks to this day he served in two Iraq wars. He has been naked in the snow. He has lived homeless under a bridge..."
>
> "... Our son escaped from a mental health facility that was locked... They found him 4 days later.
>
> They dragged him into a state hospital in shackles...... when the time came for his hearing to see whether he should receive treatment, we were precluded from participating because of HIPAA..."
>
> "... Our son has been released and sent on buses, and we haven't found him for weeks, wondering if he is dead."

I felt my heart break for Mr. Kelley and his son. It's difficult enough for families who are trying to care for an adult loved one with a severe and persistent mental illness, but when the system and the laws are working against you, your family's life can easily turn into an unending nightmare.

Following Mr. Kelley's testimony, a middle-aged woman named Jan Thomas described how she lost her husband when a 24-year-old former student named Mark Becker walked into the high school where her husband was teaching and in front of 22 students, shot him at close range. Ms. Thomas said Becker had just been released from a hospital 24 hours earlier. The police had taken him there after he rammed his car into someone's garage and tried to break his way into their house with a baseball bat, ending with him leading the police on a high-speed chase.

Ms. Thomas believed her husband's murder could have been prevented, had law enforcement been notified of Becker's release as they had requested. But due to HIPAA, the hospital authorities believed they could not, and did not, share that information. The Thomas' had known Mark Becker for many years and knew his parents struggled with getting him mental health treatment.

I thought it horrifying what these two families had been through, and so sad that our laws had contributed to their pain. Others also testified about how they had tried to obtain information about a sick family member but were blocked by the system and how it compromised their loved one's health and safety. Having been through a similar experience with Cyndi, their stories struck a chord with me. I knew as I turned off the video that their stories, and mine, were not isolated examples. Thinking of the multitude of other families out there who were having the same grim struggle against our faulty system, I slipped into bed. Snuggled against my sleeping husband, I dozed off feeling more empowered on my crusade, to push for change.

While I still believed more than ever that we needed to revise our overly stringent HIPAA laws to prevent people with serious mental illness from falling through the cracks, I'd become painfully aware that alone would not fix all that was wrong with our mental health system. The flaws ran deeper than that. Just changing the language of the privacy act would be like remodeling the kitchen on a house that was already crumbling to the ground. This realization came to me over the next few weeks, though it became most clear after I watched the video of Murphy's second congressional hearing.

In his opening statement of the hearing titled, "Examining SAMHSA's Role in Delivering Services to the Severely Mentally Ill," Chairman Murphy revealed his concerns with the Substance Abuse and Mental Health Services Administration. Along with his claim that the words "schizophrenia" and "bipolar disorder" were not even mentioned in their 117-page strategic plan, Chairman Murphy disclosed that the $1B allocated to SAMHSA each year for the Center for Mental Health Services was not being used on evidenced-based approaches, but on unproven social theory. He pointed to the 2012 "Alternatives Conference" in Portland, Oregon, where in one of the workshops, titled, "Unleash the Beast," participants were encouraged to explore "animal-inspired movements, behaviors and expressions" and to "shed layers of formal conditioning to return to their primal nature."

He also questioned why SAMHSA was providing funding to organizations that were anti-psychiatry, who denied that mental illness exists and encouraged persons with mental illness to go off their prescribed medications. He claimed other groups were using taxpayer funds to lobby against Assisted

Outpatient Treatment (AOT) laws when AOT had been shown to reduce hospital readmissions and rearrests of persons with serious mental illness.

The chairman's words had certainly grasped my attention. But when his subcommittee began to question SAMHSA's administrator, Pamela Hyde, it was jaw-dropping what they uncovered. I learned some troubling things about how the government was spending our money in addressing mental health.

As he inquired about the grants they awarded to the organizations he mentioned, Murphy asked, "… is it the policy of SAMHSA that the majority of people reviewing grants have advanced degrees and academic credentials and license credentials in reviewing these grants?" the chairman asked.

Ms. Hyde, a woman with short, cropped hair, replied in a kind, yet assertive, voice, "It is our policy, Congressman, to have individuals with the experience and—"

"But that is a no? It sounds like—"

"I will repeat—"

"That is a no."

"… I don't have the information about what their degrees—"

"That would be a major issue because that is a major part of your work. Do you fund competitive or discretionary grants that are part of the mission of SAMHSA, or do you also fund grants that run diametrically opposed to the mission of SAMHSA?"

"I think all of our grants and all of our efforts, whether grant-based or not, are working toward our mission," Ms. Hyde answered.

Mr. Murphy pressed on, "What kind of evidence did SAMHSA use in approving funding for an advocacy group that encourages the mentally ill not to take their medication?"

"… I don't think we fund advocacy efforts explicitly to tell people not to take the medication," she replied.

"You just told me that you don't fund things that run counter to your mission, and we will hear today from people who have evidence that SAMHSA does fund organizations that encourage people not to take their psychiatric medication… One of those that you fund is the National Empowerment Center whose director espouses anti-science, anti-psychiatry views, and your agency also funds the alternatives, which is that in your workshop or symposium which regularly features workshops and speakers who advised people with serious mental illness to go off physician-prescribed medication…"

Ms. Hyde interrupted him. "Congressman," she said, "there are a number of ways to provide treatment and services, and we fund a number of conference efforts and others. We do not go inside each individual presentation to identify whether or not we agree with each individual—"

"But you continue to fund it—" Murphy said.

I'd never heard of the National Empowerment Center and found it appalling that their advocates would have such audacity to advise someone seriously ill to go off their prescribed medication. This felt more than disconcerting. It felt dangerous. And already I'd been wondering how acting like animals in an effort to return to our primal nature was going to help persons with serious mental illness.

As the hearing progressed, I remained fully engrossed while Representative Marsha Blackburn, from Tennessee, exposed another questionable decision by SAMHSA. In her slightly southern accent, Blackburn inquired about an expenditure of $22,500—for a painting.

"What value do the American people obtain from SAMHSA's funding of a piece of artwork such as this?" she asked.

"We have a responsibility to get the word out about behavioral health to all kinds of populations…. the tribal populations are very clear that the way to do that is to use people from their tribes and nations. This was a tribal—"

"$22,500 for a piece of art?"

"That number is not correct, but the tribal leader is actually a person in recovery…"

While I do have an appreciation for art and artists, with this disclosure I was again wondering about our government's spending priorities, given that too many of our big cities were teaming with seriously mentally ill people sleeping on their streets.

After two hours the time for questioning SAMHSA's administrator was up. I had stirred from my chair, expecting only a few final words chairman, but when he returned to the podium it was not to wrap up the hearing. Instead, he appealed for more of Ms. Hyde's time. He wanted her to hear testimonies from a panel, including Dr. Torrey from the Treatment Advocacy Center and a man named Joe.

"Joe is going through something that no parent or husband should ever have to experience…" Murphy said.

I looked over my shoulder at my computer screen and saw a mature-looking man in a suit and tie lean into the microphone and begin reading from a script: "On February 6, 2006, my son William Bruce, age 24, was involuntarily committed to Riverview Psychiatric Center in Augusta, Maine. On April 20, 2006, with help from federally funded patient rights advocates from the Disability Rights Center of Maine (DRCM), Will was discharged early from Riverview without the benefit of any medication…"

In a flash I was back in my seat listening to Joe Bruce go on to tell how William returned home to live with his parents after his release from the hospital. Two months later, Mr. Bruce returned home one day to find the bloody body of his beautiful wife, Amy. In "a state of deep psychosis," William had murdered his mother with a hatchet.

Earlier, William had been committed to Riverview by a criminal court, and during that time he'd been told that without his consent, "his parents had no right to participate in his treatment or have access to his medical records." Believing there was nothing wrong with him, William did not consent. Mr. Bruce said he and his wife had been excluded from William's treatment due to the privacy laws and the inability to get permission from their son. The doctor who ultimately released William from the hospital made the decision "without the benefit of all of Will's history or any input from Amy and me," Joe said.

When Mr. Bruce was finally able to obtain guardianship over his son and receive access to his son's medical records, he soon discovered what the patient advocates had done to get William the "least treatment and the earliest release." Mr. Bruce said he began to learn how the DRCM and the PAIMIs (Protection and Advocacy for Individuals with Mental Illness) "are so concerned that one person may be inappropriately treated involuntarily that they seek to prevent anyone from being medicated…" and "… unfortunately, William was only able to get treatment by killing his mother."

What I'd heard so far about SAMHSA disturbed me, but Mr. Bruce's account of what happened to his son and his wife was astonishing. The system had failed them in an egregious way. It was another tragedy that could have been preventable.

As the hearing continued I heard even more on how SAMHSA was neglecting the most seriously mentally ill from Dr. Sally Satel, a psychiatrist and scholar at the American Enterprise Institute. In her testimony, Dr. Satel referred to "The Recovery Model," to which SAMHSA espouses, to guide individuals in improving their health and wellness and to live a self-directed life. She underscored how inappropriate this model is for severely ill patients.

"We're talking about individuals who are too psychotic to participate in their own self-directed life, too paranoid, too terrorized by hallucinations, too lost in delusional thoughts. Fifty percent of them don't even recognize they have an illness, and if they don't have insight into the problem, there is no way they are going to be able to collaborate in creating a detailed life plan..."

Dr. Satel emphasized that SAMHSA's Center for Mental Health Services only hears from consumers who are able to direct themselves and that it never hears from the "sickest silent minority who languish in back bedrooms and jail cells and homeless shelters." Dr. Satel said they should get rid of the Recovery Model and instead, listen to "parents, clinicians, and the sickest but improved patients who have something constructive to offer..."

What I was learning about some of our government programs through these hearings were things I would never have known otherwise. It showed me that federal dollars are not always spent in the manner in which we, the taxpayers, believe. I wondered how many Americans beside me were listening...

42

No Agreement In Sight

Reading articles online always led me from one to another, and that's how I came to a posting by Pete Earley on December 12, 2013. I recognized his name from his book, *Crazy*, about his son's mental illness, which I had read some years ago. I saw that Earley had since become well known as an advocate for mental health reform. In this post Earley commented on Murphy's bill, sharing sentiments exactly aligned with mine on how important it was that we change our HIPAA and Family Educational Rights and Privacy Act (FERPA) laws. Mr. Earley said, "While it is important to safeguard privacy, HIPAA has been used to prevent parents from helping someone who they love… parents and other caregivers need to be part of the recovery team, not seen as adversaries or enemies, and in too many cases that is how they are treated."

Like me, Earley also believed that involuntary commitment laws needed "to focus on a 'need for treatment' standard rather than requiring dangerousness."

With prominent people like Pete Earley in favor of Murphy's bill and its healthy support of 110 cosponsors, I was startled by the backlash to the "Helping Families in Mental Health Crisis Act." Angry opponents wanted to preserve the status quo. One such person was John M. Grohol, Psy.D., the founder, and CEO, of Psych Central. Grohol was offended by the very name of the bill. "This is about helping families deal with a family member who has an apparent mental illness—not about helping the actual people with a mental illness," he said in an article he wrote for Psych Central. Grohol complained that the bill is a "less-than-subtle attempt to gut SAMHSA, coerce states to pass new forced-treatment laws (even if their citizens don't want them)…"

Grohol also objected to the part of the bill that required states to implement Assisted Outpatient Treatment (AOT) to receive Community Mental Health Service Block Grants. He was likening this to "telling docs that they can get reimbursed for treating cancer—but only in the way they dictate."

I didn't understand Grohol's comparison. Most doctors followed protocols of evidence-based medicine in treating cancer, though I'd noticed people often used cancer as an example when they wanted to argue against forced treatment for persons with severe mental illness.

"People who have cancer have the right to refuse treatment," they'd say.

Of course, we have the right to refuse treatment for any affliction; however, there is no comparison of cancer, or any other physical disease, to mental illness. We do not have masses of people suffering from cancer sleeping on city sidewalks. They are not being transported to hospital emergency rooms by the police, nor do we have an overabundance of persons with cancer committing crimes and overpopulating our prisons.

When Grohol stated that this bill "seeks to force a particular patient-hostile ideological agenda down everybody's throat," it was as though he believed this bill advocated that *anyone* with any kind of brain disorder must be forcefully medicated. Grohol said he was against the "Helping Families in Mental Health Crisis Act" because it didn't provide what was really needed: "—more money and resources to states with no strings attached."

What I really wished was that we didn't have to be debating this topic at all. The idea of forcing people to take medication was unpleasant under any circumstances, and I conceded, in America, forcing people to do *anything* did not align well with "land of the free." But there were some things that couldn't be ignored under the guise of liberty.

What came to my mind was what happened in a New York subway station back in January 1999. The story was all over the news. Eyewitnesses saw a young woman, leaning against a pole, reading a magazine while she waited for the train, and nearby, a man who was furiously pacing up and down the platform, mumbling to himself and making people nervous. As the speeding train approached, the man suddenly pushed the woman so violently that she flew from the platform onto the tracks. She was killed instantly by the train. For weeks afterward, New Yorkers felt uneasy and leery about using the subway.

The images are still vivid in my mind. The woman was Kendra Webdale. The man, Andrew Goldstein, was suffering from schizophrenia. Goldstein had a history of violence and over the previous 10 years he had been in and out of psychiatric institutions, and on and off psychotropic medications. At the time of the incident he was off his medication.

As a result of this horrific event, New York passed Kendra's Law, which allows a court to order an individual with a history of arrests, incarcerations, or hospitalizations due to serious mental illness to undergo community based treatment. This was precisely what Murphy's bill proposed to do nationally.

Since Kendra's Law was passed, there are still those who oppose it, maintaining that it violates individuals' civil rights. This argument might never go away, but what can't be argued away are the statistics and research showing that Kendra's Law has had positive results in reducing homelessness, suicide attempts, substance abuse, and hospitalizations. In light of this, it's hard to argue that AOT is not a good thing.

* * *

While the Colorado bill on civil commitment remained off the table, the debates continued through the spring. It seemed there was no agreement in sight. As I followed the arguments online, I saw that it was not only legislators and politicians who were differing. Consumers of mental health treatment were not of one mind on the subject, either. In *The Denver Post*, Moe Keller, vice president of public policy and strategic health initiatives for Mental Health America of Colorado, said, "… Some people will tell you (commitment) is the best thing that's ever happened to them. They didn't know how much they needed help. Others will tell you it's the most traumatic thing that ever happened to them. It exacerbated their illness, and they did not seek treatment for years because of it."

Of course, I believed there would always be some who felt harmed by their experience, but the larger purpose for changing the law was to protect the health and safety of individuals and the public. Given the amount of attention the media gave to the recent mass shootings and the increased awareness it brought to the issue of untreated severe mental illness, I had thought this bill would surely pass. The fact that it didn't made me less optimistic about its chances in the future. It seems the voices of those worried about abuses of individual civil rights are no less quiet today than they were in 1967.

Meanwhile, summer had arrived and I was distracted by my own problems. Unexpectedly, our household of two had become a party of three. We had a house guest, a woman I rescued from eviction. The three days in which I told my husband she would be with us had turned into three months. Shauna's search for a new place to live had turned into *my* search, and suffice it to say, it was not going well.

I was up to my elbows in papers and notes from hours of phone calls, learning about the housing market, something I'd known nothing about until Shauna moved in. I was discovering that not only did we have a lack of housing options for homeless people with serious mental illness, the situation was equally dismal for low-income seniors and those with disabilities, which included Shauna. Inquiring about availability, I heard the same answer from each facility: "We have no vacancies. Our waiting list is up to two years long."

Rents for apartments and single-family homes were skyrocketing in Colorado, and homes for sale were out of Shauna's price range. The newly passed law allowing legalized marijuana in our state hadn't helped the housing shortage. Thousands of people were moving into our state to take advantage of the opportunity to buy and sell cannabis. I wondered where all these new people were going to live. Too many were already sleeping on the streets.

The outlook was bleak, and I was getting nervous. While Shauna, slept like a princess with fresh summer air flowing into her guest room at night and tended to her potted plants by day, I worried. Where was she going to live, and when was she moving out?

* * *

My anxiety increased with each day that Shauna was still with us. While she consumed my time and attention at home, she seemed content and settled into a routine when I was out. She sunned herself in the morning, read in the afternoon, and watered her plants in the evening. It didn't appear to be as critical to her that she find an alternate place to live as it was to me.

Her "homelessness" was not bad compared to those with fragile minds, who because of our faulty laws, were roaming the streets without mental health treatment, or languishing in prisons because there was nowhere else for them to go. Shauna did not fall into the category of "homeless and gravely disabled," according to some definitions. She took care of herself. In fact, she strove daily toward peace of mind. She devoured psychology books, trying to learn how to release all thoughts, cleanse her mind from negativity, and release bad energy from her body. While I succumbed to the frazzled struggle of maintaining work and family, house, cars, and pets, she sat yogi style in my living room, striving to achieve nirvana without drugs. She practiced daily to become a master. I might have learned something from her about how to lessen anxiety, but I didn't want to. I just wanted her out. My sanity was at stake.

* * *

If changing our mental health laws reduced the revolving door of homelessness, arrest, hospitalization, or prison for those with serious mental illness, I believed it would reduce the anguish and turmoil for their family members as well. Assisted outpatient treatment had been shown to reduce all of these things as well as reduce costs for taxpayers. Who could argue that these were not good things?

So, too, I believed that modifying HIPAA and the FERPA laws would have beneficial effects on our educational system. Had it not been for the strict privacy laws, what happened at Virginia Tech University, and at the Safeway parking lot in Tucson, Arizona, most likely would not have occurred. In both situations, if campus personnel at Virginia Tech and Pima Community College hadn't been afraid of violating privacy laws, most likely they would have communicated better amongst each other and the police regarding students who were exhibiting strange and threatening behavior. There could have been earlier intervention for both Seung-Hui Cho and Jared Loughner. In short, their unspeakable crimes could have been prevented.

I'd started my career interpreting in the educational system. In K–12 there was teamwork among the professionals working with challenging students, and it worked. It made life easier for everyone involved and the consistency helped the student. In higher education it was different, due to the adult age of students and our privacy laws. I'd experienced the negative effects. When interpreters were not given information regarding a student who exemplified emotional and psychological problems, we were left to make our own assessments and decisions on how to handle them. I worked with one of these students, a deaf woman named KT.

KT had a challenging personality. She had no difficulty with the coursework, rather it was other students in the classroom she had problems with. There was one student in particular that she didn't like, and everything that student did annoyed KT—like when the woman wore sunglasses in class one day, or when she arrived late, or when she asked the instructor a question. Little things most people barely noticed upset KT. She would position my chair where she wanted me to sit, and then tell me to "stay."

Once, I let KT know that I was going out of town for a week and she would be having a substitute interpreter. She began shaking, visibly upset. KT often complained about other interpreters she had, one for how many bathroom breaks she took and another for how she wore her hair. KT would ruminate and complain about them for days and weeks, expecting me to do something about them. Of course, there was nothing I could do about these things. I would say something positive to try to get her to stop obsessing about them, or change the subject entirely, hoping she'd forget about them while I went back to interpreting, but it never worked. KT couldn't let go of things. My job turned into a psychological mind game I had to play with her every day. I dreaded going to that class.

KT built annoyance upon annoyance in her mind, to where she could no longer concentrate on the class at all. All the interpreters who worked with her were nervous wrecks. Nobody wanted to be the target of her annoyance, but sooner or later, each of us was. When KT couldn't contain her irritation anymore at who she was currently mad at, she would confront that person. The result was usually detrimental, but she got what she wanted, the removal of her annoyance, including her interpreters, one by one.

I witnessed two semesters of this until, finally, I became the annoying object. I found this out when KT insisted on walking with me to my car one day after class. I was in a hurry because I had to get to another assignment. Quickening her steps to keep up with me, she demanded to know why I had interpreted for another deaf student, named J, another individual with whom she didn't get along. I knew KT had seen me interpreting for J in the library earlier that afternoon. "She had a question for the librarian," I explained.

KT became enraged. "You can't interpret for her. You have to stand up to her," she scolded, as if she had exclusive rights to my interpreting services.

I was not going to take this unreasonable attack out on the street. "We don't ignore Deaf people," I fired back, signing and speaking at the same time.

"Are you yelling?" KT signed, more as an accusation than a question.

"Yes, I am," I signed.

"Why?"

I let out an exasperated sigh.

KT had told me in the past that I was her favorite interpreter, but I knew that was over. I was convinced this woman was mentally ill.

As she had gotten rid of each of her other interpreters, she eventually got rid of me, too. It seemed that the school administration, afraid of lawsuits, gave in to her every whim. Later, still questioning whether I had been in the wrong somehow with this student, wondering if she suffered from some kind of emotional disorder, I asked my daughter, a licensed clinical social worker, and therapist, "What is borderline personality disorder like?"

"People with borderline personality disorder are the clients that get under your skin the most," she explained. "There's nothing you can say or do to get them to change their mind or quit obsessing about the thing they've made into a giant problem for no reason. They believe they have a reason to be upset, although we may be unable to understand."

My daughter validated my suspicion about KT. Had I known, I probably would not have allowed myself to get sucked into her manipulative requests, or get so rattled by her irrational behavior. I doubted that the other interpreters would have either. I eventually left that job, though I never stopped thinking that the school administration should have communicated to the interpreters what was going on with this student if they knew. I believe they did, but due to FERPA, this was a situation that ended badly for all involved.

43

Too Few of Us

Controversy had been brewing for months over Congressman Murphy's bill. Opponents had their heels dug in the argument that involuntary treatment was coercive and that changing the law to make it easier to commit persons against their will would cause people with mental illness to avoid seeking care completely.

Their argument was weak. With or without an involuntary commitment law, the seriously mentally ill avoided care most often because their illness prevented them from understanding they even had an illness. The whole point of having an involuntary treatment law was to help those who were unable to help themselves. But rather than concede the point, the opposers in Congress had come up with their own bill titled, "Strengthening Mental Health in Our Communities Act of 2014," or "Barber's Bill," named after one of its authors, Representative Ron Barber of Arizona.

Ron Barber had been a congressional aide to Congresswoman Gabby Giffords and was among those wounded at the "Congress on Your Corner" event in Tucson. For this reason alone, I would have guessed that "Barber's Bill," like Murphy's, was proposing a solution to homelessness, incarceration, and violence for individuals with untreated serious mental illness, but it didn't.

Instead, Barber's bill proposed to increase funding for veterans and active-duty service members. It did not mention involuntary treatment for persons with dangerous and severe mental illness, nor did it address any revision of the privacy laws to allow parents to be informed and involved in the care of an adult child with mental illness. And, unlike Murphy's bill, Barber's bill did not include any reform of the Substance Abuse and Mental Health Services Administration (SAMSHA).

While I was not opposed to increasing funding for our veterans and service members, it seemed like Barber's Bill was an attempt to take our eyes off the ball, away from looking at the real problems and the issues uncovered by Murphy's investigation. I was not swayed. I'd since become aware of some of the organizations that SAMSHA was funding. Groups like: MindFreedom, which held the premise that, "There is not conclusive evidence or consensus that mental illness exists," and The Icarus Project, based on the belief that, "psychiatric conditions are mad gifts needing cultivation and care, rather than diseases or disorders." Another was the National Coalition for Mental Health Recovery, which upheld the idea that "psychiatric labeling is a pseudoscientific practice of limited value in helping people recover."

A fourth group that was violating the law while receiving SAMSHA support was PAIMI, (Protection and Advocacy for Individuals with Mental Illness) that I mentioned earlier. While the purpose of PAIMI was to protect patients from abuse and neglect in treatment facilities, Murphy's subcommittee had uncovered instances where patient advocates had used the government's funds for litigating and lobbying. PAIMI agents were also found to be influencing seriously mentally ill patients to refuse treatment, which they had done with William Bruce, who then went on to murder his mother with a hatchet.

As I was learning of the background stories and all that had inspired the work that went into the creation of the "Helping Families in Mental Health Crisis Act," I came across the exhibit Joe Bruce submitted to the court on the day he testified before Congress, more than a year and a half ago. It was the written transcript of his call to 911 in which he told the dispatcher, "My son has killed my wife." I read the five-page transcript with tears in my eyes, seeing the picture of what Joe Bruce and too many other families with a mentally ill loved one have had to endure because of our messed-up laws.

We should never have to hear another one of these horror stories, and this is why I supported Murphy's bill. Having Barber's bill and Murphy's bill competing in Congress, causing divisive debates and further delays in reforming our mental health system seemed like an extraneous waste of time and energy.

I hoped that our elected officials would soon figure out that their delays were only increasing the chances of more tragic occurrences.

December 15, 2014

Keetah settled into my lap, where I snuggled on the couch with a book and a cup of coffee. The sun had not yet risen and the colored lights from the Christmas tree blinked silently in the dark. The house felt so peaceful now that Shauna had moved on. The permeating tension that had built up between us dissipated the day she left. Home is a place to rest, recuperate, and refresh. It's the place where we receive comfort and love. I didn't feel that way about my home when Shauna was here.

In the quiet of the room, I opened my book, *When Madness Comes Home*. On the inside cover it said, "Over 100 million Americans have a close relative—a parent, a sibling, or a child—who suffers from some form of identifiable psychiatric disorder." 100 million is a lot of people. I imagined those families, worn out from trying to help their mentally ill loved ones when over and over their efforts are thwarted by a system that's broken and unsupportive. I imagined them suffering from guilt, shame, and alienation, often in silence, which made it easy for legislators to ignore that we had a problem with untreated serious mental illness. Those who are ill cannot advocate for themselves, and too few of us were speaking loudly enough for Congress to hear.

There was no nationally known "Race for the Cure" for mental illness like there was for breast cancer. Rallies to raise awareness of the prevalence and seriousness of mental illness were small, and galas and fundraisers to address the need for housing, treatment, and research were too few. It felt like our individual efforts in trying to help someone mentally ill were fruitless. When we did try, we worried whether we were doing the right thing.

My mind drifted back to the time when I reported my concerns about Cyndi to the social worker. Cyndi became angry with me after she found out. "Friends don't do that to friends," she accused. I believe I did the right thing, but I never found out what happened as a result. I never learned if what I did actually helped her.

December 16, 2014

The sun glare on the windshield blocked my view, slowing me around the curve. Every morning I drove these six winding miles from home to the highway. By the time I reached the highway and merged into the traffic, the car had warmed, and the frost had disappeared from the windshield. I reached for my apple in the bag beside me. With the first juicy crunch I heard this news on the radio, "Colorado is receiving a $65 million federal grant for mental health. The money will be spread out over the next four years to help bring mental health treatment into primary-care doctors' offices."

It sounded like a good thing, though I'd been receiving my medication for depression and anxiety from my primary care doctor for nine years. So, what was really up with this grant? Did our state need $65 million just for people to get their psych meds from their primary care doctor?

After dinner when the dishes were clean, I searched for the news online. I found an article that said the grant was for "testing innovative payment and service delivery models that have the potential to lower costs for Medicare, Medicaid, and the Children's Health Insurance Program (CHIP), while maintaining or improving quality of care for program beneficiaries."

Whether improvements to the government's technology for how they handle payments would translate into helping mentally sick people, I had no way of judging.

January 6, 2015

At the start of the new year I watched Vice President Joe Biden on TV swearing in our newly elected Senators, including Cory Gardner from Colorado. The ceremony triggered a news year's resolution for me, to write to our new senator. Immediately, I set down my coffee mug and dashed to the computer.

In my letter I asked Senator Gardner to sign on to the "Helping Families in Mental Health Crisis Act," because we had a mental health crisis going on in our country and we needed to improve access to care for persons struggling with mental illness. I told him that in my professional experience I had seen the benefits for persons struggling with mental illness when they had access to effective mental health treatment, and I had seen, like most of America, the awful consequences for these individuals and their families when they did not.

But two paragraphs into the letter, I changed my mind, unhappy with what I'd written. I didn't want my letter to be something easy to dismiss. I needed a powerful, personal story to persuade him. After thinking for a while I recalled my sister telling me some time ago about her friend, Susan, whose son had schizophrenia. One day, in a psychotic state, he had started a fire in their basement. Susan became so afraid of her son, she had to kick him out of the house and change the locks on the doors to keep him away.

I could ask Susan if she would be interested in writing this letter with me. But how would I approach her about such a personal and sensitive topic? I hardly knew her. Without her help, I couldn't share her story. All I knew was that her son ended up in jail in another state and was later found dead in his cell, by hanging.

I was hesitant to reach out to Susan and debated for several weeks before deciding this issue was important enough to put my qualms aside. In a letter explaining my involvement in mental health, my work in hospitals and psychiatric facilities, and even jails and prisons, I wrote to her, saying:

> *I'm advocating for change in our laws, because our society is not dealing with the problem of homelessness, violence, and incarceration of persons with severe and untreated mental illness, but is using our jails and prisons as dumping grounds for those afflicted.*
>
> *The reason for my interest in the subject of mental illness is because it affects many of us... manifesting sometimes in ways that are not always as blatant as delusional psychosis, but in subtle ways, too, like in anxiety or depression, and alcoholism and drug addiction; illnesses that run in my family, as does schizophrenia."*

I asked Susan,

> *As a mother who lost a son who struggled with mental illness, would you be open to collaborating with me in writing a letter to our*

> *congressmen about our concern for families who are struggling to help a mentally ill loved one?*

I told her I planned to send the letter as soon as possible to Senator Cory Gardner and to Representative Jared Polis, who had not yet signed on, to ask them to support the "Helping Families in Mental Health Crisis Act." At the end I said,

> *I respect your privacy and understand if you choose not to collaborate with me.*

I hoped Susan would join my crusade. Sometimes after experiencing a traumatic event, it's cathartic to put your energies into something positive. It's better than harboring a lot of sadness. Susan replied a few days later, agreeing to meet with me. "If my son had been taken to a medical facility and treated as a patient with an illness instead of being arrested and put in jail, it's possible he would have gotten the treatment he needed and be alive today," she said. But she didn't want to meet over lunch. "Talking about my son's death is too stomach-turning, too intense to try to eat," she said.

A couple of days later Susan reached out. She'd changed her mind about meeting with me.

"It is simply too gut-wrenching for me. I can't relive the experience."

She didn't want anything more to do with mental illness.

"I understand," I said and wished her well. I was disappointed, but also partly relieved. It might have been too uncomfortable for both of us. I wrote the letter to the congressmen, wishing there was more I could do to advocate for mental health reform.

44

Not Giving Up

Winter was over. The severe storms that brought more snow to Conifer in May, with hail and tornados over eastern Colorado, had settled down. Summer, my favorite season, was finally here. In Conifer we have no spring. Just summer, fall, and winter. Winter began around mid-December and ended around Mother's Day when the snow would finally turn to rain. Then, right on schedule, in the second week of June, summer would abruptly appear. It was not my favorite season because we took exciting vacations. We didn't. It was just that it was easier, and more pleasant, living in the mountains when it was warm. And breakfast on our deck under a blue sky in a forest of trees, listening to the sounds of chirping birds, chattering squirrels, and the rush of our stream, felt almost the same as a vacation. Otherwise, our schedule in the summer was not much different from the other seasons of the year.

While I plugged along writing, advocating, and waiting for the rusty cogs of government to turn out new, more effective laws, there had been another shooting. On June 18, 2015, in Charleston, South Carolina, a 22-year-old man shot up a group of people meeting in a church. Nine people were killed.

Before he shot the people, the 22-year-old asked to sit next to the pastor, and then at some point he said, "I have to do it. You rape our women and you're taking over our country. And you have to go."

Dylann Roof, whom people described as "an introvert with few friends," had been arrested four months earlier in a shopping center after asking random employees strange questions like, "What time do you get off work?"

I didn't think it was a leap to suspect that Roof had a mental illness. Yet on the news, they were calling this "a hate/racial, crime." Truly, shooting people is hateful and horrific, but what is underneath all that hate? Could it be deluded, irrational thinking associated with mental illness?

After so much publicity on tragic murders perpetrated by young men in their twenties, why were we doing no better at recognizing symptoms of mental illness and helping these young people, (males, mostly), get intervention before their illnesses progressed to the point that they committed murders? I understood that no one had the ability to predict someone else's behavior when it came to murder, but dangerousness did not go unnoticed. In many of these cases, people had sensed danger in these young men and made reports of them previous to their shootings.

In the aftermath of these awful shootings, our lives go on. We go to work, we celebrate holidays, we celebrate a new grandson's birth, and we look forward to our son's upcoming wedding. We carry on as though these shootings don't affect us. But they do. They leave a sick feeling in our gut.

June 26, 2015

I watched President Obama and the First Lady on TV, dressed in black, wearing pain on their faces. Surrounded by secret servicemen in suits, they walked toward a church. They were going to the service for Reverend Clementa Pinckney, the pastor killed by Dylann Roof in the South Carolina church. The media were still reporting this shooting as a white supremacist hate crime. Perhaps it was. Still, I suspected we'd find out this shooter also had a mental disorder that affected his judgment.

As Dylann Roof's legal case was beginning in South Carolina, we were watching the James Holmes case in Colorado, the "Aurora Theater Shooting Trial," as it is known now. There were too many of these shootings happening, too many murder trials. This could not be our new normal. Discouraged, I turned off the TV and carried my empty coffee mug to the sink.

Whether it was out of frustration, anger, or disgust, I started a new letter to Senator Gardner, explaining with a sense of urgency why we needed to reform our mental health laws.

> *... We cannot wait until one of our own sons or daughters, or grandchildren becomes another victim of someone suffering from untreated mental illness, an individual who was allowed to roam our streets even after his desperate family members had begged medical providers and law enforcement to hospitalize him.*
>
> *Medicines can help people who are struggling with symptoms of mental illness to live more normal lives, lessening the chance that some might otherwise become dangerous to themselves or others. Right now, our laws are preventing many persons with mental illness from getting the treatment they need...*

Before I finished the letter imploring the Senator to vote for the "Helping Families in Mental Health Crisis Act," I was interrupted. An incoming email from Congressman Tim Murphy announced:

> *"A major win for millions of American families in mental health crisis..."*
>
> *The House Appropriations Committee has approved funding for a spending bill for 2016, containing part of the "Helping Families in Mental Health Crisis Act." A grant for $15 million will fund the Assisted Outpatient Treatment Program.*

This was great news! So long ago, President Kennedy signed the Community Mental Health Act of 1963, intending for community programs like this one to be established. I wondered if Kennedy were alive today if he would be happy to hear that assisted outpatient treatment (AOT) finally got funded, or would he be sad that it has taken us so long?

Going back to my letter, I clicked "Save." I no longer needed to advocate for AOT, but it was only one step of the way. The remaining parts of the "Helping Families in Mental Health Crisis" had yet to be passed, and I was not giving up.

July 4, 2015

It was a dark and soggy July 4th weekend. We stayed inside catching up on chores. The news on TV was about James Holmes and his trial in Arapahoe County. If I'd had the time, I might have livestreamed the trial, but, then again, maybe not. It was too painful, too sad, and the grinding legal proceedings were too slow. I preferred the radio sound-bites or internet headlines. I knew the prosecution had rested. It meant the defense was up next.

On day 44 of the trial, however, a headline pulled me into the trial like a magnet: *"Aurora Theater Shooting Gunman Was Psychotic at the Time, Doctor Says."*

"I knew it!" I shouted out. I hadn't been interested in the gory details of the prosecution's case, and everyone already knew that Holmes was guilty, but the defense case was different. I was curious to see if Holmes' lawyers would be able to prove that he was insane when he shot the people in the theater.

I dove into the article about Dr. Raquel Gur, a psychiatrist who had interviewed James Holmes several times, and whom the defense had called to testify. Dr. Gur said Holmes "was psychotic during the shooting…" and "All the characteristics of schizophrenia were present at the time of the commission of the crime…"

It was no surprise to me to learn that James Holmes was suffering from psychosis when he committed his violent crime. With my assumption confirmed, I was now more interested in finding out, who was Dr. Gur? A simple Google search told me she was a professor of psychiatry, neurology, and radiology at the University of Pennsylvania and had spent her academic career studying brain function in individuals with schizophrenia. I was suddenly fascinated by the doctor and started clicking on links to read more about her. What I came to, was a recorded video of the day's trial proceedings. I was tempted to push "Play," but it was late and I had to get up early the next morning. Instead, I bookmarked the website.

Thirty-six hours later with a mug of coffee and the house to myself, I watched the video of the trial. It opened to a courtroom filled with law enforcement officers and attorneys seated at tables. Someone with a gruff voice was speaking with an accent. I felt uncertain of the voice's gender until I saw a woman with blond hair sitting on the witness stand. It was Dr. Gur. The attorney at the podium was asking her about the common features of schizophrenia spectrum disorders and asked about delusions and whether there were different kinds.

"Yes, there are," Dr. Gur replied. As she described them, I was drawn in. "Common, are persecutory delusions where the person believes they are being followed or planned against, or some forces outside are operating against them, most commonly in this country it's going to be the FBI, the CIA, or somebody in authority…"

Dr. Gur described referential delusions, like when a person sees or hears something on TV and believes it's a secret code meant specifically for him. And somatic delusions, like when a person believes he has something physically wrong and goes from doctor to doctor when there is actually nothing wrong. She described religious delusions, too, and said that thoughts become delusions when they grow out of proportion or turn bizarre.

The questioning defense attorney was Mr. Daniel King. He asked Dr. Gur about another kind of delusion, the nihilistic type, and whether James Holmes' references to "human capital" had a nihilistic flavor to them.

The doctor agreed and said, "This is something in detail he described, and in his writing, that the world is coming to an end…those thoughts became his preoccupations." The doctor spoke about the bizarre quality of Holmes' delusions, "… the symbols he has presented in his writing and he described, I have never seen before. They did have a bizarre and pervasive nature…the most higher-functioning people, namely those who have greater intellectual capacity, are the ones who come up with the most bizarre delusions."

My attention did not waver from her answers, nor the long explanations in her foreign accent. Mr. King posed a question regarding the five domains of schizophrenia, two of which are hallucinations and delusions. "Is the third domain disorganized thinking or speech?" he asked.

"Yes… people with schizophrenia, when they talk and you listen to them…at the end of the sentence you say, What were they saying? How did the beginning of the sentence connect to the end of the sentence?…Philosophical ideas are expressed in writing and less verbally because it is harder for them to talk…but when you read it, it doesn't make sense…"

I assumed Dr. Gur was speaking about his notebook, the one we heard about on the news that was so controversial. People had said Holmes' notebook contained information showing that he was homicidal and because of that Dr. Fenton, his psychiatrist, should have ordered a 72-hour hold on him. Instead, Mr. King referred to a videotape that Dr. Gur reviewed of James Holmes in the police department interview room after his arrest.

"Did you find in that videotape evidence of disorganized thinking or behavior?" he asked.

"Yes," Dr. Gur replied. "He was sitting in the cell. On his hands he had bags, brown bags, and he was moving the bags as if he was popping—this is not purposeful behavior, it's bizarre behavior. I've watched other inmates in cells, and it's not common. Most people just sit, sit quietly."

I understood that the bags she was referring to were put on his hands to preserve gunshot residue.

Mr. King then asked her about the notebook. "… Did you review the writings that Mr. Holmes made both in the notebook before the crime and the writings from the jail afterward?"

"Yes, I did," Gur replied.

"Did you find evidence of both delusions and disorganized thinking?" he asked, and again she replied, "Yes."

I watched Mr. King as he approached the witness and handed her something. "… do you recognize that as some of Mr. Holmes' writings?"

"Yes," she said.

"Are those the writings you reviewed when he was in the jail following his arrest?"

"Yes."

"Are those the writings that you were talking about in your report as evidence of his delusions along with the notebook, as evidence of delusions and disorganized thinking?"

"Yes."

"Did they help form the basis for your opinion?"

"Yes, they did."

So mesmerized by Dr. Gur's testimony, I had almost forgotten that I was not sitting in the courtroom with them. I was in my house, at my desk. I glanced at my empty coffee mug, at the ring of cold sticky cream sitting at the bottom, and realized I had not yet eaten breakfast. I remembered I had an appointment that day and saw the time slipping away, yet I couldn't pull myself away from listening to Dr. Gur describing James Holmes' delusional thinking. I kept watching, and before I stopped the video I heard the defense establish that it was possible for someone with schizophrenia to experience delusions and still be highly functional.

"... was the ability to plan, buy weapons, scout out the theater, and assemble components—incendiary devices in your apartment, was he capable of that?" Mr. King asked.

"Yes, he was."

"Does that mean that Holmes was not psychotic, under the influence of delusion?"

"Under the beliefs he was holding at the time, the mission that he was bound on

accomplishing, he was able to do that."

"Is that uncommon in schizophrenia?"

"Fortunately, most people are not like that, but high-functioning people are able to do that."

* * *

It was several days later when I got back to the video of Dr. Gur's testimony. I tuned in where Mr. King was questioning her about the research she conducted on the brain structures of healthy subjects compared with persons with schizophrenia. At this point, Dr. Gur had been on the stand for three hours. Typically, I had little patience for long, drawn-out talk, but I hadn't found a minute of this testimony boring. When the topic of heredity came up, Dr. Gur pointed out that Holmes' paternal aunt had schizophrenia and both of his grandfathers had been hospitalized in the past for psychosis. I found this particularly interesting, as if it was more validation that mental illness was not a weakness of character, but more a matter of biochemistry and genetics.

As for Holmes' psychotic thinking, Dr. Gur revealed that he told her he was helping people by shooting them. She shared that he'd said, "I'm going to put them out of their misery. Life is miserable for everybody."

The crux of her testimony came when Mr. King asked, "Do you have an opinion, as to whether, but for this psychotic illness, there would have been a shooting at all?"

"I agree," she said. "There would not have been a shooting at all."

Dr. Gur reiterated her diagnosis of James Holmes, saying what I had suspected all along, that he was psychotic during the shooting. And when King asked, at last, "What is the appropriate diagnosis?"

I heard what I'd been waiting for the entire testimony: "Schizophrenia."

45

Unfounded Fears

While Congress dragged its feet on mental health reform, I read stories online about desperate parents struggling to get help for their mentally ill adult children. One story was from

Virginia State Senator Creigh Deeds, whose own son stabbed him multiple times before he killed himself. Senator Deeds had testified before Congress on June 16, 2015, in support of the Helping Families in Mental Health Crisis Act. During the hearing he said this about his son:

"He was brilliant; everyone in this room would envy his adeptness in picking up languages, his knowledge of religion, his ability to play any instrument he'd pick up, and his kindness and gentleness to his fellow man. My world was shaken to its core when he began showing signs of delusional thinking and sporadic behavior. I was not equipped with the knowledge or the information to help him.

HIPAA prevented me from accessing the information I needed to keep him safe and help him towards recovery. Even though I was the one who cared for him, fed him, housed him, transported him, insured him, I was not privy to any information that could clarify for me his behaviors, his treatment plan, and symptoms..."

Further along in his testimony Senator Deeds said, "We have to do better. Not for me, not for the countless other families who have already buried their loved ones. But for those who still struggle with mental illness and the families that struggle to help them."

I wished to tell him, "I hear you, Senator Deeds."

But more importantly, was Congress listening?

***

Having engaged with Senator Deeds' story, I hadn't realized he was speaking to Congress that day to support a newly revised, "Helping Families in Mental Health Crisis Act." Unbeknownst to me, the original bill died in the last session of Congress, right along with Barber's Bill. Had I known at the time, I would have suffered a great amount of distress and disheartenment, believing that the time and effort that had gone into creating the bill had been for naught. Fortunately, not all was lost. The fighters soldiered on with their mission to reduce barriers to individuals needing treatment. They made concessions and reemerged with the new "Helping Families in Mental Health Crisis Act of 2015," which they had introduced 12 days before Senator Deeds gave his testimony.

After reading the new version I thought it was even better than the original regarding HIPAA. It allowed caregivers access to information, provided the individual being treated had a diminished capacity to fully understand or follow a treatment plan, and that the absence of such information or treatment would contribute to a worsening prognosis.

Likewise, with FERPA, disclosure of information of a student, over the age of 18, would be allowed if a physician, psychologist, or another mental health professional reasonably believed the disclosure to a caregiver was necessary to protect the health and safety of the student or others.

These were the two elements I looked for in the bill, though it contained much more that was positive, including tighter regulation of SAMHSA to prevent the agency from giving away taxpayer money to its friends and not following up on how the money was being spent. There were also tighter regulations for PAIMI.

The new bill seemed fair and right to me, yet I saw online how others disagreed. One was Noel Hunter, a clinical psychologist who specialized in psychosocial approaches to healing from trauma and emotional distress. She said, "Recently, the Murphy bill in the United States Congress has resurfaced as a tangible threat to the civil liberties of individuals labeled 'seriously mentally ill'… Having defeated the bill once, it is back like herpes."

In a "Letter of Concern" Ms. Hunter and her supporters accused Tim Murphy of ignoring the voices of patients living with mental illness and only considering what their families had to say. They worried that Murphy's bill would defund complementary and alternative approaches of treatment for mental illness. They claimed that Murphy and his supporters had financial ties to pharmaceutical companies that would benefit from this legislation while there was evidence that psychotropic drugs were ineffective and extremely toxic. They were also concerned that an individual being forced to take lifelong drugs, without the ability to defend oneself in a court of law and not having control over decision making, could result in increased mental health difficulties or violence.

I could not accept their point about individuals being locked up in hospitals with no ability to defend themselves. Patients do have the right to a review of their certification or treatment by a judge or jury and are appointed public defenders if they're indigent. They also have patient representatives to assist them in processing complaints. While I didn't doubt there were individuals who had experienced otherwise, in my experience working in treatment facilities, patients were given and did avail themselves of these rights. Murphy's bill did not propose to take away these rights.

The fears expressed by Hunter and her followers seemed irrational to me. The bill did not state that all persons with mental health issues *need and must* be given pharmaceutical therapies and would be forced to take them for life. Neither did the bill propose to defund all non-pharmaceutical therapies. Nor did it mention removing the safeguards already in place to prevent individuals from being falsely accused of being mentally ill and locked up against their will. My sense was that some were afraid the programs they believed in would be dismantled if the bill passed.

I thought their fear was unfounded. Helping someone whose illness was so severe that they were incapable of realizing it, to access care, did not automatically mean they would be locked up and forced to take medication. It did not mean that then, and it would not mean that under the "Helping Families in Mental Health Crisis Act." It could be the person would get an "involuntary" psychological evaluation. In Cyndi's case, for example, a psychological evaluation could have been very beneficial for her. She was not dangerous to others because of her delusions, but she was dangerous to herself. She was in denial of her delusions and even of her physical limitations. She was making poor decisions about her own health and safety. Moreover, she was being taken advantage of by someone she "liked." Recognizing the peril she was in, I reported her. From there I could only hope that Cyndi would get from the state the kind of supervision her mother had given her before she passed away.

I had no expectation that a psychological evaluation would have forced Cyndi into an institution. She was neither homeless nor a threat to others; she was just sick. She was convinced her delusions were real. Whatever result an evaluation would have shown, she still would have had the right to refuse medications and to keep her delusions, if that was her wish, provided she was no threat to others. My wish and hope had been for her to receive intervention resulting in supervision so she would not be a danger to herself or vulnerable to those who were trying to take advantage of her.

A petition against H.R. 2646 was attached to Hunter's "Letter of Concern." I did not sign it. Differing views have validity, though it seemed the political fights were always over taxpayers' money and defending one's turf. I had no turf to defend. I just wanted solutions that would help families who were struggling with mental illness.

46

Advocating for Reform

July 15, 2015

The defense had rested their case in the James Holmes trial, and now it was in the jury's hands. During the trial, the jurors witnessed the nonsensical ramblings Holmes wrote in the notebook he sent to his psychiatrist. They also saw where he wrote, "The obsession to kill since I was a kid, with age became more and more realistic..." Holmes said in his writings that as early as middle school, he believed his mind was broken. Holmes knew something was not right with his mind—or his brain.

Would the jury agree? Their charge was not to determine whether James Holmes was the person who murdered the people in the Aurora theater. Rather, they were to deliberate whether James Holmes was sane or insane at the time of the crime. The prosecutors tried to prove that he was sane—that he knew what he was doing, while the defense has maintained that Holmes was suffering from schizophrenia and hearing voices that told him to kill. I agreed with the defense. Holmes was not sane.

It was hard to predict how long it would take the jury to come to their decision after the emotional 10-week trial. I assumed it would be a few days and tried to put it out of my mind. The next day was my birthday, and I'd planned to focus on more pleasant things.

* * *

I spent my birthday driving around in a rented black sports coupe. I'd like to say the racy car was part of a slick mini-vacation with my husband, but the truth was, I was using it to get work. My own car was in the shop getting extensive bodywork and new paint after being hit the previous week by an avalanche of rocks flung from the back of a truck.

I'd been traveling at 65 mph on the highway when the truck on the opposite side of the highway swerved out of control and lost the load of rocks it was carrying. The rocks flew through the air like a spray of meteors coming toward me. Instinctively, I closed my eyes, expecting a terrific blow to my face and torso. The rocks hit the windshield with a boom and a splash, creating a hole the size of a baseball. Glass spattered over the dash and onto my lap. By the time I was able to pull over and realize what had happened, the truck had disappeared. It amazed me that I hadn't crashed and only suffered some scratches on my arms.

I realized I'd been lucky that day.

The day of my birthday, my assignment was at the Department of Corrections, interpreting for a repeat offender, another individual caught in the revolving door syndrome that was plaguing the system. It was late in the day when I finished and trod through the sweltering heat emanating from the asphalt parking lot. But the heat outside was nothing compared to the suffocating air that greeted me inside the car. I quickly buzzed down the windows, craving a Diet Coke with ice for the ride home. Soon, though, I was on the highway, letting the breeze flow through the open windows. Rather than rehashing the assignment in my mind as I drove, as I sometimes did, or in this case, allow the inmate's dismal situation to ruin my mood on my birthday, I was celebrating.

I was alive and well, and I'd made it to age 62 and grandmahood with my husband of 40 years. I was thinking of the nice dinner we would have that evening to celebrate when I heard an announcement on the radio. The verdict of the James Holmes trial was about to be read.

I turned up the volume and noted the time. It was 4:15 p.m. when Judge Carlos Samour began to read the verdict: "Verdict form count one, murder in the first degree after deliberation, Jonathan Blunk. We, the jury, find the defendant, James Egan Holmes, guilty of murder in the first degree after deliberation. Verdict form count two, murder in the first degree after deliberation… guilty… Count three… guilty… four…guilty… "

The judge was still reading 35 minutes later when I arrived home. The reading of all 165 counts took more than one hour. After an 11-week trial, Holmes was found guilty of all counts. The jury did not find that Holmes was insane. It was inconceivable to me that he wasn't. Had the prosecution won them over or was it just impossible after all they had to witness for them not to see him as anything but guilty? Either way, in prison or a mental hospital, James Holmes would be put away for a long time. The sentencing hearing was still to come.

That was one birthday I'd never forget.

Identifying myself as a senior citizen felt odd, yet gratifying to have reached this stage of life. As the youngest of three sisters, with one older brother and one younger, I'd always thought of myself as young. At work there were always older, more experienced colleagues that I looked up to. When I started my career, I said, "I'm going to work for 30 years and then I'm going to take care of my grandchildren." Ten more years than that had passed and I was still working. Most of my colleagues were now younger than me. Some were not even born when I started interpreting. Nevertheless, I still enjoyed my work.

When I looked back on my six decades, successes and failures streamed through my mind. I couldn't name any particular outstanding or extraordinary achievement I'd made. Then I thought of Mr. Rousseau. I recalled the two of us sitting on a bench out in the sun one day with Colin, waiting for our ride back to the care center after one of his medical appointments. Pausing between words, Colin said to me, "I have to tell you… we've had other deaf people here before. And you are… "

His pauses got my adrenalin flowing, my heart pounding in my ears. What was he going to say?

"Without a doubt… by far, the best interpreter we've had at the care center."

This unexpected compliment set my brain into a spin, flashing back to not one, but two recent assignments where I'd thought my performance had been less than stellar. In my mind I was saying to Colin, *oh, no, I'm not—by far, anything like that. You should have seen me last week.* I had returned home after each of those days kicking myself. In the first job, I had embarrassed myself in front of my peers when I spoke, voicing for a deaf person at a public forum, blurting out something totally different from what the woman had actually said. A peer corrected me, which is always a humiliating experience.

The second awkward experience happened on a different job when I had to advise my team interpreter about an ethical situation he was getting us into. He volunteered us to take a walk with a deaf client who has a mental illness and a history of "running away." The interpreter said he'd done this with this client before.

Red flags waved in front of me. "No, we can't go without staff because we can't be responsible for him."

I had to say this in front of our client because he was standing there with us and the young lady on staff. Apparently, this facility had previously allowed this, but in my 40 years of interpreting I'd gained some insight that young people who are new to the workforce hadn't acquired yet.

"I never heard that rule," the young lady said.

It wasn't exactly a rule, nor was it something we'd been taught in interpreter training. Instead, it was something I'd learned 20 years earlier while I was interpreting for a quadriplegic deaf man at a long-stay rehabilitation center. He had permission to go to a nearby grocery store to return some videos he'd rented, and I went with him, walking alongside as he drove his electric wheelchair over uneven sidewalks. I remember how nervous I was about his heavy chair looking so unbalanced on the tilted sidewalk. I was afraid he would tip over in his chair. Fortunately, he didn't, and we returned safely from our short errand. A month later, however, I heard that he had gone out from the rehab center by himself and had fallen over in his wheelchair. His head hit the pavement and cracked open, killing him.

I'd felt uncomfortable telling the other interpreter that we couldn't go for a walk with our client. It seemed inappropriate, to say it in front of the client, but there wasn't the opportunity to say it in private as we were one step from being out the door. All of this flashed across my mind as Colin was still speaking.

"Yes," he said, "in every way you are top-notch. The other interpreters just sat reading their electronic devices. One was so dramatic when she spoke for the deaf person, it was insulting to us. We can see for ourselves…"

Listening to him, my head cleared from the side thoughts, though my adrenalin was still making it hard for me to breathe. I finally got some words out. "Well, um, thank you... I appreciate you saying that."

I didn't know what else to say, but in my awkwardness I started telling Colin about an assignment I'd had years ago in an operating room interpreting for a woman getting an epidural before a cesarean section. As she sat on the edge of the table, rolled forward over her bulging abdomen, I squatted down in front of her, so she could see me signing what the doctor was saying. The doctor stood behind her feeling for the proper spot along her spine to insert the needle. Just before that, I had started feeling light-headed like I was going to pass out.

As I think about this now, I realize that light-headedness was probably a budding sign of my growing anxiety disorder that worsened over the next few years until I finally hit a crisis point, but on that day I was just telling myself, *don't faint, don't faint*. Luckily, for the operating room staff who already had their hands full, bending down the way I was, most likely helped me avoid passing out.

After the deaf woman's baby was delivered and the surgery completed, I was taken aback when the anesthesiologist said, "You're really good at your job."

My heart fluttered. "Really?"

"Yeah, we really hate having interpreters in here," he added.

"Why is that?" I asked.

"It's just their cocky attitude. They're arrogant and they get in the way. You're not like that," he said.

"You're very kind to say that. Thank you," I said, too embarrassed to mention the fact that I had been trying the whole time not to pass out. I told Colin this story about the anesthesiologist because it reminded me of what Colin had just said.

Colin smiled. "Yes, there's just something about you."

To this day, I don't know what that something is, but it meant a lot to me, what Colin said, as so many days I felt defeated by Mr. Rousseau's lack of progress, leaving me feeling like I was in the wrong place. Colin's comment reassured me that there are places where I belong, where I do my best work. I guess I'd been in the right place after all.

July 29, 2015

James Holmes' mother, Arlene, spoke at her son's sentencing today. She said she hadn't been aware of the severity of her son's mental illness and that she and her husband had not been informed about his violent thoughts. She didn't even know that he had been diagnosed with schizophrenia until she heard this during the trial. I couldn't help wondering if she and her husband had known how sick their son was, could they have done something? Would things have turned out differently?

August 7, 2015

Since the day the verdict was announced, I'd learned why the jury found Holmes guilty instead of not guilty by reason of insanity. Back in April, on the day of opening statements, Judge Samour informed them that if the prosecution showed that Holmes "… acted with deliberation and intent—willfully taking actions that he knew would kill people—then even if he had mental problems, he should be found guilty of murder." So that was it. He was guilty and would go to prison.

We could close the book on the James Holmes story, but until we made some major changes in our laws, the grim reality was, this would not be the last story of its kind. Again, I wrote to my Congressmen, wishing there were more I could do to advocate for mental health reform. All I could do was tell my story.

The letter took 90 minutes to write. I was signing my name when the verdict on the Holmes' sentencing trial was announced over the radio online, "James Holmes is sentenced to life in prison without parole…"

* * *

Representative Jared Polis responded to my letter, acknowledging the inadequacies of our mental health system and the fact that too many people dealing with mental illness are ending up in prison. I was pleased that he recognized this reality, but disappointed by the solution he offered. He said,

> *I am proud to co-sponsor H.R. 1877, the "Mental Health First Aid Act," which would expand the resources available to mental health first aid training programs that focus on issues such as the safe de-escalation of crisis situations, the recognition of signs and symptoms of mental illness, and timely referral to mental health services for people in the early stages of developing mental health disorders.*

I saw no problem with the "Mental Health First Aid Act," but was it going to assist families who were struggling to help a severely mentally ill loved one get off the streets? I didn't believe so. "Referring" an individual who was seriously mentally ill, but who did not believe himself to be so, would not automatically ensure that the person would receive the assistance, supervision, or treatment he needed.

Did the "Mental Health First Aid Act" address the shortage of mental health providers and the shortage of psychiatric beds for people who needed long-term supervision and treatment? Did it address the overcrowding of jails and prisons with persons suffering from mental illness?

Could "the Mental Health First Aid Act" prevent more tragedies like the Aurora theater shooting? I didn't believe so, and I couldn't accept the Representative's reply as final.

I wrote him back, asking him to please support H.R. 2646, in addition to the First Aid Act, stressing that family members are currently prohibited from being involved in their adult loved one's mental health care, without their permission. By this I said:

> *… we have created the bulk of the problems we have today with the mentally ill and homeless population… With untreated mentally ill individuals being unsupervised and roaming the streets, the odds increase that one will become so psychotic, he becomes dangerous and potentially violent—increasing the possibility of a tragic event…*

H. R. 2646 is the only bill, currently, that gives families the tools they have been lacking to assist their mentally ill loved one access and comply with treatment and thereby decrease the probability of that person becoming homeless or incarcerated.

To continue warehousing the untreated mentally ill in our jails and prisons is immoral, and allowing psychotic, potentially violent, individuals to roam the streets is dangerous for all of us.

115 Congressmen and women have signed onto this bill. I ask you again, Congressman Polis, to please sign on to H.R. 2646—for the health and safety of all Americans…

* * *

Legislators send form letters in reply to our letters. They don't have time to write personal replies to the hundreds of letters they receive. They have one letter prepared for each issue that constituents write them about, even when a constituent writes them a stream of letters demanding answers to critical issues. The only way to get real answers was through face-to-face meetings.

I had met with legislatures on Capitol Hill in Washington, D.C., a decade earlier, when I was a member of the National Breast Cancer Coalition (NBCC). We spoke to Representative Perlmutter, requesting his vote to fund breast cancer research. The following year when the NBCC gathered on Capitol Hill, I returned and met with the Senator from Colorado along with Carolina Hinestrosa, one of NBCC executives, and fellow breast cancer survivor, whom I greatly admired. As part of the NBCC, Carolina was on a mission, challenging the status quo of scientific research in breast cancer. While petite in stature, Carolina exuded knowledge, confidence, strength, and grace.

Out of the 700 NBCC advocates on Capitol Hill that day, I was the only one from my district in Colorado. When we all separated to go meet with our representatives, Carolina accompanied me so I wouldn't have to speak alone to the senator. I felt honored to be in her presence, totally unaware at the time that she was fighting a recurrence of her breast cancer.

Carolina passed away a couple of years later. The day I spent with her in Washington, D.C., had a lasting impact on me. With the image of her strength and perseverance in the back of my mind, I waited for a reply from Representative Polis and followed the progress of H.R. 2646 by reading Murphy's E-News.

The bill was gaining support with endorsements by national organizations, and an editorial in the *National Review* praised Murphy's efforts on the assisted outpatient treatment program. It all sounded promising. It was something to feel positive about.

Then, as if enough tragedy hadn't happened already to get Congress to act, I heard that two young journalists were shot and killed during a live interview on TV. It happened at a shopping center in Moneta, Virginia. The gunman was a former employee of the same television station where the journalists, Alison Parker and Adam Ward, worked. He'd been fired from the station because of aggressive and inappropriate behavior. He'd also been urged to get help for his condition but had not.

Representative Murphy's words to a reporter about what happened spoke for many of us when he said, "This is extremely frustrating, and at this point I have to put part of the blame on Congress for inaction. Putting this off and hoping it would go away just means we are enabling this type of problem to continue. People with serious mental health issues need serious mental help."

I did not see any television coverage about the killing of Alison Parker and Adam Ward. I only learned of it from reading Murphy's E-News. Though I was weary of hearing about shootings and killings on TV, I wondered why the news stations were being silent about this. If the media didn't report these occurrences, maybe people would start to think our lack of intervention with individuals exhibiting signs of mental illness and threatening behavior was no longer a problem. Perhaps Congress would agree. I was on board with Representative Murphy. Our legislators' inaction was enabling more of these grievous events to occur.

September 3, 2015

Senator Cory Gardner responded to my letter with words much like those of Representative Polis. He, too, supported the "Mental Health First Aid Act of 2015." However, because neither Congressman mentioned the "Helping Families in Mental Health Crisis Act," I was not convinced they were committed to mental health reform.

47

Something to Feel Good About

October 1, 2015

Congress had been in session for one month following the summer recess. Despite 123 co-sponsors for the "Helping Families in Mental Health Crisis Act" and an endorsement by the American Jail Association representing 3,800 correctional facilities across the United States, there had been no vote on the bill. All we had was another shooting. A 26-year-old gunman had opened fire on the campus of Umpqua Community College in Oregon, killing nine people and wounding eight others before killing himself.

Like many of us, President Obama had seen enough. I listened to him speak on television, as I rocked my grandbaby in the living room. His tone was scolding. "As I said just a few months ago, and I said a few months before that, and I said each time we see one of these mass shootings, our thoughts and prayers are not enough. It's not enough," he repeated.

Obama was mad about the guns. "It cannot be this easy for somebody who inflicts harm on other people to get his or her hands on a gun," he said, adding that, "... anyone who does this has a sickness in his mind."

I agreed with the President about the sickness of mind part. He then went back to the guns. He said the problem was that we had too many guns in America. He asked us, the American people, to think about how we could get our government to change the gun laws.

Most of the television coverage that day was about the young students who were killed and others who were feeling freaked out. The question kept coming up. Why does this keep happening? Everyone wanted to know. As Corbin fell asleep in my arms, I silently asked the President, why do you say this is about guns? Dangerously, mentally disturbed individuals are the ones committing these horrific murders and other violent acts. The question should be, how can we help these individuals, stop them before they become murderers? Aside from his comment about a person who does this having a sickness in his mind, the President didn't mention mental illness again in his address.

After Corbin's nap, we drove to the preschool. Toting him on my hip into the building, we came out towing three-year-old Emerson by the hand.

"Where is Grandpa?" she asked with the snap of the seat buckle, as Corbin gleefully kicked in the car seat beside her.

"Grandpa's at work."

"Why?"

I started the car, answering, "He had to go do some work at Herb's house."

"Why?"

"Because Herb needs help fixing his house, so Grandpa went there to help him." Through the rearview mirror I admired Emerson's bright blue eyes, her petite features, and her inquisitive mind.

She pressed on. "Is Herb old?"

"Yes, he's kind of old."

"Why?"

"Because he lived a long time, and he just got old."

"Does he need to go to Heaven?"

"No, he's not ready to go to Heaven."

"Why?"

"Because he's fine. He's going to stay here."

Finally, she was satisfied. I had a hard time answering all of her questions, sometimes, telling her the truth about things in our world that were not always pretty and nice. Corbin, who'd been fussy all morning, now giggled with his sister. There is no better sound in the world than children laughing. Emerson's day at preschool seemed to have gone well. Better than her first day when she candidly told one of her classmates, "I don't like you."

* * *

The Treatment Advocacy Center (TAC) was aware, fortunately, that legislative action is impossible for people like me to keep up with. So, they sent us alerts and reminders. If not for TAC, I would probably miss opportunities to make my voice heard. On October 29, 2015, they called on me to ask my member of Congress to support the "Helping Families in Mental Health Crisis Act." The bill now had 154 co-sponsors, and it was headed to the committee markup in the House the following week. That meant committee members would be able to offer amendments to the bill before it went to the floor for a vote.

I couldn't quit now, expecting others to put the pressure on Congress. Washington, D.C., needed to know that we, the people, were paying attention. I wrote my letter.

November 13, 2015

I picked up the kids on my babysitting day at 7:45 a.m. After I got them safely strapped in their car seats, Emerson asked, "Grandma, can I have my music?"

"Yes, Sweetie, after I buckle my seatbelt."

The kids liked to listen to toddler tunes while riding in the car. It made the trip back to Conifer go faster. I started the CD, watching Emerson in the rearview mirror singing along with her hands doing some of the signs I'd taught her. Corbin rode facing backward, with his big brown eyes on his sister as long as he could before the lull of the motor drew him to sleep. I wished to watch longer, but forced my eyes back onto the morning's traffic, as I was carrying precious cargo.

Partly through "Mary Had a Little Lamb," Emerson stopped singing.

"Grandma, where is Heaven?"

I paused, turning down the volume for this important conversation, noticing that Corbin hadn't yet fallen asleep. "Heaven is waaaaay up there, Honey," I said, pointing through the windshield toward the sky.

"Up in the sky?"

"Yes, way up there."

I contemplated how I would answer her next question, which was probably going to be, "Where in the sky?" We'd had the Heaven conversation before, a couple of times, after she asked where my mother and father were, but instead, she asked a different question.

"How do we get to Heaven?"

This one was tougher to explain to a three-year-old, whom I wasn't sure she understood the concept of death. Perhaps the explanation was better left to parents, but I gave it a shot.

"Well, your spirit goes up there after you die." I took a breath, anticipating the next question, to be, "What is a spirit?"

But she outsmarted me. "We could take an airplane," she said.

"Yes," I agreed, smiling. "Maybe we could do that."

The death conversation was saved for another day, as Corbin's eyes gently closed.

***

The woman who succeeded me as president of our branch of the NLAPW sent out an email to let the group know that one of our ladies had passed away.

"Suki had been suffering from depression," our president said.

I hadn't known that about Suki. I didn't know her well, but I'd liked her. She was friendly, always well dressed, and smart. She read to us a few times—some engaging short stories she'd written. I was sad to learn that Suki was gone. I wondered if her death had been a suicide, perhaps an overdose of medication?

A date was set for a celebration of Suki's life. My husband and I were in Cancun for our son's wedding and unable to attend. Though, some weeks later I learned that my suspicion about Suki had been correct. "She took her own life," our branch president said, without further explanation.

My first thought upon hearing this was, *how could Suki do that?* She had a husband, a family. Her obituary said she had "a long career… was a real estate broker… was passionate about the arts… dancing and music…" How could someone who appeared to love life so much end her own? Then I remembered how I'd felt before I got treatment for depression.

That horrible struggle with insomnia and anxiety. When your brain chemicals are so out of whack, you can't sleep, you can't eat, and you can't think. You feel like hell, and when nothing is working to break you out of the black hole, you think you can't go on. Death seems like the only way to find relief. Yes, I knew that feeling. That awful time, after my breast cancer surgery, when I hadn't been able to sleep for days on end, dragging into months, when every task felt way too hard. I recalled saying to a friend, "Life is too hard," with a fleeting thought of wishing I had a gun. I hadn't realized then it was a suicidal thought. I thought everyone felt the way I was feeling—that life was too hard.

It didn't seem like a strange thought at the time, but now I know it was. I'd never touched a gun in my life. Guns were as foreign to me as eating bugs. If my friend had thought more about my statement, she might have realized it was a cry for help. But she didn't say anything. No one around me did.

Finally, I realized I needed help. When the physician's assistant asked me, "Are you thinking of hurting yourself or someone else?" I didn't tell her I'd had a few suicidal thoughts. Instead, I said, "No. I would never do that," and I meant it, probably because I believed in that moment she was going to help me.

I could imagine what Suki was going through. With depression, life *is* too hard. Suki must have lost hope, and it saddened me that she was unable to get the help she needed in time.

September is National Suicide Prevention Month. That year it passed unnoticed by me. However, I wouldn't be so oblivious to it in the future. After a loved one has attempted or committed suicide, families are in turmoil. Their emotional pain can be devastating. Some people need counseling or other support to aid in healing and their recovery.

I love the word *recovery*. It gave me hope when I was diagnosed with melanoma at age 33, then breast cancer at 46. Hope helped me later with my anxiety and depression. When I was broken and in pain after surgeries, hope gave me the belief that I could recover. And believing gave me the strength to recover.

Recovery is the word that came to me while reading *Cracked, Not Broken*, written by a young man named Kevin Hines. When he was 19, Kevin jumped off the Golden Gate Bridge in San Francisco trying to kill himself, except he survived. Kevin had been suffering from bipolar disorder with psychosis. In the book, Kevin described his battle with disordered thinking and irrational behavior, which led to his suicide attempt.

After his failed suicide attempt, Kevin no longer wanted to end his life and was working very hard to live mentally healthy. In the book he admitted, "It's very hard work to live mentally well, but it's possible with medication, exercise, and eating well… going to bed on time and staying with the routine…" Now an internationally known public speaker, Kevin tells audiences that living mentally well doesn't mean that you don't have relapses. He admits that he does, but he believes that he can always get better. He tells his audiences, "I should've died when I jumped from the Golden Gate Bridge. Instead, I lived and for that, I'm eternally grateful."

I wished I'd been able to share Kevin's book with Suki. Maybe it would have saved her, as Kevin says he's heard from hundreds of people who live by his words, "Stay here, stay well, stay alive."

December 15, 2015

Waking up to our seventh snowstorm since fall began, winter had us clutched in her grip. It was 12 degrees Fahrenheit, and the schools had declared it a snow day. Jim said I should stay home from work, but the place I was scheduled to go never closed.

"I have to go," I told him.

He plowed the driveway for me, so I could get my car out. It was days like these that made me think I was getting too old for mountain living, or at least for commuting.

With few cars on the snow-packed roads, I had no worries of anyone spinning out in front of me, so I allowed my mind to drift to other matters as I drove, like what we should do about my mother-in-law. Several months previously, she had two minor car accidents, both on the same day, and she couldn't remember either one. Since then, we'd been taking turns driving her to appointments and the grocery store. It was time to make the decision about transitioning her to assisted living. For someone who had worked as a nurse for many years and had been a nursing home administrator, it was not easy for her to relinquish her independence. Taking care of an elder with early signs of dementia was a challenging new phase of our life.

December 18, 2015

The car engine warmed while I stood outside in the freezing weather, scraping ice off the windshield. I cleared a circle big enough for me to see out over the steering wheel and left the rest, hoping the ice would melt by the time I got down to the highway.

It was my turn to drive my mother-in-law to her speech therapy appointment, and I didn't want to be late. The therapy was supposed to help with her short-term memory loss.

When we arrived, the therapist took us to a tiny conference room where we sat around a small table. The questions she asked my mother-in-law were intended to stimulate the part of the brain responsible for memory.

When asked, "What kind of animal is an unusual pet?" My mother-in-law answered without hesitation, "A kangaroo."

Her answer made me laugh. I saw that there was humor to find in dementia. After speech therapy, I suggested we go shoe shopping. My mother-in-law had been wearing the same pair of worn-out tennis shoes for too long. She was easy to shop with. She bought the second pair she tried on. Since the shoe shopping went so well, I asked, "Would you like to do more shopping?"

"For what?" she asked.

"Maybe some shirts or blouses?" I'd noticed many of hers were old and stained.

"I don't think so," she replied.

She probably hadn't noticed the stains, but I didn't want to press the issue. So, we went to eat lunch.

Afterward, she said, "There are a few things I need to get at the grocery store. Let's see, what were they?" She thought for a minute as we drove. "Tomato juice, that's what it was, and something else. What was it?" She said she couldn't remember things these days, but she came up with it a few minutes later. "Oh, bananas."

I was proud of her for remembering what was on her shopping list. Half the time I couldn't remember what was on *my* list, the one I often forgot to bring into the store. At the checkout counter, the girl bagging groceries spoke loudly to the checker. Her speech wasn't clear, though her tone sounded belligerent.

"What's she saying?" my mother-in-law asked, swiping her credit card through the terminal.

The checker, a tall man with kind dark eyes, and I looked at each other with knowing smiles. "She's special needs," he said, referring to the girl, but my mother-in-law didn't hear him and kept asking, "What is she saying? Why is she acting like that?"

I whispered to her, "She has special needs."

"Well, good God, she shouldn't be taking it out on everyone else," my mother-in-law complained, a bit too loudly herself.

I was a bit shocked and embarrassed by her reaction to the girl who wasn't even talking to us. My mother-in-law had never acted this way before. When she finished her transaction and slid her wallet back into her purse she said, "Well, this is the last time I'll come here," as we turned to walk out of the store, but not before the checker and I exchanged smiles, knowing we were both managing individuals with special needs.

Besides my mother-in-law's new shoes, there was something else to feel good about that day. Congress approved an omnibus spending bill that included funding for parts of the "Helping Families in Mental Health Crisis Act," The Assisted Out Patient Treatment Program, (AOT), and the Recovery After Initial Schizophrenia Episode (RAISE) Project. This was positive news for these individuals and their families. It was also good news for taxpayers, as these programs help reduce hospitalization, incarceration, and victimization of individuals with serious mental illness.

Further legislative action on Murphy's bill was still pending, and though we were nearing the end of 2015, I was optimistic. With current bipartisan support at 172 co-sponsors, I was willing to bet the remaining parts of the bill would pass in the next year.

48

Sense of Accomplishment

March 1, 2016

When people asked me what I was currently writing about, I told them it was about advocating for mental health reform. I often saw their faces go blank. I'd start to explain how our health privacy laws have failed us regarding seriously mentally ill adults. I said our overly restrictive involuntary commitment laws have been partly responsible for many of the mass shootings and we needed to reform the laws. I longed for them to jump into the discussion with me with a passion equal to mine, but usually, they just nodded and changed the subject.

I'd come to realize, though, there was a second reason I was writing on this topic. It was my longtime yearning to understand my own brain. The fact that I experienced migraines and dealt with anxiety and depression when other people didn't, indicated something was wrong with me, but that "something" had always eluded me.

Over the last few years, the answer to why I had these problems had become more clear, and it was not as complex as I'd believed. It was not some deep, maladaptive character flaw left over from childhood deficiencies from being raised in a dysfunctional family. It was more simple. It was genetics, perhaps something as simple as a misplaced nucleotide of a "C" instead of an "A," or a "T" instead of a "G," in one of the codons in a strand of nucleic acid. Or a deleted segment in my DNA. Some kind of alteration in the normal sequence of amino acids in my DNA had rendered me prone to migraines and anxiety and depression. Genetic abnormalities were responsible for drug and alcohol addiction, anxiety and depression, and schizophrenia, among my relatives.

Scientists engaged in studying genetics related to myriad physical and mental health disorders are publishing interesting research. The studies are interesting to read, though difficult for non-scientists like me to fully understand. However, the strides they've made in discovering specific genes and mutations have given us a much better understanding of genetics today than back in the 1950s when my mother told us what she had learned in Al-Anon about what was wrong with my dad.

"He has a disease," she said.

Actually, it was my sister who was three years older than me, who told me when I was 10 that our dad was an alcoholic. The words stunned me, for even at age 10 I knew what an alcoholic was. In my mind it was a disheveled homeless person who slept in doorways downtown on Larimer Street. I felt conflicted because my father was not like those people. My father dressed in pressed suits and polished wingtips and went to work downtown in the Equitable building. Hearing my 13-year-old sister say this put a stick in my heart. How could it be true? Yet, as young as I was, I knew she was right. Our father did have a terrible drinking problem. My mother softened the blow by calling it a disease. My young mind understood that it wasn't a kind of disease like cancer that was going to kill my father, but it meant that he couldn't help that he had the craving to drink and to keep drinking until he passed out.

My father couldn't help all those times he came walking home from a bar after work, having left the car somewhere, sometimes not remembering where, or stumbling home with a dripping gash on his forehead from a drunken spill. He couldn't help it all those nights when he sat glassy-eyed and sloppy in the living room chair, with his bottle of gin lying underneath while he forced my mother to sit and listen to him talking nonsense.

There were other things about my father's drinking that my siblings and I kept secret. We didn't know at the time that people suffering from mental disorders often become addicted to alcohol. We also didn't know that many other families across the United States were dealing with the same problem we were, and they were keeping it a secret, too.

Luke Longstreet Sullivan wrote about growing up in the '50s with an alcoholic father in *Thirty Rooms to Hide In*. I started reading this book and couldn't put it down. Luke's father, Dr. Roger Sullivan, was an orthopedic surgeon at the Mayo Clinic in Rochester, Minnesota. He was a brilliant and talented doctor who, unfortunately, became addicted to alcohol. According to Luke, his father's drinking turned him into a nightly raging monster. His violent rants toward his wife and six sons often had the boys running to all corners throughout their Millstone mansion, looking for hiding places from their father. Sometimes, the family went fleeing to a motel to spend the night. One Thanksgiving, fleeing from their father's drunken vitriol and verbal lashings, they abandoned him and their freshly baked turkey.

Even after sobering up in a psychiatric facility, Dr. Sullivan went back to drinking. His alcoholism eventually caused him to lose his job, his family, and finally his own life. He was found dead in a motel. People suspected it was a suicide.

The raging monster that Luke described in his book made Dr. Sullivan sound like a very bad man, born with poor character. In reality, he was a brilliant surgeon who suffered from the disease of alcoholism caused by a genetic flaw in his brain.

My father, too, had a fine mind. He graduated from high school at age 16. When World War II began he was drafted into the Army and as the second lieutenant of an anti-tank unit he fought in Germany. After the war he went to college and earned a law degree. But, early into his career with a wife and four young children, he began slipping into the mire of alcoholism and all the problems that came with it.

As a child, I wanted to know why my father was this way and why he didn't take us on family vacations like other kids' dads. My mother explained that it was the trauma of the war that led our father to drink. Was that true? Was it the atrocities that he witnessed that caused him to drink? All I know about my father during the war is that he lived in a foxhole during the winter months, wearing the same uniform day after day.

As a mature woman, I don't believe that the war caused my father's alcoholism. I believe he was born with a genetic predisposition to this disease. What emotional trauma he experienced during the war likely contributed to his drinking, but the genetic makeup in his brain was there before he went to war.

My dad's father was also an alcoholic. I don't drink, but I knew I inherited migraines from my father. He suffered from them and so did his mother. There were a lot of things I wished I could ask my father about his family history relating to our genetics, but I hadn't become interested in learning about them until after my father passed away. Perhaps it wasn't even necessary to know who I inherited what from, as researchers know that alcoholism runs in families, and science is getting closer to identifying specific genetic links between migraines, anxiety and depression, alcoholism, and drug addiction. Studies today, which increase our understanding of gene mutations and their related biochemical effects, will hopefully lead to new and better treatments for tomorrow.

More effective treatments, better access to care, and laws that don't prohibit family members from assisting an adult loved one with a severe mental illness, are reasonable goals to help decrease the number of lost souls who sleep on park benches and street corners. Congress can help, and this is why I sat watching video clips of the week's C-SPAN coverage of Congressman Murphy leading a bipartisan group of lawmakers in a special order on H. R. 2646. Would they move to a vote?

February 6, 2016

A friend sent me a flyer about the Legislative Education and Advocacy Day sponsored by Mental Health America of Colorado. Participants would have the opportunity to meet individually with policymakers to give them input on issues that were most important to them. I decided to attend.

I didn't want to be late, so that morning I got up early, expecting traffic to be heavy downtown. It turned out I needn't have worried. I arrived before almost everyone else, finding the room set with round tables. A gray-haired woman sat at one. Thinking that it might be good to be with persons of my same generational experience, I went to sit at her table. Another woman, seeming of like mind, came and joined us. As more people arrived, others filtered to our table with cups of coffee and breakfast muffins. Soon, all the tables were filled with more than 250 people.

As we sipped coffee, I introduced myself to the others. "What brings you all here today?" I asked.

It was amazing how quickly each one opened up. One said she was here because her mentally ill adult son lived with her, and she had a concern about where he was going to go when she couldn't take care of him anymore. Though we were all connected to the issue of mental illness, we had come for slightly different reasons. I told the ladies I was interested in the causes of mental disorders and in reforming our laws, so we might better serve those who were suffering.

The first speaker for the conference did not speak about either of these issues. Carol Hedges from the Colorado Fiscal Institute addressed the state's budget. She said Colorado had one of the fastest-growing economies, and our population was increasing daily. "People come here because of the beautiful Aspen trees," she said. "The scenery and the environment unite us, but what is it that Coloradans do together?" Personable and dynamic in her style, Ms. Hedges answered her own question, "Together, Coloradans adopt public policies. We do that on the ballot… the legislature doesn't decide things, the people do."

Ms. Hedges said there would be $200 million available the following year and that it could be allocated to different categories.

"We can sit back and be cynical, or we can do what's harder and get out and participate in government, in our democracy," she added.

I agreed. We need to voice our opinion of how our state's money should be spent. Ms. Hedges talked about the difference between Eastern progressives and Western progressives. "Western progressives go to church more, and they own three or more guns. I'm from Kansas. We hunt and we have guns. The third thing about Western progressives that's different from Eastern progressives is that we're more willing to show our patriotism and fly the American flag."

Ms. Hedges revved up our enthusiasm. I'd never referred to myself, a native Coloradan, as a Western progressive, but I was passionate about my country, and I wanted to help solve our mental health crisis, so I guessed I was in the right place to do that.

Michael Lott-Manier, the Deputy Director of Public Policy at Mental Health Colorado, spoke about the importance of focusing on adolescents: "We need to think of mental illness the same way we think about illnesses like cancer, diabetes, and others, which have been improved by early detection in many cases and treatment in others," he said. "About half of all adolescents experience a mental health condition in any given year… the first symptoms in young people are trouble sleeping, bad dreams, and trouble making friends…"

I believed Mr. Lott-Manier was right. Early intervention could make a tremendous difference in reducing teen suicide as well as the number who progressed to a more severe and irreversible mental illness.

At this point in the program Mr. Lott-Manier proclaimed all of us "mental health advocates." He urged us to share part of our story with our legislator at the capitol: "Share what is real, heartfelt, and emotional to illustrate your point," he said. "Talk about what you know."

Until now, I hadn't had a single thought about speaking to a legislator. What would I say? I didn't even know who my legislator was. A stir of panic swirled in my chest, but it soon subsided when Mr. Lott-Manier reminded us that we didn't have to be experts.

I began jotting down points I wanted to make: *It's not about guns, it's about the underlying problem behind the guns—untreated mental illness… families struggling…* Ideas kept coming to me as the time ran short and Mr. Lott-Manier began introducing the leaders who would escort us to the capitol to meet the legislators. One came to our table to help us polish our 30-second personal stories before it was time to go.

After I practiced my little spiel with the leader, she informed me that I would be meeting with Representative Tim Leonard. I was the only advocate from my district, so I would be speaking on my own.

As we all streamed across the street to the capitol building, I thought of Carolina Hinestrosa and how I felt sitting alongside her as we met with the senator in Washington D.C. I loved the articulate way in which she spoke, advocating for funding for breast cancer research. The thought of her gave me confidence.

While most of the advocates were flowing into the capitol, a smaller number of us proceeded across Colfax Avenue to another building. Our escort took us to the 6th floor, where carpeted hallways led us to the different offices. I overheard a couple of legislative assistants telling advocates that their legislator was not in. They were in meetings at the capitol. Many offices were dark. I continued alone through the quiet hall looking for Representative Leonard's office. My heart quickened as I approached. The room was brightly lit and through the glass door I saw two men talking. They glanced at me, shook hands, and then opened the door.

One man walked away, and the other greeted me.

"Hello. Are you here to see me?"

"Yes," I said. "Do you have a few minutes?"

The representative was tall with short hair and wore a double-breasted blue suit. He looked like an Air Force officer. I pulled a chair up to his desk and introduced myself. "I'm here to speak with you about mental health. I'm concerned about the problem of untreated mental illness in our society. Thank you for allowing me to meet with you today."

"Yes. Welcome," he said. He leaned back in his chair, crossed his legs, and folded his hands together, giving me all his attention.

"As you know, there's been these awful shootings that have been happening—the one at Columbine, where my son's soccer teammates went to school. His team was getting ready to go to a competitive soccer tournament in Cincinnati the day that the Columbine shootings happened. Those boys who did that, there was something wrong with them, mentally, and their parents seemed to have no idea what they were up to. And the other shootings—in Aurora, Tucson, and all the others. Everyone is screaming that we have to get rid of the guns!"

With his eyes on me, Mr. Leonard nodded, and I went on.

"I didn't come here today to talk about guns, but about the mental illness that is at the root of these atrocities. I'm here to speak for a friend named Susan whose son had schizophrenia. He lived with her and he was starting fires in her basement, so she had to kick him out and change all the locks in the house. She was scared to death of him. She had no power to help her son because of our overly strict privacy laws. She had no access to his health records because he was over the age of 18."

Words tumbled effortlessly from my mouth. "We need to change the law so parents and family members can help their adult loved ones with mental illness get treatment, and stay on their medications. And we need better ways to identify young people who are struggling with mental health issues and spread awareness to parents."

Without a taking breath I continued: "Untreated mental illness can lead to substance abuse and addiction. It can lead to crime and incarceration or suicide. Our psychiatric hospitals have downsized and closed, and now our jails and prisons are the new psychiatric hospitals."

Representative Leonard was listening as if he hadn't heard any of this before. He didn't stop me, so I kept going: "There was something I found interesting this morning at the conference on mental health. They showed us this list of categories to which our tax dollars are allocated."

I slid a piece of paper over the desk and showed him where we got to write in the percent of tax money we thought should be allocated to each category: schools, healthcare, jails and prisons, public safety, and others.

"I know none of these categories receive enough money. They all need more. But which category would you cut to be able to give more money to another one?" I asked.

He looked at the paper, but I spoke before he could answer.

"They didn't say this at the conference, but you see, we don't have to cut any of them to improve mental health in our society. We can change the HIPAA laws to allow families access to their seriously mentally ill adult loved one's health records, so they can assist them in complying with treatment. That way, the individual is less likely to go off his meds, less likely to become homeless or a victim of crime, and less likely to become locked in prison or a hospital."

I was aware that I had gone beyond my 30-second spiel. The representative's desk was clear of papers and files. He appeared as if he had all day to spend with me. So, I kept talking—about my family and relatives, about my anxiety and depression and how often these conditions are at the root of alcohol and drug addiction, and how medication saved my life.

Finally, Representative Leonard leaned forward. He brought up a point about prescription drugs. "You know people say that kids are overdrugged—the kids on Ritalin, and all the other drugs they're on. You hear people say, 'What are they doing to our kids?' What do you think about that?"

"I hear those things, too," I said, acknowledging his point. "Many people are opposed to prescription drugs. They have their own soapboxes."

In my mind I saw a flash of the document I had seen circulating the internet, listing all the mass shooters and the medications they were supposedly on or had quit taking, before the shooting.

"They're opposed to antidepressants, and they are antipharmaceutical companies. I'm not a teacher, and I'm not a parent of one of those kids. I cannot speak to medications prescribed for children. I can only speak about my own anxiety and depression, and the alcoholism, drug addiction, suicide, and schizophrenia in my family. Medication helps me immensely, and I believe it could have helped my father, who struggled with alcoholism and maybe could have prevented my two cousins from taking their own lives."

Representative Leonard still appeared engaged.

"I understand some people don't like to take prescription medications. And some people believe that pharmaceutical companies are evil and just trying to make a lot of money. My father was one of those people, but when my mother had Parkinson's disease and had to take several medications, he helped her with them, and took care of her."

I realized then I was talking way too much, going in all directions, and I apologized to Representative Leonard. "I'm so sorry, we were told not to talk too long, and here I am rambling."

"Oh, no," he said. "Please, go ahead, tell me things I don't know."

The Representative's kindness made me feel comfortable and before I knew it, I was saying things I hadn't even thought about.

"I watched my father over the years. I remember when I was a child and there were times when he was so miserable when he was not drinking. My mother would say, 'He's dry drunk.'"

Thinking of that now, it sounds ridiculous. He was probably experiencing anxiety and cravings for alcohol.

"When I was 13, my father quit drinking. He quit working, too, shortly after that, but he was healthy. He played golf and seemed happy for many years. Late in his life, however, he showed signs of an obsessive-compulsive disorder. He liked to joke and have fun, but he had so much anxiety and agitation that it got in the way. I loved my father, and I think medicines could have helped him. It still pains me to think that he suffered for maybe no reason.

"I know nobody *wants* to take medicines, and we certainly don't want to be forced to take them, but sometimes if we're willing to try them, we can see the benefits."

I didn't how long I'd been talking, while the congressman was taking it all in. It could have been 20 minutes, or 40. I felt I should wrap up, even though Representative Leonard was giving no hint that he wanted me to leave.

"So, that's why I believe treatment for persons struggling with mental illness can be beneficial—for them and for society. And one solution I have doesn't cost a thing. Change our privacy laws to allow caring and competent families to be involved in the care of their seriously mentally ill adult loved ones."

With that, I sat back in my chair.

"You've made your point!" he said. "Thank you for opening my eyes."

I left the representative's office feeling a sense of accomplishment and pride for having had the courage to speak up about difficult things. I spent the rest of the week cleaning the house to prepare for our family's Easter celebration. When the day arrived, we had an Easter egg hunt for the grandchildren before our dinner of ham and scalloped potatoes. Afterward, I glanced at the baskets of candy and dirty dishes piled on the counter. The kitchen smelled of smoke from the overflowed liquid that had burned in the oven. It was still making me cough. The doors to the outside were open and Jim had fans blowing, trying to clear out the smoke. The kids ran in and out, oblivious to the chilly air.

Plopping down on the couch next to my mother-in-law, I let out a deep sigh.

"Whew! I've had a busy two weeks," I exclaimed.

"What have you been doing?" she asked.

"Cleaning, mostly." I didn't mention work, or the visit I had with Representative Leonard. I hadn't even told Jim about it. I wasn't sure why. Maybe because I didn't think they would understand. "This house was so dirty, I just had a lot to do to get ready for the party. It wore me out."

"Are you always so overwhelmed?" she asked, like she was puzzled.

I laughed. If she only knew how true her question was. I'd never shared anything with her about my anxiety and depression, or my work writing this book.

"I guess I so," I replied.

49

To The Finish

June 10, 2016

It had been seven months since the updated "Helping Families in Mental Health Crisis Act, 2015," passed out of the Health Subcommittee in Congress. That vote followed a grueling 10-hour markup during which congressmen argued over 50 amendments that unsuccessfully sought to overturn the bill. On this day Congressman Murphy's E-News announced that H.R. 2646, (now referred to as "Helping Families in Mental Health Crisis Act, 2016") would be up for committee markup on June 15th, in advance of moving to the full House.

Congressman Murphy promised that he wouldn't stop fighting for families in crisis.

"Delivering evidence-based treatment for serious psychiatric conditions is how we will finally conquer stigma surrounding mental illness," Murphy said in his e-news blast. I was grateful for the Congressman's news blasts. Without them, I would not know what was going on with this bill.

On June 15th, with a 53-0 vote, H.R. 2646 passed through the House Energy & Commerce Committee and Chairman Murphy proudly delivered his remarks. "… This bill calls for a complete overhaul of the current federal system, refocusing resources on helping those with the most serious mental illness by getting them treatment before, during, and after a psychiatric crisis…"

This vote was a victory for the 200 bipartisan co-sponsors who had fought for this bill. Family members of individuals with serious mental illness from various parts of the country flew in to be present when the votes were being called. When they announced the final tally, the audience gave Representative

Murphy a standing ovation. I felt the victory, too, but we were far from the finish line.

July 5, 2016

A bulletin from Mental Health Colorado let me know that the full House of Representatives would be taking action on H.R. 2646 the following day. It urged advocates to voice our support by contacting our representative and gave the phone number. I was busy all day but committed to call tomorrow.

When I woke in the morning, I gambled that I could get my two cats to their veterinarian appointment and still have time to make my call to Representative Polis before it was too late. With 26 pounds of meowing felines hanging in carriers from my shoulders, I looked like I was running late to the airport. Pushing through the door of the animal hospital, I credited myself for my conniving skill this morning in outsmarting the cats, making it look like any other morning, while I schemed on how to get each of them cornered and into their carriers before they outsmarted me. Hoolie could easily tell when I had something in mind that included him. He could elude me for hours. It was not a game for either of us. For him, it was fight or flight, and the chase became worse when I was in a hurry.

With Keetah the challenge wasn't so much in trying to catch her. It was trying to keep her from escaping the carrier once we were in the car. I had to turn her carrier upside down so she couldn't squeeze through the small opening at the top. The carrier wasn't designed for determined cats like her. Hoolie hadn't yet figured out that he could do the same, but they both let me know in loud cries how unhappy they were about going for a ride.

"Whew, we made it," I said to the receptionist as I set the carriers on the floor.

"I understand. It's stressful for them, coming to the vet."

"You mean it's like this for everyone, not just us?"

"Oh yeah, there's been books written on how to make it easier," she said, making me feel better.

In the exam room, I let the cats out of their carriers and checked my cell phone for the time as we waited for the doctor. It was 8:40. That meant it was

10:40 in D.C. I worried that I might already be too late. I dialed the number for Representative Polis, expecting to leave a message on an answering machine if it was not already full.

After one ring, a man with a young-sounding voice answered. "Good morning, this is Ryan Burke. How can I help you?"

I assumed Ryan was Representative Polis' legislative assistant. "Hello, this is Diane Chambers from Colorado calling to urge Representative Polis to vote for House Resolution 2646, the "Helping Families in Mental Health Crisis Act."

I knew to keep my request short and got straight to the point: "It's so important that we pass this Act because untreated mental illness leads to such heartache for families and tragedy and expense for society when someone untreated turns violent. We all know this from these terrible shootings."

"Yes, yes, that's right," Ryan agreed.

"Do you know how Representative Polis plans to vote on this resolution?"

"Um, no, he hasn't given us any talking points on this," Ryan said.

Ugh, not a good answer, my friend.

"Well, I want to stress how important this is. Untreated mental illness is a very high cost to society when these individuals end up incarcerated, or when they do something violent. I'd like you to please pass this information on to him."

The veterinarian and his assistant entered the room and the doctor spoke to me as if he didn't notice I was on the phone. I wasn't great at multitasking, but at least I heard Ryan say, "I'll do that."

Later, I realized I forgot to tell Ryan that he needed to tell Jared Polis immediately. If he was already on the floor, they may have been ready to vote at any moment. I guess I had assumed that a legislative assistant would know his representative's schedule and how he was going to vote. I should have known better. Never assume. Ryan probably didn't know.

It turned out that my sense of urgency was unnecessary. The majority of representatives apparently didn't need any more convincing. They passed the "Helping Families in Mental Health Crisis Act, 2016" by a 422-to-2 vote. The bill would now go to the Senate. On behalf of the most vulnerable mentally ill who were unable to advocate for themselves, who lacked the insight to seek care, and for the safety of society, I prayed for this bill to pass quickly through the Senate and get signed by the President.

December 2, 2016

The fall months had slid by in the breeze, and it was already December when a special edition of E-News arrived with the headline, "In Case You Missed It." My intuition told me I probably did miss it, whatever it was.

It said:

> On Wednesday, November 30, 2016, the House passed the 21st Century Cures bill, which included mental health reforms from the "Helping Families in Mental Health Crisis Act." The bill now goes to the U.S. Senate for a vote next week."

My gosh! What was this? I hadn't even heard of the "21st Century Cures Bill." When did this emerge I wondered? Did the name of Murphy's bill get changed? Looking at the date on the headline, I eventually figured out that the "Helping Families in Mental Health Crisis Act, 2016" had morphed into one giant healthcare reform package with a fancy new name. This was huge! Why didn't I know about this? Where had I been?

I felt like Rip Van Winkle, awakening from a long sleep. I could scarcely recall the last two months. The blur must have started on that Saturday evening back in October when we last saw our beloved Keetah. She was perched on the back deck off from the kitchen. Jim was grilling burgers. I could still see her in my mind, hunched down on all fours, peeking out, looking over our land through the thick of trees where a herd of elk had waited out a storm. Through those trees you could hear the neighbor's ducks quacking and their rooster crowing.

It wasn't until an hour after Jim and I had finished dinner and cleaned up the kitchen when we noticed Keetah was missing. Maybe she had gone to check out the family of deer that graze on our property. Jim and I searched our property, calling her name, but it was getting dark outside and hard to see through the trees. We went back inside, and Jim pulled up a chair in front of the sliding glass door. He sat down to wait for her, as he'd done many times before, while I readied myself for bed.

Jim was still sitting in that chair when I went to bed. When I got up in the morning and heard that Keetah hadn't returned, I knew it was bad news. Running outside, I called her name, searching in vain. When I came back in, Jim and I broke down in each other's arms. We searched again later, all three acres, up the stream and down, afraid of what we might discover. Still, there was no trace of her. Nor did she appear that night or the next. Despite our fear that a mountain lion had taken her, we put up signs on the road, describing our lost 9-year-old gray tabby, with our phone number. We called and visited animal shelters. None had Keetah. Her brother, Hoolie, was as distraught over her absence as we were.

Losing a pet is painful, but I had so much work I didn't have the luxury to sit and grieve. Jim couldn't stop thinking of Keetah. He searched the internet for lost pets in our area. He called the shelters again, in case someone had just found her. Ultimately, he began looking for a new kitten to adopt—a gray tabby, just like Keetah.

That's when he found Willa.

"We have an appointment at 8:00 on Friday, to go see her," he said.

I didn't want to tell him, but I wasn't ready for a new kitten. I had work and my advocacy, and the grandkids to take care of. I felt overwhelmed as it was, but Jim was set on getting a kitten, so I went along.

With grandson Corbin in tow, we drove to a warehouse in Denver that also served as a feline shelter. We met tiny Willa and her brother, falling in love with both kittens. Jim and I looked at each other and knew we couldn't take Willa without taking her brother. So, we brought them both home in a box.

Hoolie was not happy to see two newcomers. He'd never liked strangers of any kind coming to the house. We had to separate the tiny kittens from him for two weeks until he got used to them. Like new babies, the kittens consumed a good deal of our attention. Kittens and grandkids had taken over matters of importance in our home. And, there was the election! Yes, we'd had a roller-coaster presidential election, with results that surprised much of the country when Donald Trump was elected as our new president.

Now, I saw where I'd been. Scattered.

Recognizing it was only my attention that had been elsewhere lately was a relief. I thought for a moment I'd lost my mind. But now I had to figure out what I'd missed with these bills. Searching for an explanation, I came across mentions of the "Mental Health Reform Act of 2016," the "Mental Health and Safe Communities Act," and the "21st Century Cures Act," which had me totally confused. In an overwrought voice I asked my trusted computer, "What are all these different bills and what happened to the 'Helping Families in Mental Health Crisis Act, 2016,' that the Senate was supposed to be voting on? Are people just calling the one bill by different names?"

I longed for someone to explain it all to me, instead of having to sort through massive amounts of online articles to learn what happened. After some work, I ultimately stumbled upon a commentary by Dr. Jeffrey Lieberman, a psychiatrist and schizophrenia research scientist, from Columbia University in New York City. On December 6, 2016, Lieberman wrote, "… the week after Thanksgiving, something totally unexpected happened that has almost restored my faith in government. Congress has orchestrated a visionary, clever legislative process to push some sweeping legislation over the goal line… something that could be not only beneficial but actually transformative."

Like an angel speaking directly to me, Leiberman answered my questions about these bills. They were indeed separate and distinct bills. The "Mental Health Reform Act of 2016" arose in the Senate, parallel to the "Helping Families in Mental Health Crisis Act" in the House. Also from the Senate came the "Mental Health and Safe Communities Act." While these bills were being debated, another bill, co-authored by Diana DeGette, a congresswoman from my state, aimed at boosting funding for scientific research and accelerated development of new drugs and therapies was introduced. It was the "21st Century Cures Act."

I couldn't discern if these were fabulous developments or if it was complete craziness coming from our legislators.

"Meanwhile, the presidential election took place," Leiberman said, "The aftermath of the election brought a tectonic change in expectations that could have completely derailed any possibility that these bills would be addressed during the lame-duck session, and if that were the case, everything would have had to start over again in the new Congress after January 2017."

Instead, something amazing happened. The leaders of the House and Senate came together. In a bipartisan effort they took the best parts of the three bills, and integrated them all into the "21st Century Cures Act."

I felt eternal gratitude to Dr. Leiberman for helping me understand. Though before I could fully rejoice over the Cures Act, I had to know: How was it going to help individuals and families who were in an immediate mental health crisis?

December 7, 2016

Holding Corbin snuggled in a blanket, the two of us waited in the car for Emerson to get out of school. Looking into his brown eyes, my heart swelled with warmth despite the 12-degree outside. Corbin reached up with his dimpled fingers and touched my face.

"Nose," he said.

His smile showed two new teeth breaking through alongside the two in front. We didn't care about the temperature outside, because snuggling together was so much fun. With a ping of a new email on my phone, our game was interrupted.

I saw the email was from John Snook, the Executive Director of the Treatment Advocacy Center.

"You told Congress it was time to finally fix our broken national mental health system. You told them that families couldn't wait for reform any longer. And they heard you," he said. "Today, the Senate voted to pass Mental Health Reform. Now the bill goes to President Obama for his signature!"

I was stunned.

"The 21st Century Cures Act passed," I announced to Corbin.

It happened so quickly, I didn't even have a chance to read it. I didn't know what the new provisions would be for mental health reform, but I felt a glow all over. Corbin was smiling, too. The long haul to the finish was over.

Epilogue

President Obama signed the 21st Century Cures Act into law on December 13, 2017. In addition to its intention to streamline the development and delivery of medicinal therapies, accelerate research into serious illness, it would also address the opioid crisis in our country. Though changes to HIPAA were not included, the law has many provisions intended to improve our nation's mental health services. I will never know if my voice made a difference in advocating for these changes. Many other people gave powerful testimonies along the way. The opportunity to say what I believe and to be able to play a part in creating our laws is a freedom and a right for which I am forever grateful.

Epilogue

Acknowledgments

First, I would like to thank the ladies of the National League of American Pen Women (NLAPW). Since 2001, these professional women of the arts have inspired me, taught me, and encouraged me in my creative endeavors. It has been this organization that has enabled me to grow and gain the confidence to call myself a writer. I would especially like to thank the members of the Intensive Critique Group of the Denver Branch of the NLAPW who have stuck with me over the years offering me constructive suggestions on my manuscripts, including *Fragile Minds*: Juliana Adams, Andrea Antico, Erika Christiansen, Donna Clark, Kelly Ann Compton, Carol Ehrlich, Shelley Harding, Patricia Kennedy, Neeli Lambert Thompson, Sue Luxa, Juanita Pope, Sydney Popovich, Atlanta Sheridan, Kay Taylor, Kathleen Visovatti, Linda Volin, Adrianna Voss, Cathy Wield, and Ruthy Wexler.

I wish to thank all the mental health professionals with whom I've worked alongside during my career, who for privacy reasons shall remain unnamed, but who shared their knowledge and insight with me while modeling how to treat all humans with dignity and respect. I give thanks to the patients of the psychiatric facilities and to the residents of the care centers where I worked, who allowed me to share space in their private worlds for a time. I also wish to thank my instructors in mental health interpreting, which, spanning three decades of continuing education, are too numerous to name. From them, I earned the credentials by which I was able to gain entrance onto locked wards, where I would never have been permitted otherwise.

I would also like to recognize Alexandra O'Connell, who helped me with the focus and structure of the manuscript for this book, and Diana Ceres, my editor, for her patience, skillful guidance, and editing of *Fragile Minds*. I am indebted to Jeff Grober and to my friend Emily, both of whom helped me cope with the challenging circumstances we faced together, but also for their part in helping me (unknowingly) to find the clarity I was looking for at that time of my life. I am grateful to Representative Tim Leonard, who gave his time to listen to me as a concerned constituent and made me feel that my voice was heard.

Most of all, I want to thank my husband for his patience and support of me in my writing journey, and my grown children, Heather Porter and Matthew Chambers, for their love and encouragement as well as that from my siblings and extended family.

About the Author

With an undergraduate degree in Therapeutic Recreation, Diane Lane Chambers has enjoyed a career as a professional sign language interpreter for over 45 years. Her focus for the last 20 years has been in the medical and behavioral health arenas.

Active in the National League of American Pen Women, she has served as the Denver Branch vice president and president. In her free time, she follows legislation and advocates for reform of our nation's privacy laws and involuntary commitment statues to remove barriers to treatment for persons with serious mental illness.

Diane is the author of two other nonfiction books: *Words in My Hands: A Teacher, A Deaf-Blind Man, An Unforgettable Journey* and *Hearing the Stream: A Survivor's Journey into the Sisterhood of Breast Cancer*. She is the producer and narrator of a DVD about Support Service Providers for persons with hearing and vision loss titled, *SSPs: What Are They and Why Are They Necessary?* She lives in Conifer, CO, with her husband.

Notes

1. Baur, Susan. *The Dinosaur Man, tales of Madness & Enchantment from the Back Ward.* Edward Burlingame books, 1991, p.83.
2. Kessler RC, Chiu WT, Demler O, Walters EE. "The Numbers Count: Mental Disorders in America," *The National Institute of Mental Health, Kessler Prevalence. Prevalence, severity, and comorbidity of twelve-month DSM-IV disorders in the National Comorbidity Survey Replication (NCS-R). Archives of General Psychiatry,* 2005 Jun; 62 (6):617-27, http://www.nimh.nih.gov/health/publications/the-numbers-count-mental-disorders-in-america/index.shtml#.
3. Cullen, Dave. "The Depressive and the Psychopath, At last we know why the Columbine killers did it," *Slate,* April 20, 2004, http://www.slate.com/articles/news_and_politics/assessment/2004/04/the_depressive_and_the_psychopath.html.
4. Augé, Karen. "Psych Units Shutting Doors," *News Headlines, The Denver Post,* January 24, 2009, http://www.denverpost.com/2009/01/24/psych-units-shutting-doors/.
5. "Pima County Sheriff Clarence Dupnik Calls Out Vitriolic, Hateful Rhetoric," *tucson.com,* https://tucson.com/pima-county-sheriff-clarence-dupnik-calls-out-vitriolic-hateful-rhetoric/youtube_1395c4f0-1ba9-11e0-9425-001cc4c03286.html.
6. Loughner, Jared Lee. "Genocide School," *Rant Video, You Tube,* January 15, 2011, https://www.youtube.com/watch?v=bLYeSwMVg_0.
7. Whitney, Eric. "Governor Pitches $18.5 Million for Mental Health," *CPR News,* December 12, 2012, http://www.cpr.org/news/story/governor-pitches-185-million-mental-health.
8. Long, Liza. "I am Adam Lanza's Mother," *The Blue Review,* December 15, 2012, https://thebluereview.org/i-am-adam-lanzas-mother/.
9. Rosin, Hanna. "Don't Compare Your Son to Adam Lanza," *Slate,* December 17, 2012, http://www.slate.com/blogs/xx_factor/2012/12/17/i_am_adam_lanza_s_mother_liza_lang_essay_libels_her_son.html.

10. Clayton Cramer. "Reforming Colorado's Mental Health Law," *Independence Institute Issue Paper*, August 16, 2012, http://www.claytoncramer.com/scholarly/ColoradoMentalHealthReform-1.pdf.

11. Bridget O'Shea. "Psychiatric Patients With No Place to Go but Jail," *The New York Times, Health*, February 18, 2012, http://www.nytimes.com/2012/02/19/health/in-chicago-mental-health-patients-have-no-place-to-go.html?_r=0.

12. Armat, Virginia, and Isacc, Rael Jean, *Madness in the Streets: How Psychiatry and the Law Abandoned the Mentally Ill*, The Treatment Advocacy Center, 1990 p.253.

13. Armat, Virginia, and Isacc, Rael Jean. *Madness in the Streets: How Psychiatry and the Law Abandoned the Mentally Ill*, The Treatment Advocacy Center, 1990, pg.11 from Interview, Edward Holder (pseudonym), May 7, 1988.

14. Seager, Stephen B. *Street Crazy, America's Mental Health Tragedy*, Westcom Press, Redondo Beach, CA, 2000. 193.

15. Sarah Garrecht Gassen and Timothy Williams. "Before Attack, Parents of Gunman Tried to Address Son's Strange Behavior," *The New York Times*, March 27, 2013, http://www.nytimes.com/2013/03/28/us/documents-2011-tucson-shooting-case-gabrielle-giffords.html?_r=0.

16. "Washington Navy Yard shooter's mother 'so, so very sorry'," *Fox News*, September 18, 2013, http://www.foxnews.com/us/2013/09/18/navy-yard-shooter-mother-so-so-very-sorry.html.

17. Tim Murphy. "Op-Ed: Overhaul of mental health care long overdue," *The Philadelphia Inquirer*, January 26, 2014, https://murphy.house.gov/uploads/Philly%20Inquirer%20Op-Ed.pdf.

18. "Does HIPAA Help or Hinder Patient Care and Public Safety?," *Energy and Commerce Committee Hearing*, April 26, 2013, https://www.youtube.com/watch?v=AJq9Hn8WGyg.

19. Joe Bruce. "Examining SAMHSA's Role in Delivering Service to the Severely Mentally Ill," Testimony, *Energy and Commerce Committee Hearing*, May 22, 2013, You Tube, https://www.youtube.com/watch?v=rI6e83RGGX4.

20. *Mental Illness Policy Org.* "SAMHSA Fails seriously mentally ill," http://mentalillnesspolicy.org/samhsa.html.

21. Creigh Deeds "Examining H.R. 2646, the Helping Families in Mental Health Crisis Act," *Congressional Testimony*, June 16, 2015, http://docs.house.gov/meetings/IF/IF14/20150616/103615/HHRG-114-IF14-Wstate-DeedsC-20150616.pdf.

22. Noel Hunter, Psy.D. "The Murphy Bill: People are Afraid," *Mad in America*, May 26, 2015, https://www.madinamerica.com/2015/05/the-murphy-bill-politics-and-playing-a-new-game/.

23. Sadie Gurman, "Trial Tries To Look Inside Theater Shooter's Unstable Mind," *Associated Press*, April 27, 2015, CBS Denver, http://denver.cbslocal.com/2015/04/27/trial-tries-to-look-inside-theater-shooters-unstable-mind/.

24. Assisted outpatient treatment (AOT), *Treatment Advocacy Center Backgrounder*, Updated 1/2012, http://leg.mt.gov/content/Committees/Interim/2013-2014/Children-Family/Committee-Topics/SJR20/sjr20-tac-aot-backgrounder-jan2014.pdf.

www.ingramcontent.com/pod-product-compliance
Lightning Source LLC
Chambersburg PA
CBHW031404290426
44110CB00011B/251